The Mac Internet
Tour Guide™

The Mac Internet Tour Guide™

Cruising the Internet the Easy Way

Michael Fraase

VENTANA
PRESS

The Mac Internet Tour Guide™: Cruising the Internet the Easy Way
Copyright © 1993 by Michael Fraase

Library of Congress Cataloging-in-Publication Data

Fraase, Michael.
     The Mac Internet tour guide : Cruising the Internet
     the easy way / Michael Fraase. --1st ed.
         p.   cm.
     Includes bibliographical references and index.
     ISBN 1-56604-062-0
     1. Internet (Computer network) 2. Macintosh (Computer)
     I. Title.
     TK5105.875.I57F73 1993
     384.3--dc20
                                   93-4482
                                   CIP

Book design: Karen Wysocki
Cover design and icons: John Nedwidek, Sitzer:Spuria
Editorial staff: Ruffin Prevost, Pam Richardson, Cabell Smith
Production staff: Brian Little, Midgard Computing, Marcia Webb, Karen Wysocki

First Edition 9 8 7 6 5 4 3
Printed in the United States of America

Ventana Press, Inc.
P.O. Box 2468
Chapel Hill, NC 27515
919/942-0220
FAX 919/942-1140

Trademarks

Trademarked names appear throughout this book. Rather than list the names and entities that own the trademarks or insert a trademark symbol with each mention of the trademarked name, the publisher states that it is using the names only for editorial purposes and to the benefit of the trademark owner with no intention of infringing upon that trademark.

About the Author

Michael Fraase is the proprietor of Arts & Farces, a multifaceted communications and professional services business specializing in hypermedia production, technical writing, desktop/electronic publishing, general Macintosh consulting and software interface design.

Fraase is the author of numerous books, including the three-volume *Macintosh Hypermedia* series (ScottForesman, 1990-1991), *Farallon's MediaTracks* (Business One Irwin, 1991), *Groupware for the Macintosh* (Business One Irwin, 1991), *Structured Publishing From the Desktop: Frame Technology's FrameMaker* (Business One Irwin, 1992) and the 15-volume *Rapid Reference Series* (Business One Irwin, 1992-1993).

Acknowledgments

This is my twenty-second computer book, and the first one in a long time that has been a load of fun. Writers don't make much money, so most of us insist that what we do be fun. At least I do. My most heartfelt gratitude is offered to my wife, Karen Caldwell Fraase who continues to make my life fun.

While the task of writing is a solitary one, the act of creating a book isn't. Thanks to everyone at Ventana Press for proving what I suspected: small publishers can make a Big Difference.

Thanks to Joe and Elizabeth Woodman for seeing the potential in this project. Thanks especially to Elizabeth for recognizing that Mac users needed this book and Joe for a rich sense of humor. I will forever carry the image of a "spaghetti book" in my mind's eye.

Thanks to Pam Richardson for routing and scheduling everything. Thanks to Diane Lennox for publicity and promotion. Thanks to Fran Phillips and Larry Levitsky for sales. Thanks to Karen Wysocki for the interior page design and managing a feverish production schedule. Most of all, thanks for reminding me, with your design, that I'm a writer and not a designer. Thanks to Brian Little and Geoff Reiss for the desktop publishing.

Thanks to John Nedwidek, of Sitzer:Spuria for the cover design and icons. Everyone who's seen the cover has had the same reaction: "Wow! That's really neat. I like it...." then a sideways glance and "Do you like it?" Anyone who can evoke that kind of reaction is doing something right.

And finally there's Ruffin Prevost, my editor. Writers' nightmares are populated with bad editors. Ruffin is the exception that proves the rule; he's a real writer's editor, and approached this project as a true collaboration. He made this a better book with a reasoned, even hand. The world would be a better place if there were more editors like Ruffin.

■ ■ ■

The publisher would also like to acknowledge a number of individuals and organizations who made invaluable contributions to this book.

For advice, support, technical expertise and general friendly assistance, thanks goes to a number of people at MCNC's Center for Communications in Research Triangle Park, North Carolina. Thanks especially to Naomi L. T. Courter and Alan Clegg at the CONCERT Network and Jane Smith and Kevin Gamiel at the Clearinghouse for Networked Information Discovery and Retrieval.

Thanks also goes to Paul Jones and the staff at the University of North Carolina's Office of Information Technology in Chapel Hill for their cooperation and support.

For their help in testing, reviewing and otherwise trying to crash various Internet client applications and software resources and verifying tons of tips, tricks and inside information, thanks goes to Mac Internet cybergeeks Rob Terrell and Shea Tisdale.

A special thanks also goes to Aladdin Systems (makers of the StuffIt Expander utility), Steve Dorner and the University of Illinois Computing Services Office (author of the Eudora e-mail program), and Jim Matthews of Dartmouth College (author of Fetch FTP software) for graciously allowing their excellent Mac applications to be included on the companion disk. Thanks also to InterCon Systems for their assistance and advice regarding their TCP/Connect II integrated Macintosh Internet software.

For advice on telecommunications and modems, technical information and hardware support, special thanks goes to Hayes Microcomputer and Global Village Communications.

About the Images in this Book

The graphic images shown on the opening pages of each chapter of *The Mac Internet Tour Guide* are from the OTIS ("The Operative Term is Stimulate") Project. OTIS is an electronic art gallery containing hundreds of images and animations. According to OTIS Project founder, Ed Stastny, OTIS exists "to distribute original creative images over the world's computer networks for public perusal, scrutiny and retransmission, and to facilitate communication, inspiration, critique and to set the foundations for digital immortality."

According to Stastny, "The basic idea behind 'digital immortality,' is that computer networks are here to stay, and anything interesting you deposit on them will be around nearly forever. The images of today will be the artifacts of an information-laded future. Perhaps the images will be converted into newer formats when the current formats become obsolete—perhaps only surviving on forgotten backup reels. But they'll be there, and someone will dig them up—data-archeologists sifting through the cobwebs of an old storage room."

The OTIS Project is currently accessible by anonymous FTP at three sites:

- no-name-broadband.med.umich.edu in the /projects/otis/ directory
- sunsite.unc.edu in the /pub/multimedia/pictures/ OTIS/directory
- aql.gatech.edu in the /pub/OTIS/ directory

For more information about the OTIS Project, contact:

OTIS Project
Ed Stastny
PO Box 241113   ed@cwis.unomaha.edu
Omaha, NE 68124   ed@sunsite.unc.edu

A special thanks goes out to those OTIS artists who generously allowed us to reproduce their images. Thanks to: Ed Stastny (Information Web, Chapter 1; VR2, Chapter 5; ©1993 Ed Stastny, used with permission); Tom Nawara (Stigmata, Chapter 2; Eye See U, Chapter 8; ©1993 Tom Nawara, used with permission); Michael Maier (Future Culture, Chapter 3; ©1993 Michael Maier, used with permission); David Anjo (No Roof, Chapter 4; ©1993 David Anjo, used with permission); Barrett Ryker (Fractal Moon, Chapter 6; Castle Spirit, Chapter 7; ©1993 Barrett Ryker, used with permission).

Contents

Introduction   xvii

Chapter 1 What is the Internet?   1
It's Easier Than You Think 2
Finding Your Way Around 2
Cruising the Easy Way 3
A Sense of Place 4
Internet Benefits for the Average User 5
A General Overview of the Internet 6
   Internet Governance 7
A Brief History of the Internet 8
The Future of the Internet 10
   Commercialization 10
   Privatization 11
   Bandwidth 11

Chapter 2   Getting Connected   13

Where to Sign Up   14
University Users   14
Government Users   16
Business Users   17
Individual Users   18

Types of Connections   19
Dedicated Connection   19
SLIP & PPP Connection   20

Other Types of Connections   22
Service Providers   22
Resource Requirements   26
Macintosh   26
Network Interface Card or Modem   27
MacSLIP or MacPPP   28
MacTCP   28
Client Application Software   29

Making the Leap   30

Chapter 3   Network Infrastructure   31

An Information Democracy   32
The Internet Rosetta Stone   33
Transmission Control Protocol (TCP)   33
Internet Protocol (IP)   34

Where.Is.That.Thing@On.the.Net?   35
Have Your .Org Call My .Gov About That .Com   37

When in Rome... Don't Tie Up the Phone Lines   39
Acceptable Use Policies   40
Security Issues   41

First Names Are Lousy Passwords   41
Usage Courtesy   42

Chapter 4 Electronic Mail 45

What is E-Mail & How Does it Work? 46

E-Mail Etiquette & Courtesy 48

E-Mail Privacy 50

How to Send E-Mail Anywhere 53

Internet to UUCP & Back 53

Internet to CompuServe & Back 55

Internet to MCI Mail & Back 55

Internet to America Online & Back 56

Internet to AT&T Mail & Back 57

Internet to AppleLink & Back 57

Cross-Network E-Mail Addressing Quick Reference 59

Quick Guide to Using Eudora 59

Configuring Eudora 60

Using Eudora 67

Retrieving and Reading E-Mail With Eudora • Creating an E-Mail Message
With Eudora • Replying to E-Mail Messages With Eudora • Sending E-Mail
Messages With Eudora • Managing E-Mail With Eudora

Quick Guide to Using TCP/Connect II 76

Configuring TCP/Connect II Mail Module 77

Using TCP/Connect II Mail Module 81

Retrieving & Reading E-Mail With TCP/Connect II • Creating an E-Mail
Message With TCP/Connect II • Replying to E-Mail Messages With
TCP/Connect II • Managing E-Mail With TCP/Connect II • Working
With E-Mail Filters

Finding Addresses 94

Using Finger 94

Using MIT's USENET User List 95

Using Whois 96

Using the PSI White Pages 97

Future Directory Services 98

E-Mail Address Starter Kit 98

Electronic Mailing Lists 99

Subscribing to Mailing Lists 100

Cancelling Subscriptions to Mailing Lists 102

E-Mail & Attached Files 103

Sending Files in E-Mail Messages 103

Receiving Files in E-Mail Messages 105

Files in E-Mail Caveats

Chapter 5 **Network News & Newsgroups 109**
What Is Network News & What Are Newsgroups? 109
An Overview of Newsgroups 113
Interesting Newsgroups 113
Macintosh Newsgroups 115
A Primer on Newsgroup Etiquette 116
Flames, Flame-Bait & Flaming 119
Selecting a News Reader 121
Configuring Nuntius 121
Configuring TCP/Connect II News Module 127
How to Read, Post & Reply to Articles 131
Using Nuntius 132
Reading News With Nuntius • Posting a News Article With Nuntius
Using TCP/Connect II News Module 137
Reading News With TCP/Connect II • Posting a News Article With TCP/Connect II

Chapter 6 **Transferring Files 147**
What is FTP? 148
Why Would You Want to Transfer Files? 148
A Primer on Software Resources 150
Public Domain 151
Freeware 151
Shareware 151
Making Shareware Work
A Primer on File Types 152
A Disinfectant for Viruses 154
Using Disinfectant 155
Using Fetch to Transfer Files 156
Configuring Fetch 158
Downloading Files With Fetch 164
Uploading Files With Fetch 169
Using TCP/Connect II to Transfer Files 170
Configuring TCP/Connect II FTP Module 171
Downloading Files With TCP/Connect II 177
Uploading Files With TCP/Connect II 182

Chapter 7 Using Gopher 185

What is Gopher? 185

What Can I Use Gopher For? 186

Why Should I Use Gopher Instead of FTP? 187

Using TurboGopher 187

    Configuring TurboGopher 188

    Browsing Information With TurboGopher 193

    Downloading Files With TurboGopher 195

    Using TurboGopher Bookmarks 200

        Sharing Bookmarks

Gopher Servers 206

TurboGopher Tips 207

Chapter 8 Other Internet Resources 211

What Is TELNET? 212

    Using NCSA TELNET 212

        Configuring NCSA TELNET • Opening an NCSA TELNET Session

    Using TCP/Connect II's TELNET Module 216

        Configuring TCP/Connect II's TELNET Module • Opening a
        TCP/Connect II TELNET Session

Knowbots 221

Netfind 221

Finger 222

WAIS 226

World Wide Web (WWW) 229

Archie 231

    Using the Macintosh Archie Client 232

    Using TurboGopher for Archie Searches 233

RFCs 236

FAQs 238

Internet Organizations 238

    Electronic Frontier Foundation 239

    Internet Society 241

Neat Stuff 242

Clearinghouse for Networked Information Discovery and Retrieval (CNIDR) • Colorado Alliance of Research Libraries (CARL) • Computer Professionals For Social Responsibility (CPSR) Mailing List • Current Cites • Dictionary Server • E-Mail Address Locator • Earthquake Information • Electronic Frontier Foundation (EFF) Mailing List • Electronic Serials List • FTP Sites List • Geographic Server • Hot off the Tree (HOTT) • HPCwire • Hytelnet Server • Incomplete Guide to the Internet • Internet Maps • Internet Monthly Report • Internet Society Archive • InterNIC • Introduction to TCP/IP • IP Address Resolver • Law Library • LawNet • Library of Congress LIBS • MacPGP v2.2 Encryption Utility • Mailing Lists List • MELVYL MicroMuse • Mining the Internet • Music Server • Network News Mailing List • New Users' Guide • NorthWestNet User Services Guide • NREN Information • Project Gutenberg • Public Network News Servers • Special Internet Connections • Sports Schedules • Travel Information • University of North Carolina LaUNChpad • US State Department Travel Advisories VAX Manual • Washington University Gateway • Weather Maps Weather Service • White House E-Mail • White House Press Releases • (More) White House Press Releases

Appendix A Electronic Updates & Visitors Center 261

Updates Are Just a Postcard Away 261
The Electronic Visitors Center 262
How to Subscribe to a Full Year of Updates 264
A Note about Privacy 264

Glossary 265

Bibliography 281

Index 283

Introduction

These are the days of lasers in the jungle
Lasers in the jungle somewhere
Staccato signals of constant information...
—Paul Simon

Part of the experience of using a Macintosh is a sense that there's a collection of actual places behind the screen—places you can't see, but know are in there. Or, rather, out there. This feeling really hit home for me when I saw a photo a friend used to replace his usual Macintosh desktop pattern. It showed his face and hands scrunched up against a window pane, creating the illusion of someone *out there* trying to get *in here*. If you've ever used your Macintosh to connect to another computer—either by network or modem—you know this experience, and you know it's real. Tapping into the Internet not only confirms, but *validates*, this feeling.

These days, it's hip to call this collection of not-quite-real places *cyberspace*. William Gibson created the term in his novel, *Neuromancer*, to represent a universe sustained by a vast network of computers and telecommunications lines.

"People jacked in so they could hustle. Put the trodes on and they were out there, all the data in the world stacked up like one big neon city, so you could cruise around and have a kind of grip on it, visually anyway, because if you didn't, it was too complicated, trying to find your way to a particular piece of data you needed."

But cyberspace isn't some wild future dream; it's here now. John Perry Barlow—sometimes Wyoming cattle rancher and sometimes lyricist for the Grateful Dead—describes cyberspace as where you are when you're on the telephone. Think about that for a minute, and then realize that cyberspace is also where your bank accounts, credit history and tax records are. And in the near future, cyberspace is also likely to be where you earn a good portion of your income.

This book is about the Internet—a vast computer network of many component networks. Think of it as a web. Think of it as the first *really real* cyberspace.

For too many years, the Internet has been the playground of propeller-heads and spooks, inaccessible to mere mortals. But lately, the Internet has changed, becoming a critical tool for millions of computer users. Powerful but simple software tools have made the network accessible to practically anyone—especially anyone with a *Macintosh*. And that's what this book is all about: making the Internet as friendly and familiar as everything else you do with your Mac.

Explosive Growth

The past few years have seen the Internet expand at an astonishing rate. Individuals and businesses are rushing to the Internet in droves for a good reason: it's an invaluable resource for anyone who works with information. Its power and potential are practically limitless. Just a few of the most popular features of the Internet include

- **Electronic mail.** Send electronic mail (e-mail) to virtually any networked computer user. Internet e-mail reaches its destination—practically anywhere on the planet—in a matter of a few minutes.

- **Network news.** Participate in a wide variety of electronic discussion groups on just about any topic you can think of. There are literally thousands of in-depth discussions on topics ranging from the essential to the arcane. Molecular biology, politics, comic books, the stock market, computers and practically anything else you can think of are all covered in the Internet's network news.

- **File transfer.** Transfer any kind of file between your computer and any other computer on the Internet. The Internet boasts the largest collection of Macintosh software and shareware in the world, and its libraries are growing every day.

- **Information browsing.** You can browse through a never-ending collection of information resources available throughout the Internet. Weather reports, electronic information databases and electronic journals (and much more) are available—free to anyone with access to the Internet.

Who Can Use The Mac Internet Tour Guide?

If you use a Macintosh and already have Internet access, or if you're interested in obtaining Internet access in the future, this book is for you. If you subscribe to one of the commercial information services (such as CompuServe or America Online), you can use this book for exchanging electronic mail with Internet users, subscribing to mailing lists and retrieving files available on the Internet via electronic mail.

This *Tour Guide* is written for Internet newcomers. No knowledge of the Internet is assumed (although experienced Internet users are sure to find plenty of interest here as well). I do assume, however, that you're comfortable finding your way around a Macintosh. You should be able to copy files from a floppy to your hard drive, launch application programs, work with control panels, and connect peripherals to your Macintosh. If you haven't yet mastered these simple skills, don't despair. A couple of hours with your Macintosh manuals (or a beginning Macintosh tutorial) will bring you up to speed.

Although the *Tour Guide* will help you navigate the Internet and lead you through its vast resources, regardless of what hardware or software you have, you'll need a few things to get the most out of this book:

- A Macintosh with at least 4mb of RAM.

- An Internet account (or an account with one of the commercial information services, if you want to exchange electronic mail with Internet users).

- An appropriate network connection. To make the most of the tools and techniques discussed in this book, you should have a SLIP or PPP connection or direct connection to the Internet. If you have a dial-up connection, you will find many of the tips and resources useful, but you won't be able to make full use of the companion software.

- MacTCP, properly configured and installed. MacTCP is provided on the disk that comes with this book. See your service provider or network system administrator for specific configuration information for your network connection.

- The floppy disk that comes with this book.

If some of this sounds Greek to you, don't despair. Information on joining the Internet can be found throughout these pages, with specifics in Chapter 2.

The Mac Internet Tour Guide will not only show you the most fascinating and helpful places on the Internet, it will also give you the tools and techniques you need to navigate the vast landscape of information out there. The software on the enclosed companion disk will bring new power and simplicity to everything you do on the Internet. Best of all, every detail of configuring and using the companion software is discussed in detail throughout the book—using real-world examples to show you how to get the most out of your time on the Net. Here's a brief look at what you'll find in the *Tour Guide* :

What's Inside?

Chapter 1: **What Is the Internet?** (And Why Should I Use It?) covers network benefits for the average user and provides a general overview of the Internet for beginners. It also includes information about the history, growth and future of the Internet.

Chapter 2: **Getting Connected** (The Big Plug-In) provides information for all different types of users about how to physically connect to the Internet. If you work for a medium or large organization, you may want to talk with your system administrator; you may already have an Internet account and not even know it. If you're with a smaller firm, or simply an individual looking to "plug in," this chapter also covers the basics of all the various kinds of Internet connections.

Chapter 3: **Network Infrastructure** (Electronic Alphabet Soup) offers background on how the Internet is organized, what you need to know about networking protocols, and the parts of an Internet address. We'll also go over some basic information about being a good Internet citizen. This chapter is a must-read before venturing out into the Net—it will make future chapters easier to understand.

Chapter 4: **Electronic Mail** (The Pony Express Goes Digital) covers everything you need to know about sending, receiving and replying to electronic mail (e-mail). You'll learn how to send e-mail from the Internet to virtually any other networked computer. You'll also learn how to use Eudora (an invaluable e-mail program included on the *Tour Guide* companion disk) and TCP/Connect II, a favorite commercial mail program used by thousands of Macintosh Internet enthusiasts. Finally, you'll also learn how to find addresses, participate in mailing lists and send and receive attached files with your e-mail messages.

Chapter 5: **Network News & Newsgroups** (Broadsheets of the Broadband) offers information on reading, posting and replying to the tens of thousands of news articles available via the Internet. This chapter shows you how to quickly and effectively browse, track and search newsgroups and articles using Nuntius (a program you'll download as part of a step-by-step tutorial) and TCP/Connect II. A brief discussion of posting etiquette and a general overview of available newsgroups are also provided.

Chapter 6: **Transferring Files** (The Mother Download) provides complete instructions for using the File Transfer Protocol (FTP) for downloading and uploading files on any of the thousands of publicly accessible file archives on the Net. Again, two excellent software products are covered: Fetch (included on the companion disk) and TCP/Connect II. We'll also cover the basics of computer viruses and how to use the popular Disinfectant antivirus shareware program.

Chapter 7: **Working With Gopher** (Burrowing for Information) covers the details of using the powerful and user-friendly TurboGopher software to browse information resources and download files on any Gopher server on the Internet. Information on creating and sharing TurboGopher bookmarks (electronic crumb trails through vast amounts of information) is also included.

Chapter 8: **Other Internet Resources** (Geez, What Is This Stuff?) offers information on various Internet resources, both human and electronic. Just as the Internet promises something for everyone, so will this eclectic chapter. The Electronic Frontier Foundation (EFF) and Internet Society, for instance, are bountiful organizations that provide a wealth of information for Internet users of any level of expertise. This chapter also includes information about relatively "minor" or esoteric Internet services that sometimes get overlooked, including time- and money-saving gems like: know-bots, Netfind, Network Information Centers, Finger, the Internet Business Pages, Archie, RFCs, FAQs and the World Wide Web (WWW). This chapter also features an overview of dozens of other fascinating information sources.

A complete glossary, bibliography and index are also included in the last sections of the book.

But perhaps the best thing about *The Mac Internet Tour Guide* is that you can't get lost or left behind—just follow along at your own pace. Everything is covered in simple, step-by-step detail. Even if you've never used the Internet before, you'll find the software and instructions in this *Tour Guide* as easy to use as all your other favorite Macintosh applications.

And to keep the trip interesting, our tour will take frequent sidetrips to visit some of the most fascinating people, places and resources throughout the Internet. Keep an eye out for these "scenic route sidebars"—they'll feature people profiles, file reviews, resource listings, and fun and intriguing examples of the kinds of information you'll find (by chance or design) as you cruise the Internet.

So forget what you've heard about how complicated and frustrating the Internet can be. With the right software and a few pointers from a pro, it's a lot easier than you think—in fact, it's actually fun. Hop aboard, our tour is about to begin!

Michael Fraase
Arts & Farces
2285 Stewart Avenue
Suite 1315
Saint Paul, MN 55116
mfraase@farces.com

CHAPTER 1

WHAT IS THE INTERNET? And Why Should I Use It?

Imagine down-loading Dante's *Inferno* from a computer in Massachusetts or California, just as quickly as if you were copying the file from a floppy disk. Imagine corresponding with anyone on almost a billion different computers, anywhere in the world, as easily as typing a letter with a word processor. Imagine reading the latest news practically as soon as it's written, or cruising through a web of connected computer networks and information resources so vast that no one knows for sure how big it is or how many people it reaches.

Need to know what the weather is like for your trip to New England this weekend? No problem—weather reports and even weather maps are only a few mouse clicks away. Want to find out who wrote a particular book or article? You don't even have to leave your chair to browse the holdings of the Library of Congress. This isn't a scenario from some commercial for a futuristic telephone company or a guess at what television will be like in the year 2050. This is a snapshot of the Internet as it exists right now.

It's Easier Than You Think

Forget everything you've heard about how complicated it is to use the Internet. Tools with a familiar Macintosh interface are available for just about every Internet service. You don't need to know any arcane UNIX commands or have an office next-door to a mainframe computer. The myth is still there, but it's all smoke and no fire. Oh, sure, you can still plod around the Net the hard way, pecking out abbreviated gibberish on your keyboard like so much secret code. But there's a much easier way to cruise the Internet—one that will make your time online more fun and more productive—and that's what this book is all about.

I grew up in cities when I was a kid, and my cousins all grew up on farms in the country. Whenever I went to visit, they would tease me because I didn't know much about driving a tractor, saddling a horse or tossing a cowpie. I couldn't tease them about not knowing how to play stickball or dodge traffic, because I was on their turf—my city experiences weren't relevant. It's sort of like that on the Internet, but now the turf is common to everyone. If the UNIX fans and command-line aficionados want to pump water by hand, that's fine. Smile at them politely while you turn on your Macintosh faucet.

The main reason my country cousins teased me was because I wasn't familiar with their turf. I didn't have a tour guide or a map of the territory. The same is true for new Internet users. It's a daunting task to navigate new terrain without a guide to point out the landmarks.

This book is a tour guide to the Internet, designed to provide you with the tools and information you need to effectively navigate its vast information resources. You'll also find step-by-step tutorials for using a wide array of Macintosh software tools that help you effectively communicate with people and travel to both the "cities" and the "rural areas" that make up this vast information resource. In fact, many of these tools are included on *The Mac Internet Tour Guide Companion Disk*.

Finding Your Way Around

Also included in our *Tour Guide* are what information designers and cartographers humbly call *wayfinding elements*, little signs that help you find locations of interest. Being a Macintosh user, you'll know them simply as icons. Look for these four icons throughout this book for interesting landmarks and tidbits of information.

People profiles are snapshots of how real people use the Internet. These are the true stories of real people, not techno-nerds. With luck, these vignettes will stimulate you to use the Internet in ways you may have never thought of. Look for them to provide insight about the general workings of the Internet, not necessarily relevant to the surrounding text.

Software reviews are brief overviews of some of the best public domain, freeware and shareware software programs available on the Internet. Because space is limited, only the best or most interesting software is mentioned. The archive location and pathname for each program is also provided. All of the programs mentioned can be downloaded to your computer using FTP. (For information on FTP, see Chapter 6, "Transferring Files .")

Hot spots and **cool resources** are short descriptions of both the most popular and the more offbeat information resources available on the Internet. Complete connection information is provided. These resources usually require you to use a specific software program or Internet client for access. Refer to the appropriate chapter for more information on using the right software tool for the job. Any passwords required to access these resources are provided in the sidebar.

Found text excerpts are brief passages of network news exchanges, electronic mailing list information, amusing conversations, general tips and tricks and other information morsels that may not fit within the context of a chapter, but are interesting nonetheless.

Cruising the Easy Way

Neal Cassady was one of the most tenacious drivers of his generation. He'd think nothing of hopping in a Buick and driving Jack Kerouac coast to coast—stopping only for gas—with only a hip flask and a pack of smokes. Cassady was a pretty lousy guide, though, especially when he was trundling along in the big Merry Prankster bus on one of Ken Kesey's intrepid trips.

This book is a tour guide of the Internet, but my pace is a little less frantic than Cassady's (then again, I'm still alive). Since getting there is half the fun, we'll be making frequent stops to wander the nooks and crannies of cyberspace. And the great thing about this bus trip is that, although I'm driving, you can take things at your own pace. If you're anxious to get moving, you can bail out and catch up with the group at the next stop. If you're a slow starter, you can slow things down to a more leisurely pace. So, before we leave the station, let's take a couple minutes to check the map and itinerary for a quick overview of where we're headed and what we'll see.

A Sense of Place

People often describe the Internet as a worldwide network of computer networks. That's as good a description as anything I can come up with, but the experience of using the Internet—*being in the Net*—is something completely different. For instance, when I log into the simple local area network in my office, I'm pretty certain of what I'll find there; it doesn't really feel like a place. It's instead sort of like insipid American hotel chains. There's hardly ever anything different—never a surprise—the same bedspreads, brown Formica, loud air conditioner and view of the interstate.

But when I login to the Internet, it feels like a real place, just as real as the bar on the corner or the deli down the street. There's always something new to explore, and usually an interesting message or two in my e-mail box. And you can no more explore the entire Internet than you could visit every country on the globe. Things change too quickly and dramatically for you to ever become bored.

In this chapter, we'll take a look at what the Internet is, what kinds of information it contains, and how you can use that information to your advantage. We'll also explore a little of the history of the Internet, and speculate about what the future might hold for network users. But best of all, we'll take a look at the places, people and things you'll discover on your tour through the Net.

If you're already familiar with the Internet and how it works, or if you're just anxious to get connected and start exploring, you may want to skip ahead to Chapter 2, "Getting Connected."

Internet Benefits for the Average User

The Internet is much more than a network of networks. It's also much more than a huge repository of information. The Internet is a virtual community, existing only ephemerally in physical reality. While all this philosophical mumbo-jumbo is a great mental exercise—something interesting to think about while you're waiting in the dentist's office or the airport—it probably doesn't have much impact on your daily life.

But the Internet provides several very real benefits that can have an enormous impact on your daily life:

▓ **Electronic mail** You can use the Internet to send electronic mail (e-mail) to virtually any networked computer user on the planet. Traditional Post Office mail ("snail mail" or "the paper net" to e-mail users) may take several days to reach its destination. Internet e-mail can be delivered anywhere on the planet in a matter of minutes, or at the most, a few hours. I used e-mail to correspond with my editor (who is also on the Internet), sending chapters back and forth during the entire writing cycle of this book. When the manuscript was finished, I used e-mail to correspond with the publisher's marketing and publicity staff—and they weren't even on the Internet.

▓ **Network news** You can participate in a wide variety of electronic discussion groups on just about any topic imaginable, from investment strategies to molecular biology, from comic books to politics. If you can think of a topic that isn't already represented by a *newsgroup*, you can start your own. As of mid-March 1993, there were more than 3,000 active newsgroups accessible through the Internet. That number continues to steadily grow, and there are hundreds of additional commercial newsgroups that are available for a fee. As I was writing this book, Apple announced significant advancements with its forthcoming PowerPC computer. This bit of news, accompanied by an extended discussion and analysis, was posted to a Macintosh-specific network newsgroup within a few minutes of its announcement—days ahead of the trade press. Similarly, when the Clinton administration announced its support for the Clipper encryption chip, lively and informative discussions on all sides of the issue were taking place in various newsgroups within minutes of the announcement.

■ **File transfer**   You can use the Internet's standard protocols to transfer computer files between your Macintosh and just about any other computer on the Internet. It doesn't matter where the other computer is located, how it's attached to the network or even if it uses the same operating system as yours. You can just as easily download a file from a UNIX-based mainframe in Tokyo as you can copy it from another Mac in the next room. Apple released QuickTime 1.6 the day I wrote this paragraph. I was able to immediately download it from Stanford University's Macintosh archive. Just for fun, I called several local dealers to see if they had it in stock. Not one did.

■ **Information browsing**   You can use specialized software tools to browse through an almost limitless collection of information resources. Everything from weather reports and electronic journals to university and government databases is available. Shortly after I began work on this book, for example, the Clinton administration began to make position papers and speeches available on the Internet.

And that's just the beginning of what the Internet has to offer. As you explore, you'll discover people, places and other resources that will become invaluable to you. Because of its size, depth and diversity, the Internet can truly be all things to all people. But if you're new to the Net, you may be still wondering exactly what it *is*. The answer is at the same time simple and complicated. And the Internet changes so quickly, it's become something of a moving target—like a lemon seed on your kitchen counter—just when you think you have it in your grasp, it slips away.

A General Overview of the Internet

If you're a technophobe and don't much care about how things work, feel free to skip this section. It contains information about the plumbing of the Internet, and you can always read it later.

The Internet is a collection of various computer networks, linked together and communicating via a common protocol known as TCP/IP (Transmission Control Protocol/Internet Protocol). Because every computer on the Internet agrees to communicate using this protocol, it doesn't matter what kinds of computers you travel to, or even what operating system they are running.

In order for your Macintosh to communicate with other computers using TCP/IP, you must have the MacTCP software installed and properly configured. This process is discussed in more detail in the next chapter.

Although most of the computers that are connected to the Internet run some form of UNIX (the software that controls the computers), as a Macintosh user, you don't need to know one whit about UNIX. Though it probably wouldn't kill you to know a little UNIX, it's important to understand that, for the purposes of basic Internet activity, you don't need to know anything about UNIX—especially if you follow the advice and step-by-step instructions in this book.

The Internet is often defined as that group of computer networks that cooperatively form a seamless network using TCP/IP. But what about those computer systems that don't use TCP/IP but appear to be part of the Internet? For example, I can send electronic mail and even file enclosures from my Internet account to any user on MCI Mail. Yet MCI Mail's computers technically aren't on the Internet. MCI Mail maintains a *gateway* that's used to transfer electronic mail between their computers and the Internet. So, if you have an MCI Mail account, you can be reached from the Internet even though you don't have a computer on the Internet.

Internet Governance

Consensual anarchy best describes the governance of the Internet. While the individual networks that make up the Internet are likely to have executive officers, there's no such person running the entire Internet. The closest thing to an absolute governing authority is the Internet Society. The Internet Society is a group of volunteers whose charter is to promote the exchange of information using Internet technology. The Internet Society appoints a subgroup, the Internet Architecture Board, that authorizes standards and allocates and keeps track of Internet resources (like unique computer addresses). Another volunteer group, the Internet Engineering Task Force, handles acute operational and technical problems.

If you've ever driven in Paris, you'll understand this notion of consensual anarchy. The French have traffic lights, but they don't pay much attention to them. The traffic sort of develops a rhythm of its own without regard to the traffic lights. Drivers take account of the weather, the time of day, the number of vehicles, but not the traffic lights. If you come to a dead stop at a red light in Paris, people will honk their horns and shout silly-sounding French epithets at you. It's hard for an American mind to grasp a situation where there's a sense of everyone doing the right thing without external rules or order. But that's the way it is with the Internet. There are only two "rules" for life on the Internet, and they're unwritten:

- Don't waste bandwidth.
- Don't do anything that threatens the network.

You can do just about anything you like on the Internet, so long as you keep these two guidelines in mind. Would that the rest of life were as easy.

Each member network maintains its own Network Operations Center. These centers communicate with each other and arrive at a consensus on how to facilitate communications and resolve problems.

Since the Internet doesn't really exist in physical reality, there's nowhere to send a check for access. Each of the component networks that make up the Internet pays for its own operations. I send payment for my organization's connection to a regional network, which in turn pays a national provider for its connection. In theory, everyone on the Internet pays for his or her share, and in practice, this actually works amazingly well.

A Brief History of the Internet

The Internet began in the early 1970s as a Defense Department network called ARPAnet. The ARPAnet was originally implemented to support military research about how to build networks that could withstand partial outages and still function properly.

This network design approach assumed that the network itself was unreliable—a very realistic approach in hindsight, bomb attacks notwithstanding. Because the original ARPAnet model called for all communication to occur between two computers directly, any segment of the network could suffer an outage and the communication would still take place using any available alternative route across the network. The *computers* on the network—rather than the *network* itself—were responsible for correctly addressing and verifying communications. In network lingo, this is called *peer-to-peer* networking.

All that was needed for two computers to communicate on the ARPAnet was a message enclosed in a standard envelope—called an Internet Protocol (IP) packet—with a correct "address" for the destination computer.

In the early 1980s, Ethernet-based local area networks were developed. Most of the workstations that made up a local area network (LAN) in the early 1980s ran the UNIX operating system. The UNIX operating system came with IP networking capabilities built-in. Organizations using these workstations wanted to connect their LANs to the ARPAnet, rather than connecting to one large timesharing computer at each site. Since all of the networks were speaking IP, the benefits of enabling users on one network to communicate with those on any other network became obvious.

In the late 1980s, the National Science Foundation (NSF) created five regional supercomputer centers, making the resources of the world's fastest computers available for academic research. Because the supercomputer centers were so expensive, only five could be created, and their resources were to be shared. A communications problem became immediately apparent: researchers and administrators at the different supercomputer sites needed to connect their centers together and also had to provide access for their clients. The ARPAnet seemed to be the solution to the communications problem but was abandoned, mostly because of bureaucratic problems.

The NSF built its own network—NSFNET—based on the ARPAnet's IP technology, with connections running at 56,000 bits per second (56 kbps) over specially conditioned telephone lines. This kind of connection was capable of sending about two pages per second across the network—slow by today's standards. Because these special telephone lines were expensive (the telephone companies charge for these lines by the mile) the NSF decided to create regional networks allowing sites to connect to their nearest neighbor, in daisy-chain fashion. Each daisy-chain was connected to one of the regional supercomputer centers, and the centers themselves were linked together. This strategy allowed any computer to communicate with any other computer by passing messages up and down the daisy-chain.

This strategy was successful—too successful, actually, and the network quickly became overloaded when the researchers discovered that the network was also useful for sharing resources not directly related to the supercomputer centers. In 1987, Merit Network received a contract to maintain and upgrade the network. Merit, in conjunction with IBM and MCI, ran Michigan's educational network. The original NSF network was replaced with telephone lines that were 20 times faster, and quicker computers were also installed. The network was subsequently opened to most academic researchers, government employees and contractors. Access was extended to international research organizations in countries that were allies of the United States.

In the early 1990s the network was opened up to a few large commercial sites, and international Internet access has also started expanding rapidly.

Today, the Internet is a collection of high-speed networks composed of the national backbone network provided by the National Science Foundation and a hierarchy of more than 5,000 attached regional, state, federal, campus and corporate networks. Links to networks in Canada, Europe, Japan, Australia, Central America and South America are in place. There are more than 750,000 computers and workstations of various sizes connected to the Internet, with millions of users.

The Future of the Internet

The Internet is growing at a rate of about 10 percent per month as more colleges, universities and businesses come online. As of April 1992, observers estimated the total Internet population at somewhere between 7 million and 14 million people. The future of the Internet lies in three key areas: *commercialization*, *privatization* and *bandwidth*.

Commercialization

Lots of large multi-national corporations have been on the Internet for years, although their access has been limited to research and engineering departments.

Corporations have recently discovered how expensive running multiple networks can be and have begun to look for ways to consolidate their separate networks. Many have discovered that the Internet is at least part of the answer to their problems. In 1992, many of the restrictions on commercial use of the network began to change. In fact, there are already more commercial sites on the Internet than educational and research sites combined.

Privatization

Internet proponents have always wanted the various telephone companies—or other commercial organizations—to provide Internet connections. They claim you should be able to order an Internet connection just like you order call-waiting or a second line for your telephone service. The telephone companies haven't jumped on this idea right away, but the recent corporate interest in the Internet has not gone unheeded, and this attitude is (slowly) changing.

But before the Internet can be fully privatized, users must find a method for funding the connections that are already in place. As soon as enough small businesses and individuals—the driving force of our economy—decide that connection to the Internet is an important asset, privatization of the Internet will occur very quickly.

One of the short-term changes likely to be brought about by commercialization and privatization is that transactions will become commonplace on the Internet. You will soon be able to order and pay for software and information via e-mail. More importantly, people will actually begin to make their livings in cyberspace.

Bandwidth

Bandwidth is the range of transmission frequencies a network can use. What this means is that as bandwidth increases (which it will dramatically in the next few years), you can transfer *more* information *faster*.

Increasing available bandwidth will not necessarily change the way many people currently use the Internet, but it will improve certain aspects of the way we use the Internet:

- Electronic mail will be richer in media type and benefit from faster delivery.
- File transfers will take much less time—a mere fraction of their current rate.
- Electronic publications—telepublications—will be richer in media type and benefit from faster delivery.
- Telecommuting (working from home via phone, fax and modem) will be more enjoyable and effective.
- Remote collaboration will become easier, more rewarding and more effective.

In short, the way we use and work with information will change drastically. More than ever before, information will take on new value and urgency, while at the same time becoming more accessible and available.

Moving On

This chapter has introduced you to the basic aspects of the Internet as well as its history and future. By now, you're probably ready to get connected and see for yourself what the Internet is all about. Don't worry, we'll get there. But first, you should know how to establish an Internet account and learn a little bit about the mechanics of the network. The next chapter explains how to establish your actual account on the Internet.

The road ahead is long and winding, and it's not without its pitfalls. But if you stick with the group and follow instructions, you're guaranteed to enjoy every second of the journey. Let's get started!

CHAPTER 2

GETTING CONNECTED
The Big Plug-In

Before actually
starting our tour of the Internet, we'll spend this chapter covering the
details of how to get connected. If you already have an Internet connection, you can probably skip all this and go straight to Chapter 3, "Network Infrastructure," where you'll learn about how the places and
pathways of the Internet are constructed and connected. Getting connected to the Internet traditionally has been either exceptionally easy or
almost impossible. If you're with a university, government agency or
corporation that already has computers connected to the Internet—or
"on the Net," as veteran netters say—your task is remarkably easy:
sweet-talk the folks in your computer support department to create an
account for you. It will take them less than 15 minutes, but they'll
probably tell you it will take anywhere from a few hours to a few
weeks. Don't argue; bite your tongue, smile pleasantly, thank them for
their time and efforts, and count your blessings—you are one of the
lucky few. If you're not a part of an organization that's already on the
Net, don't worry; it's not nearly as hard to get connected as it was just a
few years ago.

Where to Sign Up

Because the Internet is not a single computer system—it's not even centrally managed—there is literally no "where" to sign up. For years, it was nearly impossible to get connected to the Internet. Most people talked to a friend of a friend, or found someone inside an organization who could provide them with a news and mail *feed*, sending packets of electronic mail and a limited number of newsgroups.

MacPGP v2.2 encryption software.

Encryption is an important way to assure privacy and authentication of e-mail messages. MacPGP v2.2 uses the non-NSA approved IDEA cipher patented in Switzerland.

You can download the current version of MacPGP by FTP at soda.berkeley.edu in the /pub/ directory.

In those days when "real people" could only wheedle their way onto the Internet, there was always a feeling of dealing with an "information black market." People passed around secret tips and covert instructions for bluffing your way into getting an account on the sly. Invariably, these instructions were to approach a sympathetic librarian in the musty basement of the local university computer center and imply that you were either a student or on the faculty. (The feeling was always one of begging for an audience with a scribe in the Holy Roman catacomb.) If luck was with you, your account would be activated later that day, and you were off to explore the nether regions of the Net, hoping nothing would go wrong and you wouldn't be found out.

These days, it's much easier. The following four sections provide general instructions about who to befriend and what arcane terms to utter so you'll sound like a seasoned expert. You'll be able to obtain your very own Internet connection, regardless of what type of user you are—academic, government, business or individual.

University Users

If you're a university user—faculty, staff or student—you're in luck. Chances are, your college or university is already directly connected to the Internet. Contact anyone in the computing center and ask them for—or perhaps tell them you *must have*—access to the network. After you've been shuttled to the right person, he or she will probably ask you a series of questions like the ones shown in Figure 2-1: "University users Internet information." Note that these questions are general in nature and the responses are merely examples, so your mileage will surely vary depending on your situation. But since half the game of getting the kind of Internet connection you want is just knowing what to ask for, the table shows you how to ask for the most and best of everything. If you sound like you know what you're talking about, most people will assume that you do. Don't worry about what it means; that's all explained later.

Figure 2-1: University users Internet information.

They'll Ask	Your Response
Do you want a full or partial connection?	I need a connection to both my department's local area network, the campus wide area network and the Internet.
What kind of computer do you have?	I have a Macintosh IIci with 8mb of RAM running System 7.0.1, with a LocalTalk connection to my office's LaserWriter.
Do you want a dedicated, SLIP/PPP, UUCP or dial-in connection?	Preferably both a dedicated and a SLIP/PPP connection. I have a second Macintosh in my home office, and I'd like to have a PPP or SLIP connection to the network.
Do you want LocalTalk or Ethernet for your dedicated connection?	I'd prefer an Ethernet connection, but I also need to connect to my office's LaserWriter.
What speed modem do you need for your home office connection?	I need a V.32bis/V.42/V.42bis modem and the appropriate software to make the network connection.
Do you want a PPP or a SLIP connection?	I'd prefer a PPP connection.
What do you want for your username?	I'd like my username to be jsmith, which is my first initial and last name with no punctuation.

After all that, the odds are in your favor that you'll get at least some of what you asked for; and at this point you'll probably be scheduled to have your office computer network connection upgraded. Your account should be activated in a day or two. You will probably be given a packet of software, an instruction manual and the name, telephone number and e-mail address of your network administrator (often known as a "net ghod"). Most important, you'll probably get the telephone number of the campus help desk for any problems you have while using your connection. That's it—you're now an Internet citizen.

Today's baseball schedule.

You can get today's schedule for any major league baseball team (during the season, of course) by TELNET to culine.colorado.edu port 862. Press the Return key for today's schedules. You'll be prompted to enter a team. Here are sample schedules for the Minnesota Twins and the Chicago Cubs:

MLB schedule for Minnesota on Wednesday, 5/12...

Minnesota at California

MLB schedule for Cubs on Wednesday, 5/12...

Los Angeles at Chicago

Government Users

If you work for a government agency, it's likely your agency is already connected to the Internet. Begin by asking your supervisor (or the appropriate computer techie) if your office has an Internet connection. He or she may not know but will probably be able to point you toward someone who can help. The person responsible for maintaining Internet accounts within your agency may or may not be affiliated with your local office.

In any case, finding the right person to help set up your connection is probably the hardest part. The questions—and your responses—will likely be similar to the ones shown in the university table in Figure 2-1. It's not likely that you'll be able to request a dial-in connection—government agencies are fairly stingy with that type of connection, which is usually reserved for work-at-home types or people who travel extensively. But who knows; maybe you'll get lucky.

You'll probably have duplicate requisition forms to fill out, you may have to demonstrate that you have a direct need for an Internet account (a little creativity goes a long way here), and it will probably take you several attempts to fill out all the forms properly.

When your forms are correct and complete and your access has been authorized, someone will wire your computer for the network connection. This person will install a network card if necessary and provide you with software and an instruction manual.

Here's an important tip: try to get the installer to test the connection for you. The installation person will also give you the name, telephone number and e-mail address of your local network administrator. You probably won't be provided with a help desk telephone number (but you can always call the nearest university help desk and try to sound professorial). You'll also be instructed where to report network problems. Once that's done, you're all set.

Business Users

Many large businesses—especially those involved with the computer industry—are old-timers when it comes to the Internet. Here you may find one person (or even a whole department) in charge of maintaining Internet connections. These are the people you want to seek out: ask your supervisor or refer to your corporate employee manual or inter-office directory. If you've been using a local area network within your department, ask the person who comes to fix your computer when it breaks or when the network goes down. (Odds are, they'll be so happy to hear from someone who isn't reporting a problem, they'll be happy to hook you up to the Net.)

The procedure for acquiring an Internet connection within most businesses usually falls somewhere between the looseness of a university connection and the structure of a government connection. You may be able to get a dial-in connection, depending on your organization and its corporate culture. But as a starting point, you should be able to use the responses from Figure 2-1.

If the company you work for isn't on the Internet, you may have to look into opening an individual account on your own and seek reimbursement from the company (for more information on this approach, see "Individual Users" later in this chapter). Alternatively, you may be able to generate enough interest within your workgroup or department to have management look into connecting existing local and wide area networks to the Internet.

Flame wars, affirmative action and babies (oh my!).

People love to carry out heated debates via the electronic messages they can post throughout the Internet. Here's a great "net.story" from Mikki Barry:

"In 1991, a huge flame war [a heated debate carried out via electronic messages] erupted over affirmative action in the soc.women newsgroup. The flames were exchanged for many months, tensions getting higher and higher. Not being one to let anyone else have the 'last word,' I helped fuel this war with my obviously eloquent articles, made increasingly virile through the evil hormones prevalent through late pregnancy. However, nobody on the Net knew I was pregnant, since I was at work until the day I went into labor.

"Just as the flame war reached it's peak, however, I had the strange feeling that I wasn't going to be able to participate for awhile. So I posted a message saying, in effect, 'Sorry, I can't respond to this thread anymore. I have to go have a baby now.' Morgan Elizabeth Baumann was born later that night."

The procedure for establishing an Internet account varies widely from business to business. Some firms create an account for all new employees, while others offer accounts only to "critical" employees. In most medium and large businesses, there will be a help desk (or at least an MIS specialist) available if you have any questions or problems with your Internet account.

Individual Users

Unlike universities and large companies, individuals and small business users rarely need a full-time connection and are well served with only a dial-in connection. With a *dial-in* connection, you use your Macintosh and a modem to dial another computer or server where your Internet account is stationed. This is less convenient (but usually cheaper) than a standard connection, where your Macintosh is always connected directly to the Internet. For more information on the advantages and disadvantages of a dial-in connection, see "Types of Connections," later in this chapter.

Individuals and small businesses typically have the hardest time establishing an Internet account. Until recently, the Internet has been geared for users within large organizations communicating only with users inside other large organizations. Thankfully, this is changing rapidly, and now it's fairly common to find individuals and small businesses with full Internet access.

The main difference in individuals and small businesses using the Internet is that *you (or your business) have to foot the complete bill for your account*. Needless to say, this affects the kind of connection and level of service you select. But Internet access is not nearly as expensive as it used to be—usually well within the means of most small businesses.

Take a quick look at the next two sections, "Types of Connections" and "Resource Requirements," before you jump in and order the most expensive Internet connection offered by your service provider. You run the risk of buying a fully loaded Cadillac with power windows, sunroof and Corinthian leather interior when a more sensible Saturn or even a VW microbus will do.

Types of Connections

This book assumes that your Internet connection is a "full" connection— one that includes electronic mail, TELNET, FTP (File Transfer Protocol), network news and all the other network niceties. "Partial" connections with only some of the features of a full connection are also available from some institutions and service providers, but they are not powerful enough to be of much use to the dedicated Internet cybernaut. With that understanding, there are only two types of individual or small business connections you need concern yourself with: a dedicated connection and a SLIP (Serial Line Internet Protocol) or PPP (Point-to-Point Protocol) connection.

Dedicated Connection

If you have a dedicated Internet connection, your Macintosh—or the local area network to which your Mac is connected—is directly connected to the Internet. These connections are most common for users within universities, government agencies and large corporations; they're usually too expensive for individuals and small businesses.

Dedicated connections offer three distinct advantages over SLIP or PPP connections:

- You can set up an FTP server, allowing anyone else on the Internet to access your files when it is most convenient for them (be careful, this can also be seen as a disadvantage in some organizations).

- You don't have to connect to the network each time you want to use it—you're always connected. Wherever you go, there you are.

▓ Your file transfers (and any other work you do on the Internet) will be accomplished much faster.

When you contract for a dedicated Internet connection, your service provider will lease a dedicated telephone line at the speed you specify and will install a *router* at your site. The faster the telephone line you specify, the more you'll pay.

The only disadvantage to a dedicated connection is that it's expensive; but like most everything else, you get what you pay for. If you need convenient, constant access or lightning-fast file transfer and data throughput, you won't be happy with anything less than a dedicated connection. But that performance comes at a great cost. As of summer 1993, a dedicated Internet connection would cost most small businesses between $15,000 and $20,000 for the first year and about $5,000 to $10,000 each subsequent year. Organizations with more than 50 employees pay fees tied to their usage rates, but the average per-employee cost is as much or more than for small businesses.

SLIP & PPP Connection

Luckily, access to the Internet needn't cost several thousands of dollars. Using a modem, you can get most of the benefits of a dedicated connection at only a fraction of the cost. SLIP and PPP allow you to establish an Internet connection over standard telephone lines via high-speed modems. If you have a SLIP or PPP Internet connection, your Macintosh is also directly connected to the Internet—*but only while the SLIP or PPP link is active.*

Although SLIP is currently the more common protocol, PPP will probably surpass SLIP in the near future. PPP offers more features and better throughput during interactive sessions where small bits of information are passed in both directions. Additionally, PPP is a recognized Internet standard for transferring IP information over serial lines (SLIP isn't). If you're given a choice, you're better off to go with a PPP connection—it's the up-and-coming standard.

Intercon Systems Corporation has released SLIP software for the Mac-intosh—InterSLIP—as freeware. It's available by anonymous FTP at ftp.intercon.com in the /pub/sales directory. While you may have a hard time retrieving Inter-SLIP through the Internet if you need it to log onto the Net, you can always have a friend or your network administrator download it for you.

MandelTV.
MandelTV is one of the slickest Mandelbrot set (fractal) generators available for the Macintosh. It's implemented as a desk accessory and requires color QuickDraw and a math coprocessor. You can download it by FTP from mac.archive.umich.edu in the /mac/system.extensions/da/ directory.

MacPPP is available as freeware by anonymous FTP at merit.edu in the /pub/ppp directory. (For information on using FTP, see "Using Fetch to Transfer Files" or "Using TCP/Connect II to Transfer Files" in Chapter 6, "Transferring Files.")

SLIP or PPP connections lack many of the features of a dedicated connection:

- Because you're using a modem rather than a direct network connection, getting files from here to there (and back again) will take significantly longer over a SLIP or PPP connection than with a dedicated connection.

- You cannot offer a reliable, constant FTP archive, so other users can't directly access your files at any time.

- Your connection to the Internet is active only while the modem connection is active; when you hang up the modem, you are no longer on the Internet.

- The connection isn't fast enough to support more than two or three users.

- You have to pay for at least one high-speed modem.

The biggest advantage to a SLIP or PPP connection is that you pay much lower connection costs. And unlike a less powerful dial-in connection, you are actually on the Internet while the connection is active. With the exception of offering a full-time FTP archive (something most individuals and small businesses would have limited use for anyway), you can do anything on the Internet with a SLIP or PPP connection that you can do with a dedicated connection at a literal fraction of the cost.

As of summer 1993, an individual commercial user can get SLIP or PPP access at a one-time startup fee of about $150 and monthly charges of about $65 for 80 hours of service. If you use more than 80 hours of connect time per month, you can expect to pay about $2 per hour for each additional hour.

SLIP or PPP access is usually the best alternative for individuals and is the method I use to connect myself and my very small business to the Internet.

Other Types of Connections

You can dial in to gain access to the Internet if you have an account on a computer that has a dedicated connection to the Internet (a university mainframe, for instance). Dial-in access to another computer is not as useful, powerful or easy to use as a SLIP or PPP connection, but it's much easier (and usually cheaper—sometimes free) to set up. Unfortunately for Macintosh users, dial-in access methods most often require you to use the archaic UNIX commands to traverse the Internet. And your dial-in connection may limit which Internet services you can use.

UUCP (UNIX to UNIX Copy Protocol) can also be considered an alternative type of connection. Every UNIX system supports UUCP as a method of moving information across standard telephone lines. You can usually find a service provider or an existing UUCP site that will allow you to use UUCP to transfer Internet mail and network news to your Macintosh—via a modem—but you won't really be "connected" to the Internet itself.

While this *Tour Guide* is geared for users with dedicated or SLIP/ PPP connections, if you only have limited dial-in access, you'll still find much of the information on electronic mail, network news and other Internet resources highly useful.

Service Providers

The following table shows contact information for some of the major service providers in the United States.

Figure 2-2: Internet service providers in the United States.

Service Provider	Region	Connections Offered
Advanced Networks and Services (ANS) 2901 Hubbard Rd. Ann Arbor, MI 48105 313/663-7610 info@ans.net	World	High-speed dedicated connections
BARRNET #115 Pine Hall, Stanford University Stanford, CA 94305-4122 415/725-1790 info@nic.barrnet.net	San Francisco, Calif.	Dedicated connections; SLIP/PPP
CERFnet PO Box 85608 San Diego, CA 92186 619/455-3900 help@cerf.net	Southern Calif.	Low- and Medium-speed dedicated connections; SLIP/PPP
CICnet 2901 Hubbard Dr., Pod A Ann Arbor, MI 48105 313/998-6103 info@cic.net	Midwest	Medium- and High-speed dedicated connections
Colorado Supernet Colorado School of Mines 1500 Illinois St. Golden, CO 80401 303/273-3471 gkolin@csn.org	Colorado	Low- and Medium-speed dedicated connections; SLIP/PPP
CONCERT PO Box 12889 3021 Cornwallis Rd. Research Triangle Park, NC 27709-2887 919/248-1999 info@concert.net	North Carolina	Medium-speed dedicated connections; SLIP/PPP
JVNCnet Global Enterprise Services 3 Independence Way Princeton, NJ 08540 609/897-7300 market@jvnc.net	Northeast	Low- and Medium-speed dedicated connections; SLIP
Netcom On-Line Communicaitons Services 4000 Moorpark Ave., Suite 209 San Jose, CA 95117 408/554-8649 info@netcom.com		

Service Provider	Region	Connections Offered
Merit 2200 Bonisteel Blvd. Ann Arbor, MI 48109 313/764-9430 info@merit.edu	Michigan	Low- to High-speed dedicated connections; SLIP/PPP
MIDnet 29 WSEC University of Nebraska Lincoln, NE 68588 402/472-5032 dmf@westie.mid.net	Lower Midwest	Low- and Medium-speed dedicated connections
Minnesota Regional Network (MRNet) 511 11th Ave. South, Box 212 Minneapolis, MN 55415 612/342-2570 hasting@mr.net	Minnesota	Low- and Medium-speed dedicated connections; SLIP
MSEN 628 Brooks St. Ann Arbor, MI 48103 313/998-4562 info@msen.com	Michigan	Low- and Medium-speed dedicated connections; SLIP/PPP
BBN Systems and Technologies (NEARnet) 10 Moulton St. Cambridge, MA 02138 617/873-8730 nearnet-join@nic.near.net	New England	Low- to High-speed dedicated connections; SLIP/PPP
netIllinois Bradley University 1501 West Bradley Ave. Peoria, IL 61625 309/677-3100 joel@bradley.edu	Illinois	Low- and Medium-speed dedicated connections
NorthWestNet 15400 SE 30th Place Suite 202 Bellevue, WA 98007 206/562-3000 ehood@nwnet.net	Pacific Northwest/ Northern Plains/ Alaska	Low- and Medium-speed dedicated connections

Service Provider	Region	Connections Offered
NYSERNet, Inc. 200 Elwood Davis Rd., Suite 103 Liverpool, NY 13088-6147 315/453-2912 info@nysernet.org	New York State	Low- and Medium-speed dedicated connections; SLIP/PPP
OARnet 1224 Kinnear Rd. Columbus, OH 43212 614/292-9248 ruth@oar.net	Ohio	Low- and Medium-speed dedicated connections; SLIP/PPP
Performance Systems International (PSI) 1180 Sunrise Valley Dr., Ste. 11800 Reston, VA 22091 703/620-6651 info@psi.com	World	Low- and Medium-speed dedicated connections; SLIP/PPP
PREPnet 305 South Craig, 2nd Fl. Pittsburgh, PA 15213 412/268-7870 twb+@andrew.cmu.edu	Pennsylvania	Low- and Medium-speed dedicated connections; SLIP/PPP
PSCnet 4400 Fifth Ave. Pittsburgh, PA 15213 412/268-4960 hastings@psc.edu	Eastern U.S.	Low- to High-speed dedicated connections
Sprint International 13221 Woodland Park Dr. Herndon, VA 22071 703/904-2156 mkiser@icm1.icp.net	World	Low- and Medium-speed dedicated connections
SURAnet 8400 Baltimore Blvd. College Park, MD 20740 301/982-4600 info@sura.net	Southeast	Medium- and High-speed dedicated connections
UUNET 3110 Fairview Park Dr., Ste. 570 Falls Church, VA 22042 703/204-8000 800/488-6383 info@uunet.uu.net	World	Low- and Medium-speed dedicated connections; SLIP/PPP

Service Provider	Region	Connections Offered
VERnet Academic Computing Center, Gilmer Hall University of Virginia Charlottesville, VA 22903 804/924-0616 vernet-info@ver.net	Virginia	Low- and Medium-speed dedicated connections; SLIP/PPP
Westnet 601 South Howes, 6th Fl. South Fort Collins, CO 80523 303/491-7260 pburns@yuma.acns.colostate.edu	West	Low- and Medium-speed dedicated connections
WiscNet 1210 West Dayton St. Madison, WI 53706 608/262-8874 dorl@macc.wisc.edu	Wisconsin	Low- and Medium-speed dedicated connections; SLIP/PPP

Resource Requirements

Hang on, you're almost there! Now that you know about the different types of available connections, and assuming you have an appropriate network connection and your account has been activated, let's explore exactly what hardware and software resources are required to connect to the Internet.

Macintosh

You'll need a Macintosh of course. Almost any Macintosh will do, although you'll be hard-pressed if your Mac doesn't have a hard drive and at least 4mb of RAM. (As in all things Macintosh, you can never have too much hard drive space or memory.) If you don't have enough RAM to run System 7, you should at least be using the most recent version of System 6 (Version 6.0.8). *But be aware that some software programs require System 7 for full functionality.*

Library of Congress Information System (LOCIS).

It's a great spectator sport—watching Congress in action. And you can do it if you have an IBM 3270-compatible terminal emulator. Luckily, the popular Mac Internet software, TCP/Connect II, can emulate just such a terminal. TELNET to locis.loc.gov and browse through the legislation that Congress introduces.

Sometimes it's rather alarming:

OFFICIAL TITLE(S):

AS INTRODUCED: (DATA FURNISHED BY THE HOUSE)

A concurrent resolution stating that Congress supports the suspension, with respect to the leadership of Iraq, of the prohibition of Executive Order 12333 on assassinations until Iraq has complied fully with all United Nations Security Council resolutions concerning the withdrawal of Iraqi military forces from Kuwait.

COMMITTEE(S) OF REFERRAL: House Foreign Affairs

SUBCOMMITTEE(S) OF REFERRAL:

Hsc International Security and Scientific Affairs

Hsc Europe and the Middle East

COSPONSORS

Rep. Holloway

Rep. Solomon

Rep. Paxon

Rep. Inhofe

Rep. Santorum

Rep. Barton

Rep. Rohrabacher

Rep. Spence

Rep. Ravenel

Network Interface Card or Modem

You'll also need a way of connecting to the Internet: either a high-speed modem or a network interface card. If you're with a large organization, someone will probably install and configure your network card hardware for you. If you're on your own, simply refer to the instructions that came with the card.

If you plan to access the Internet by SLIP or PPP, use at least a V.32 (9600 baud) modem, although I'd highly recommend a V.32bis/V.42bis (14,400 baud) modem, assuming your service provider supports the higher speed (and most do).

Buying a modem is simple in theory but difficult in practice: purchase the modem supporting the fastest *standard* modulation protocol and the best error correction and data compression you can afford.

MacSLIP or MacPPP

If you're connecting to the Internet with either SLIP or PPP, you'll need the appropriate LAP (Link Access Protocol) driver for MacTCP. (MacTCP is special software that you install in your System Folder to allow you to access the Internet. In most cases, your service provider or network administrator will configure and install MacTCP for you.) If you have a dedicated Internet connection, you do not need either of these drivers; you can skip the rest of this section and continue with "MacTCP" (the following section).

InterSLIP is available by anonymous FTP at ftp.intercon.com in the /pub/sales directory. MacPPP is available by anonymous FTP at merit.edu in the /pub/ppp/ directory. (For information on using FTP, see "Downloading Files With Fetch" or "Downloading Files With TCP/Connect II" in Chapter 6.)

The SLIP software I use and recommend is Hyde Park Software's MacSLIP. It's usually available from your service provider or network administrator. If you are an individual user, you can order MacSLIP directly from the manufacturer for about $50.

Hyde Park Software
PO Box 7133
Austin, TX 78713
512/454-1170
info@hydepark.com

MacTCP

You'll also need to install and properly configure MacTCP, the software that lets your Macintosh communicate with other computers on the Internet. If you're dying to know the technicalities of it all, MacTCP enables your Macintosh to use Transmission Control Protocol/Internet

Protocol (TCP/IP) to communicate with non-AppleTalk devices on the Internet.

Important note: MacTCP is included on the disk that came with this book. It is required to establish an Internet connection and use Macintosh-specific TCP/IP software programs. Regardless of whether you have a direct connection to the Net via Ethernet or a SLIP or PPP connection via ordinary telephone lines, you must install and properly configure MacTCP. Even though the basic procedures for installing and configuring MacTCP are the same, the exact details (which are crucial) are always different for everyone. For that reason, it's best to work directly with your network administrator or service provider to get MacTCP up and running. It is absolutely crucial that you not misconfigure MacTCP or use bogus IP addresses.

Alice in Wonderland.

The complete text of *Alice in Wonderland* has been made available by Project Gutenberg. Project Gutenberg was formed to encourage the creation and distribution of electronic text.

You can download the complete text of this and other works by FTP at mrcnext.cso.uiuc.edu in the /etext/ directory.

Client Application Software

Unless you're part of a large organization, getting a network connection and an account on the Internet is only half the battle. You'll also need some client application software (or software that let's you navigate and take advantage of the Internet). This can be something of a chicken-and-the-egg situation, since no such software is built into the Macintosh operating system or provided with your Mac when you buy it. If you need a special program to transfer other software programs to your Macintosh (*and you do*), how do you download a program that you need the program to download?

The Mac Internet Tour Guide Companion Disk is the best place to start. Programs and utilities are provided on the disk for *using* your Internet connection, but not for *establishing* the connection. You can use the programs provided on the disk to transfer, convert and decompress virtually any other program or utility you will need for using your Internet connection effectively. Best of all, the later chapters in this book address where to find and how to use the hottest software available on the Internet.

Making the Leap

OK, you've got your account established, you've got your network connection or modem configured, you've got MacTCP installed and configured, and you've got the software that came with this book loaded. Congratulations! You're finally ready to make the leap and make your first Internet connection.

If you enjoy a dedicated Internet connection, simply launch the client software program you want to use.

If you use a PPP or SLIP Internet connection, you will have to establish a modem connection to the network before you can launch any of the client software programs you may want to use. For information on how to establish a modem connection with your PPP or SLIP driver, refer to the documentation that came with the software or talk to your service provider or network administrator, who should give you a customized settings document to use with your PPP or SLIP driver to establish your Internet connection.

Moving On

Now you know how to get an Internet account—who to talk to and what to ask for—and a little bit about what you need to actually establish the connection.

As the bus pulls out of the station, go ahead and take a nap or stretch your legs as we get up to speed; that was a long time to spend in the terminal waiting for our old bus to be gassed up and made road-worthy. But the weather ahead looks favorable—feels like we even have a bit of a tail wind.

If you're anxious to get on the road and take a quick sidetrip on your own, feel free to skip ahead to Chapter 4, "Electronic Mail," where you'll learn how to send e-mail, search for addresses and even subscribe to mailing lists. Or, you can jump to Chapter 6 and download some software. But if you want to stay with the main group, we're heading for Chapter 3, where we'll learn what we need to know about the terrain and the natives we're likely to encounter.

NETWORK INFRASTRUCTURE
Electronic Alphabet Soup

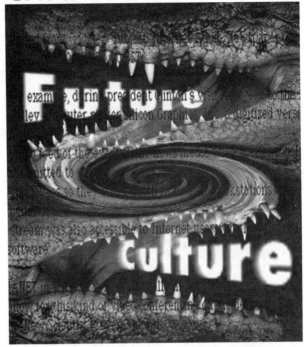

As the bus wends its way along the back-roads route (I hate the interstates—they all look the same—so this tour will follow the roads less traveled), now might be a good time to talk about the customs of the people you'll be meeting and the places you'll be visiting as we continue to explore the Internet.

I know you're eager to begin prowling the Internet, but reading this brief chapter before resuming our tour will pay off down the road. This chapter covers what absolute beginners need to know about how the Internet works. One of the most crucial aspects of navigating and using the Internet is understanding the complex and sometimes confusing addressing schemes used throughout the Net. It's important to know how Internet addresses work, not only for sending e-mail, but for locating and using the vast resources available throughout the Net. This chapter explores all you need to know about network addresses to find your way to any resource on the Internet.

We'll also cover what it means to be a good Internet citizen.

An Information Democracy

The Internet's strongest single organizing principle is the democratization of information. As open and untamed as the wild west, the Internet has no formal organization.

What organization there is can be thought of as a sort of "consensual information anarchy," a network of networks connected by everything from standard telephone lines to high-speed, dedicated, leased lines to fiber-optic links. Think of each component network as a fiefdom with its own organizational structure.

When someone talks about being "on" the Internet, their computer is connected to one of the interconnected networks that make up the Internet. Computers on the Internet talk to each other by passing notes to each other—just like we all did when we were in grade school. Only the computers on the Internet are a lot more particular about the whole process, as I'll explain shortly.

The Internet has only two practical organizing principles:

1. It serves to democratize information. Your network communications are handled in exactly the same manner, whether you are the chief executive of a Fortune 100 corporation or a junior high student.

2. Every computer on the Internet agrees to follow the same protocol—to speak a common language: TCP/IP, which is short for Transmission Control Protocol/Internet Protocol.

The Info-Mac archive.
Stanford University's Info-Mac archive is arguably the most popular Macintosh archive on the Internet. Like the University of Michigan Macintosh archive, just about any public domain, freeware or shareware program for the Macintosh is available here. The archive is accessible with TurboGopher, so use that whenever you can. Point your TurboGopher at sumex-aim.stanford.edu port 70. Alternatively, all files are available by anonymous FTP at sumex-aim.stanford.edu. A text file containing abstracts of all available files is available in the info-mac/help/ directory.

The Internet Rosetta Stone

To understand how your communications on the Internet are handled, you have to know a little bit about TCP/IP, the network's common language. Rather than bore you with unnecessary details, I'll only discuss the main points of TCP/IP. You need to know a good bit about TCP/IP to *administer* an Internet connection, but not to *use* one.

As I mentioned earlier, computers on the Internet talk to each other by passing notes, just like we did in grade school. Unfortunately, the Internet's component networks—and the computers that use the Net to communicate—aren't as intelligent as grade-schoolers. Grade-school kids can decipher just about any kind of note, folded any which way. Computers on the Internet are like a picky penmanship teacher; they require the message to be in a very specific language, and the note has to be folded just so. If the Internet note doesn't comply with the TCP/IP standard, it gets tossed faster than a school love poem intercepted by a lunchroom monitor.

So, if you want to communicate on the Internet, the software you use has to pass properly worded, carefully formatted notes. You can't just shout across the lunchroom, *"Hey! Augie! Pass me those peas!"* You have to use the proper decorum. You have to quietly pass your message in a note to your neighbor closest to Augie.

Transmission Control Protocol (TCP)

The Transmission Control Protocol (TCP)—the first piece of the protocol puzzle—controls the information you want to send across the Internet and separates it into smaller pieces that are easily managed. This allows you to send virtually any type of information, from text and graphics to sounds and video, or even actual shareware and software programs. And that information can range in size from a brief e-mail message to the complete works of William Shakespeare.

As TCP separates your information into manageable chunks, it numbers each piece, so the receiving end can put the pieces back together again in the proper order. As soon as each piece of information is received at the destination, TCP verifies it. If some pieces of your information are missing or garbled, TCP requests the originator to resend the missing or garbled pieces. When TCP has assembled all the information in the correct order, it sends it to the software program using its services. But remember, all this is going on at several thousands of bits per second, even if you're working over a modem, so the whole process is transparent to you.

Going back to Augie in the lunchroom, Augie would number each pea before putting them in a bowl and then pass you the bowl. You'd then take the bowl and eat each pea in numerical sequence. If you found a squished or missing pea, you'd pass a note back to Augie asking for a specific replacement pea. Hey now, I've seen stranger things in a lunchroom.

Internet Protocol (IP)

When you mail a paper message to a friend via the US Postal Service, you seal your message in an envelope containing both a destination and return address. When you drop your message in the mailbox, a mail carrier transports the message to a local post office where your message is combined with others bound for the same general destination. The messages are then loaded on trucks and planes and shipped off to their destinations. Once there, the sorting process is reversed, and your message is delivered.

Messages sent on the Internet (and everything you do on the Internet is basically a message) work in roughly the same way, thanks to the Internet Protocol (IP). The networks that make up the Internet are connected by special-purpose computers, called *routers*. These routers are the network equivalent of post offices; they determine how to route the information traffic on the Internet. Each router need only know what different connections are available and which is the best next destination to get a message closer to its final destination. The routers are physically linked by Ethernet networks and telephone lines—the network equivalents of the Postal Service's trucks and planes.

The Internet Protocol manages each message's addressing, working just like an addressed envelope for your paper mail.

Once again, returning to the lunchroom metaphor—and I promise this is the last time—think of the Internet Protocol as the lunchroom monitor. The monitor makes sure the bowl of peas Augie passes down the line gets routed most efficiently among all the schoolmates between the two of you, including the class bully, until it finally reaches you.

Travel advisories.

The State Department of the United States provides foreign travel advisories by FTP from world.std.com in the /obi/US.StateDept/Travel directory. I've always wanted to go to Belize; let's check out the travel advisory:

Belize—Consular Information Sheet—December 15, 1992

Embassy Location: The U.S. Embassy in Belize is located at the intersection of Gabourel Lane and Hutson Street in Belize City; telephone (501-2) 77161.

Country Description: Belize is a developing country. Its tourism facilities vary in quality.

Entry Requirements: A passport, a return/onward ticket, and sufficient funds are required for travel to Belize. US citizens who stay less than three months do not need visas. However, for visits exceeding one month, travelers must obtain permits from the immigration authorities in Belize. For further information, the traveler can contact the Embassy of Belize at 2535 Massachusetts Avenue N.W., Washington, D.C. 20008, (202) 332-9636. Or contact the Belize Mission to the U.N. in New York.

Medical Facilities: Medical care is limited. Doctors and hospitals often expect immediate cash payment for health services.

Crime Information: Petty crime, including pickpocketing and muggings, occurs. Visitors who walk alone on city streets, especially at night, or travel alone to a remote tourist site are particularly at risk.

Drug Penalties: Penalties for possession and trafficking in drugs are strict, and convicted offenders can expect jail sentences and fines.

Where.Is.That.Thing@On.the.Net?

While messages sent across the Internet may travel in a fashion similar to regular letters, the Internet addressing system looks nothing like a street address. Many beginners are intimidated by the complex and seemingly arcane—or apparently random—way Internet sites are named, or addressed. But a closer look at the process reveals a method to the madness, and learning that method will help you avoid plenty of confusion, panic and frustration.

Each computer on the Internet has two unique addresses:

- **IP address**, like 134.84.101.48 (always four numbers—each less than 256—separated by periods).

- **Domain name**, like deeper.farces.com (always at least two words—or numbers—separated by periods).

All you really have to know is the domain name (the nonnumeric one) of any computer on the Internet you want to communicate with. The Internet addressing schemes were designed so that people only had to use the domain name address, while the computers would use the IP address.

Each person on the Internet has his or her own unique address: username@domain.top domain. My Internet address, for example, is mfraase@farces.com. My machine name address is deeper.farces.com ("deeper" is the name of my Macintosh). An example of this domain name address and its structure is shown in Figure 3-1.

Figure 3-1: Example domain name address and structure.

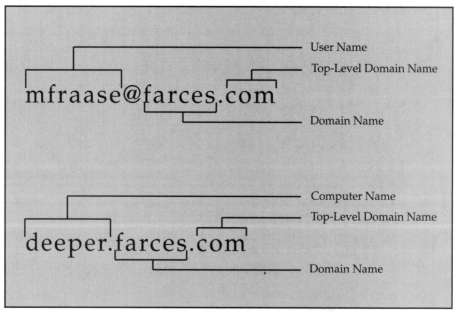

'Zine scene.

Lots of electronic 'zines are available at the Electronic Frontier Foundation's Gopher server and FTP archive. *Athene, CORE, Quanta, Unplastic News* and *ScreamBaby* are all available. Point your TurboGopher to gopher.eff.org port 70. Alternatively, you can FTP to ftp.eff.org and browse through the /pub/journals/ directory.

Domain name addresses have special pronunciation rules:

- mfraase@farces.com is pronounced "em-frazy at farces dot com."

- deeper.farces.com is pronounced "deeper dot farces dot com."

User names aren't always a first initial followed by the last name, as mine is. Sometimes they're a first and last name separated by an underscore, like Ida_Jones@idacorp.com. Others may be almost indecipherable, like mx121bc@cowcollege.edu. If you get a chance to choose your own user name, remember that people who send you e-mail will have to remember it. So pick something that's meaningful to other people as well as yourself.

Similarly, domain names aren't always a recognizable company or organization name. Domain names can be virtually anything, so long as they're unique, and they don't always refer to a specific business or other organization.

Generally, you can refer to computers on the Internet with either their IP address or their domain name address (although it's usually much easier to remember a domain name address), and you always refer to people with their domain-name address.

Have Your .Org Call My .Gov About That .Com

The last portion of a domain name address is called the top-level domain. It provides a clue about the computer or the person you're addressing. Top-level domain names are standardized throughout the Internet, as shown in Figure 3-2.

Figure 3-2: US top-level domain names.

Domain	Represents
com	businesses and commercial organizations
edu	educational institutions
gov	government institutions
mil	military organizations
net	network resources
org	other (usually nonprofit) organizations

All Internet sites outside the United States are identified by a unique two-character top-level domain name, as shown by the examples in Figure 3-3.

Figure 3-3: International top-level domain names.

Domain	Represents
au	Australia
at	Austria
bz	Belize
ca	Canada
dk	Denmark
fi	Finland
fr	France
de	Germany
it	Italy
jp	Japan
no	Norway

The top-level domain name for the United States is "us," although it's not used very often. Some Internet users identify themselves by their geographic location in their domain names. For example, the domain name username@well.sf.ca.us indicates a user on the Whole Earth 'Lectronic Link (WELL) located in San Francisco, California, United States.

Finger.
Finger is a Macintosh implementation of the UNIX Finger command. The archived file contains two programs, a Finger client and a Finger daemon. When Internet users Finger you or your machine, they'll see a report you can customize. The program is available by FTP from mac.archive.umich.edu in the /mac/util/comm/ directory.

Here are a few tips to help you deal with the alphabet soup of Internet domain-name addresses:

■ The example addresses used in this chapter are very simple. My editor's Internet address, for example, is ruffin@gibbs.oit.unc.edu. Ruffin's account is on a computer named Gibbs (gibbs) in the Office of Information and Technology (oit) at the University of North Carolina (unc), an educational facility (edu).

■ The computer networks on the Internet aren't picky about case-sensitivity. For instance, mFraase@Farces.COM, Mfraase@farces.Com, and MFRAASE@FARCES.COM will all reach me just as efficiently.

■ Make sure to write down important e-mail addresses. I can't tell you the number of times I thought I could remember an e-mail address only to have forgotten it by the time I needed it. Keep a hard-copy record of your e-mail address book. You never know when it might be accidentally deleted from the computer that maintains your account.

Eudora.
Eudora is one of the best Internet e-mail programs available for the Macintosh. Freeware and commercial versions are available. You can always download the latest release of the freeware version and its associated documentation by FTP from ftp.qualcomm.com in the mac/eudora/ directory. Information about the commercial version of the software is available by e-mail from eudora-info@qualcomm.com.

When in Rome... Don't Tie Up the Phone Lines

If your friend Augie invites you to dinner, you have to know more than just how to get to his house. You also need to know which water glass is yours (is it the one on the left or the one on the right?) and which fork to use for the salad. Before you set out on your Internet explorations, take a moment to review a few tips that may keep you from alienating anyone or making a fool out of yourself right away. We all make fools of ourselves on the Net at one time or another; here's hoping you can delay your fool debut for a while.

Acceptable Use Policies

Although the acceptable use policies of the various networks that make up the Internet are rapidly changing, we'll all probably have to deal with them at least until the mid-1990s. Instead of reprinting all of the different acceptable use policies, I'll just go over the main points.

To some extent, your category of Internet connection determines how you can use the Internet. If you're classified as an educational, research or noncommercial user, your Internet activities must be restricted to the purpose of research, education, charitable activities, government affairs, individual professional development or public service. If you're classified as a commercial user, your Internet activities are unrestricted (except, of course, for activities that are specified as unacceptable). Research and educational network traffic is routed over connections subsidized by taxpayers; commercial network traffic is routed over private connections. You don't have to worry about how your traffic is routed; that's the responsibility of your service provider.

Most service providers specify these uses as unacceptable:

- Distribution of unsolicited advertising.
- Transmission of anything that causes disruption of service to others.
- Propagation of computer worms or viruses.
- Use of the network to make unauthorized entry to any resource.

In addition, most service providers require you to abide by some general common-sense usage guidelines:

- Respect the privacy of other users.
- Usage must be consistent with common ethical practice and community standards.
- Respect copyrights and licenses of programs, information and documents.

Nuntius.
Nuntius is a Macintosh network news reader that employs the familiar Mac interface. It uses the NNTP protocol and allows you to follow message threads within the various newsgroups. The program is available by FTP from mac.archive.umich.edu in the /mac/util/comm/ directory.

Finally, some service providers may require you to comply with the NSFNET Backbone Services Acceptable Use Policy. Ask your service provider or network administrator if your Internet activity is affected by this policy.

And if your idea of a good time is to wade through pages of legalese, you can always retrieve the complete documents from various archives on the Internet. For more information on how and where to get these documents, refer to "Downloading Files With Fetch"and "Transferring Files With TurboGopher" in Chapter 6, "Transferring Files."

Security Issues

With the rapid growth of the Internet, computer security becomes a more serious issue each year, especially when you're sharing resources across the Net. While your Internet connection is active, your computer—and perhaps more important, any other resources attached to your computer via a local-area network—are all on the Internet. It is your responsibility to protect your own system.

You also have a responsibility to be a good Internet citizen. You have been granted access to a worldwide resource and should respect the privacy and property of others.

If we, as Internet inhabitants, don't manage our own security wisely, it's likely that some less-than-benevolent government agency will take it upon itself to manage things for us.

Fetch.
Fetch is currently the best Macintosh FTP client software program. Fetch is distributed as freeware for non-profit and educational users and as shareware for commercial users. You can always download the latest release of the software and its associated documentation by FTP from dartmouth.edu in the /pub/mac/ directory. Site license information for commercial users is available by e-mail from fetch@dartmouth.edu.

First Names Are Lousy Passwords

Your login password is your security key, and is the most likely way someone will gain unauthorized access to your Internet account. Guard your password with care. Don't write it down, don't allow others to use it and change it often.

A good password:

- is made up of at least six characters that do not form a word

- includes both uppercase and lowercase letters and numerals

- is easily remembered, but is something no one can guess

If you think your Internet account is being hacked—or if you suspect that your computer has been broken into—talk to your network administrator or service provider immediately.

TurboGopher.

Gopher lets you burrow through information resources using a series of easy to navigate menus that appear as standard Macintosh file folders and icons. You can use TurboGopher on the Macintosh to navigate huge dataspaces just by double-clicking the mouse button. The current version of TurboGopher is always available by FTP (or Gopher) from boombox.micro.umn.edu in the /pub/gopher/Macintosh-TurboGopher/ directory.

Usage Courtesy

Everything you do on the Internet has potential ramifications beyond the Net. The unwritten rule underlying all Internet activity is simple: *The Internet is a good thing and it must be protected.* While unwritten, this rule is enforced with impartial severity. If you screw up badly enough, you can expect to lose your access privileges. While there are no etiquette handbooks or Internet finishing schools, the same common sense and social grace you use in the real world will generally be enough to get you through most potentially sticky Internet situations.

While some of the tips and advice in this section may mean little to you now, they'll become second nature once you get your Internet legs:

- **Anonymous FTP isn't.** Always use your e-mail address as your login password when accessing remote FTP servers as an anonymous user. (See Chapter 6 for more on accessing FTP sites.) You can always make up a phony e-mail address when you visit far-flung spots on the Net, but don't bother. Cookie-crumb trails will lead back to your site, if not directly to you.

- **Leave your ethnocentricity at the door.** Many juicy Internet resources reside in foreign countries. Be careful with the cultural references you use.

- **Don't tie up popular sites at busy times.** Be aware that shared resources on the Internet may actually be in use by real people trying to do real work. Try to access the busiest resources during off-peak hours whenever possible (unless, of course, you're a real person doing real work). Be sensitive to time zones; think about what time it is where you're *going* rather than where you *are*. Try to find alternative routes to the busiest and most popular resources. Many popular archives have less crowded "mirror" sites elsewhere on the Net. Learn where they are and use them when possible.

- **Try to find the closest source for what you need.** Don't FTP or Gopher to Finland for a file you know is available a mere one or two hops away from your local site.

- **Don't use remote resources when you can use local ones.** Don't use archive space clear across the world for your personal files, just because you can't afford a bigger hard drive.

- **Log off properly.** Make sure you leave all resources in the same condition and state in which you found them. If you log off improperly, you may leave certain tasks or processes running in the background of the host machine, causing problems for other users or worse, network administrators.

Keep in mind that nothing on the Internet is really free. Somebody is paying for it. And if everyone takes a "free ride" on the most popular and expensive Net resources, it won't be long before those same resources are protected, restricted or closed to public access.

You'll find more Internet etiquette advice in the chapters that deal with specific network services.

Moving On

Now you know how the Internet works and how computers and people are identified. You've also looked at how to best get along with your fellow Internet inhabitants. The next chapter guides you through the wonders of using electronic mail on the Internet. You'll learn how to use the best Mac Internet e-mail software and how to communicate via e-mail with people who aren't even on the Internet.

ELECTRONIC MAIL
The Pony Express Goes Digital

Our tour bus has been making pretty good time, sticking to the back roads. But we've been rolling along for some time now, and some of you may want to send a message to your friends and family back home, just to let them know you're having a great time. So let's take a look at how to use electronic mail to communicate privately with individuals and small groups on the Internet.

With the exception of gestures, e-mail is arguably the most efficient means of communications yet devised by humans. Because it uses recycled phosphors on your Macintosh screen, e-mail is ecological—nary a tree and very little energy is used to create, deliver and read e-mail messages. You can choose to read your e-mail whenever is most convenient for you, not when it's convenient for someone else. You can scan an electronic in-box full of e-mail faster than you can open a single paper mail envelope. You can easily forward, store or reply to e-mail messages with the touch of a button. Sending messages to dozens of people is a snap with the multiple-addressing capabilities of e-mail. And there are a host of other features that make e-mail one of the most powerful and convenient ways to communicate.

But lots of people never get the most from their e-mail systems because they have to wrestle with arcane and obscure commands and abbreviations, just to send a simple message. Forget about all that command-line nonsense. You're a Macintosh user, and there are excellent tools available that provide an elegant Mac interface for the Internet's electronic mail services. After all, electronic mail is only effective if you actually use it, and who wants to put up with a UNIX-based, command-driven e-mail program, when simple, Mac-specific options are available?

E-mail is an incredibly powerful form of communication, and there are plenty of Internet users who do little on the Net besides send mail. Consequently, we'll be spending more time discussing e-mail than any other topic in the course of our tour. So before we get started, let's pull off to the side of the road and take a look at the map of what we'll be covering in this chapter:

- What is E-Mail & How Does it Work?
- E-Mail Etiquette & Courtesy
- How to Send E-Mail Anywhere
- Quick Guide to Using Eudora (included on companion disk)
- Quick Guide to Using TCP/Connect II
- Finding Addresses
- Electronic Mailing Lists
- E-Mail & Attached Files

We've got a long road ahead, so hang on tight and let's get started!

What is E-Mail & How Does it Work?

Most people who have never used e-mail have trouble understanding why it's touted over regular mail, fax or even phone conversations. It takes anywhere from a few seconds to a few minutes to deliver an e-mail message (complete with attached files) anywhere in the world. A postal delivery usually takes several days to reach its destination, and the telephone system is immediate, but both parties have to be on the phone at the same time. Fax was the rage in the '80s because it was fairly easy to use and didn't require a computer. But this chapter shows why so many people prefer e-mail to phone, fax or paper mail.

You can use e-mail to

- **Send text-based messages to any other Internet user.** You can also send messages to users on commercial electronic mail and information services. Soon you'll be able to send messages that contain fully formatted text, pictures, sound and even video— *between different types of computers and operating systems.*

- **Attach computer files to text messages.** You can send binary files— complete software programs or fully formatted files—to any other Internet user and users on most of the commercial electronic mail and information services. (Why send a static, dead document via fax when you can work with a live one via e-mail?)

- **Send messages and files to multiple recipients.** Where telephones tend to be useful for one-to-one communications, e-mail is useful for both one-to-one and one-to-many communications.

- **Reply to or forward messages you receive.** You can quickly and easily dash off a reply to a message, or forward it to other users around the world.

- **Subscribe to electronic mailing lists.** You can add your name to any of the thousands of mailing lists whose topics range from Macintosh hardware and software to political debates and discussions.

- **Communicate with mail list servers.** By sending e-mail queries to special addresses, you can query list servers that automatically respond to special commands by returning to you specific information, documents or other files.

Electronic mail is different from other Internet services in one important way—the sending and the receiving computers need not be able to connect directly with each other. You create e-mail messages on your computer and send them to a *mail server*. The mail server determines the best route to reach the recipient and passes the e-mail to the next closest mail server. The e-mail is passed through any number of mail servers and is eventually delivered to the final recipient's mail server. This is called a *store-and-forward* service, and it happens much faster than it took you to read about the process.

Smithsonian Institution photograph archive.
The Smithsonian Institution has begun to archive electronic versions of its photographs and art collections. The archive is accessible by FTP at photo1.si.edu in the directory /pub/images/. Unfortunately, this machine has a poor network connection. Daily updates are mirrored at the University of North Carolina and are accessible by FTP at sunsite.unc.edu in the /pub/multimedia/pictures/smithsonian/ directory.

Like the phone system and the Postal Service, e-mail isn't infallible. Occasionally, an e-mail message doesn't reach its intended destination. Any e-mail that does not reach its recipient is returned to the sender as undeliverable mail. This is called a *bounced* e-mail message. Reasons for bounced mail include (in order of likelihood)

- **User unknown** (incorrect address in the username portion of the address).
- **Host unknown** (incorrect address in the domain or top-domain portions of the address).
- **Network unreachable** (gateway limitations or problems with the network backbone).
- **Connection timed out** (software problem on the destination mail server).
- **Connection refused** (problem with the destination mail server).

The important point here is, if your e-mail message is undeliverable—for whatever reason—it will be bounced back to you. Many first-time e-mail users waste countless hours worrying if their messages are delivered, often following e-mail transmissions with faxes and phone calls to the effect of "Did you get my e-mail?" As a general rule, assume that your e-mail efforts are successful rather than figuring they don't work at all.

E-Mail Etiquette & Courtesy

Electronic mail eliminates a lot of subtle impediments to effective communication. Judgments based on appearance, voice or social position are impossible in electronic communications. E-mail's asynchronous nature—the ability to deal with a message when it's most convenient for all parties involved—is truly a boon to communications among individuals and groups.

One of the most amazing things about e-mail is the immediacy of its delivery. When you click that **Send** button, your message is delivered in seconds. This is a great advantage in most cases, but can work as a disadvantage if you have a short fuse. Unlike a letter, which may sit on a desk for hours or days before being mailed, electronic communications are usually dashed off as soon as they're completed. If you've been using e-mail for a while, you'll notice that a lot of the messages you receive (and perhaps a few you've written) shouldn't have been sent. It pays to ponder the ramifications of an e-mail message before launching it into the electronic ether—once it's gone out, there's no way to get it back.

The price you pay for e-mail's convenience and speed is a fairly high potential for misunderstanding. The best way to avoid e-mail misinterpretations and mixed signals is to follow three simple, common-sense rules of e-mail etiquette and courtesy.

1. *Don't send anything via e-mail that you wouldn't want to read in your hometown newspaper.* Invariably, that juicy e-mail message is read by the one person who was never meant to read it. There are lots of stories about the politics of e-mail, and until the law catches up with the technology, you're better off playing it safe. Assume your e-mail messages are available to anyone who wants to read them. Some companies even have a policy making e-mail the property of the company, not the individual correspondents. In early 1993, the Georgia Institute of Technology announced that it would no longer consider e-mail delivered to any of its systems on the Internet to be private. Already, landmark legal cases about trade secrets, corporate espionage and e-mail are filtering through the courts. E-mail *should* enjoy all the rights and securities of paper mail, but don't make the mistake of assuming that it *does.*

2. *Facial expressions and body language don't fit through the narrow bandwidth of e-mail.* Statements that you intend as pithy may come across as condescending or sarcastic. Some people approach e-mail as conversational; others don't. Some people never take e-mail personally, others always do. Unless you're close friends with an e-mail recipient, never expect that he or she will understand your sense of humor, wry wit or playful repartee.

3. *You can't control when your message will be delivered, so assume it will arrive at the worst possible time.* Be careful with your wording. What may seem funny or cute today may be inappropriate or rude when e-mail is read tomorrow. Just because e-mail is delivered at warp speed doesn't mean it's read at the same rate. Lots of people get more e-mail than they can keep up with; keep that in mind as you compose your missive. If you only read three e-mail messages a day, you'll probably remember them all for a few days. But people who receive dozens of messages need reminders (or forwarded messages) to help clue them in to the context of previous correspondence.

Auto-Advice From EmilyPost.

If you think you get some perplexing junk paper mail, consider receiving this automated e-mail message:

Dear Net-Mail User [o EweR-635-78-2267-3 aSp]:

Your mailbox has just been rifled by EmilyPost, an autonomous courtesy-worm chain program released in October 2036 by an anonymous group of Net subscribers in western Alaska. [o ref: sequestered confession 592864 -2376298.98634, deposited with Bank Leumi 10/23/36:20:34:21. Expiration-disclosure 10 years.] Under the civil disobedience sections of the Charter of Rio, we accept in advance the fines and penalties that will come due when our confession is released in 2046. However we feel that's a small price to pay for the message brought to you by EmilyPost.

In brief, dear friend, you are not a very polite person. EmilyPost's syntax analysis subroutines show that a very high fraction of your Net exchanges are heated, vituperative, even obscene.

Of course you enjoy free speech. But EmilyPost has been designed by people who are concerned about the recent trend toward excessive nastiness in some parts of the Net. EmilyPost homes in on folks like you and begins by asking them to please consider the advantages of politeness.

For one thing, your credibility ratings would rise. (EmilyPost has checked your favorite bulletin boards, and finds your ratings aren't high at all. Nobody is listening to you, sir!) Moreover, consider that courtesy can foster calm reason, turning shrill antagonism into useful debate and even consensus.

We suggest introducing an automatic delay to your mail system. Communications are so fast these days, people seldom stop and think. Some Net users act like mental patients who shout out anything that comes to mind, rather than as functioning citizens with the human gift of tact.

If you wish, you may use one of the public-domain delay programs included in this version of EmilyPost, free of charge.

Of course, should you insist on continuing as before, disseminating nastiness in all directions, we have equipped EmilyPost with other options you'll soon find out about....

—From David Brin's *Earth* (Bantam, 1990).

E-Mail Privacy

If I took a paper letter from your mailbox, opened it and read it, I'd be guilty of a federal offense. If I did the same thing by intercepting or retrieving your e-mail, chances are I would not be committing a crime.

Electronic communications are not given the same protection as first-class mail. As the rapid rate of change outpaces the social and legal conventions that govern how we use technology, we continue to suppose that we have freedoms and rights that simply do not exist. For example, in the past, wiretapping had to be physically carried out. A spook had to be near the person under surveillance. A tape recorder had to be in the immediate vicinity of persons recorded. With advancements in telephone switching technology, this is no longer the case. Anyone can now easily eavesdrop on conversations simply by sending the proper signal tones down the telephone wire—from anywhere.

In 1986, President Ronald Reagan signed into law the Electronic Communications Privacy Act (ECPA). The act is designed to expand the scope of telecommunications covered under the protection of the 1968 federal wiretapping laws. The ECPA protects electronic mail, cellular telephones, pagers and electronic data transmission. It also requires government agencies to obtain a court order before intercepting electronic communications.

The ECPA, as currently written, has two main goals:

1. Protecting all electronic communications systems, including e-mail, from outside intrusion.

2. Protecting the privacy of certain messages transmitted over public-service e-mail systems.

The ECPA makes it a federal crime to intercept certain electronic communications, but makes a distinction between public and internal electronic communications systems. Most importantly, electronic mail messages transmitted within internal e-mail systems that are used solely for interoffice communications are not subject to the privacy provisions of the ECPA. That means that a company can read such messages without invading the privacy of employees. Electronic mail messages transmitted within internal e-mail systems that allow outside access can be read by a company if either the sender or receiver grants permission. Reading electronic mail messages exchanged over public e-mail systems by anyone other than the sender and receiver is a felony under the ECPA. To make matters more confusing, it's not clear whether the Internet is considered a public e-mail system under the ECPA.

If this all seems a little vague and you're wondering how it relates to you as an e-mail user, a recent poll conducted by *Macworld* magazine might bring the issue into clearer focus. In its July 1993 issue, *Macworld* published the results of a nationwide poll of top corporate managers from 301 businesses of varying sizes. The poll found that 21 percent of respondents have "engaged in searches of employee computer files, voice mail, electronic mail or other networking communications." The figure was even higher—30 percent—among large companies.

E-Mail Horror Stories.

Linda Ellerbee's infamous Associated Press e-mail incident didn't so much involve eavesdropping or invasion of privacy as it did the simple misrouting of electronic communications. Ellerbee, so the story goes, sent a note to a friend through the Associated Press e-mail system. The note included some very nasty comments about her boss and the Dallas city council, as well as other Texas luminaries. An accident in the network caused the message to be distributed to every AP outlet in four states. Ellerbee lost her job over the incident, and the potential for legal action by everyone involved—including Ellerbee, her boss and the AP—was gigantic.

In the summer of 1990, the members of the city council of Colorado Springs became outraged when they discovered the mayor was secretly reading their private e-mail messages.

In August of 1990, Alana Shoars, a network administrator in charge of electronic mail at Epson America, Inc., filed a lawsuit against the company. Shoars's lawsuit alleged that her supervisor, Robert Hillseth, manager of data communications for Epson, had intercepted her MCI Mail messages on a regular basis as they were passing through the company's network gateway. Shoars claims that when she complained about Hillseth's activities, he fired her. Shoars filed an individual suit for wrongful termination and also filed a class action suit with 2,500 other current and former Epson employees, asking for unspecified damages of up to $3,000 per violation. That's $3,000 for each message that was intercepted. The class action suit was filed as an invasion of privacy under Section 631 of the California Penal Code.

Secret Service Director John Simpson admitted in a letter to California State Representative Don Edwards that the United States government has been intercepting private e-mail and surreptitiously monitoring computer bulletin boards in order to track the activities of suspected hackers.

While there are various techniques for encrypting or otherwise protecting e-mail messages, they are not always practical or convenient, and no system is completely foolproof. So until specific laws are passed and sweeping policy changes are enacted by government and business alike, the lesson here is clear: assume that your e-mail messages are being read by people other than their intended recipients.

How to Send E-Mail Anywhere

You can do anything with e-mail that you can do with postal mail, except mail physical objects. With an Internet account, you can even send e-mail to people who have accounts on one of the commercial electronic mail or information services like MCI Mail or CompuServe.

Addressing e-mail on the Internet is standardized and simple, despite how arcane or inscrutable some Internet addresses seem. Everyone's Internet e-mail address, as explained in "The Parts of an Internet Address" in Chapter 3, "Network Infrastructure," is formatted the same:

username@domain.top-domain

To send e-mail to someone on the Internet, just address the message to their Internet address.

The next six sections detail how to send and receive mail from most of the common commercial information services that provide an *e-mail gateway* to the Internet.

An e-mail gateway is software or hardware that connects networks that use different protocols. In effect, it translates between the protocols so that computers on the connected networks can exchange data. Be careful with the size of the files you send by e-mail. Most of the e-mail gateways provided by the commercial information services like CompuServe and America Online have severe file-size limitations, as indicated in Figure 4-1.

E-mail addresses are not case-sensitive, and most people don't care how you capitalize their name or domain name, as long as their e-mail gets to them.

Internet to UUCP & Back

UUCP, the UNIX-to-UNIX Copy Program, is a protocol used by UNIX workstations to communicate with each other over telephone lines. UUCP is also commonly referred to as a network, because e-mail and files can be sent to any UUCP-capable computer by specifying which intermediate computers the e-mail must pass through to reach the final recipient. Since many UUCP sites are switching over to full domain name registration, you might first check to see if your recipient has a standard Internet domain name address.

To send e-mail to a UUCP user, use the format:

user@host.uucp

or

user%host.uucp@gateway

For example, to send e-mail to Peter Piper (whose user ID is *ppiper*) at his Megacorp (*megacorp.uucp*) host, use the format:

ppiper@megacorp.uucp

Alternatively, if Megacorp uses the Performance Systems International (PSI) gateway to receive e-mail (check with Peter or his assistant if you aren't sure), use the address format:

ppiper%megacorp.uucp@uu.psi.com

Sometimes UUCP users will provide you with what's called a *bang-path address*. Bang-path addresses are easily spotted because they contain exclamation marks (!):

...!uunet!megacorp!ppiper

The exclamation marks are pronounced as "bang." The above address would be pronounced as "from bang uunet bang megacorp bang ppiper."

You can always convert bang path addresses to this format:

user%host.uucp@gateway

UUCP users with access to an e-mail gateway send e-mail messages to colleagues on the Internet using the standard domain name addressing:

user@domain.top-domain

For example, UUCP users with access to a gateway address e-mail to my Internet address as:

mfraase@farces.com

UUCP users without access to a gateway must route Internet e-mail using whatever paths are appropriate to reach a computer that is connected to the Internet.

"Dear Sysadmin, Punish your user for what he said!"

In mid-April 1993, Carl Kadie asked a variety of system administrators how they respond to the above request from Internet users. The responses were very interesting:

Ten respondents explained the value of free expression or replied that punishing users wasn't their job.

Seven respondents told the accused to "cool it" (or else).

Four respondents said the situation has never come up.

Two respondents said they judge the article and punish the user if the posting is found to violate policy.

One respondent removed the entire newsgroup in which the article was posted.

One respondent told the complainer "we'll handle it," but didn't do anything to follow up.

One respondent passed the complaint up the chain of command.

Internet to CompuServe & Back

CompuServe is a commercial information service that opened an e-mail gateway to the Internet in July 1989. CompuServe subscribers are assigned a unique identification number as a user name, in the format:

71234,5678

To send e-mail to a CompuServe subscriber, use the format:

useridentification.number@compuserve.com

For example, to send e-mail to Peter Piper (whose CompuServe ID number is *71234,5678*) use the address format:

71234.5678@compuserve.com

Note that the comma in the recipient's user identification number is translated to a period.

You should also remember that there is a 50,000-character limit on e-mail messages that pass through CompuServe's Internet gateway.

CompuServe subscribers send e-mail to the Internet using the format:

>Internet:user@domain.top-domain

For example, CompuServe subscribers address e-mail to my Internet address as:

>Internet:mfraase@farces.com

Internet to MCI Mail & Back

MCI Mail is a commercial electronic mail service that has offered an experimental Internet gateway since the late 1980s; the gateway is no longer considered experimental. MCI Mail subscribers are assigned a unique MCI ID number, an MCI ID name and a full user name, in the following respective formats:

557-4126

mfraase

Michael Fraase

To send e-mail to an MCI Mail subscriber, use any of the three following formats:

idnumber@mcimail.com

idname@mcimail.com

full_user_name@mcimail.com

For example, to send e-mail to any of the above three MCI Mail address formats, use the three following formats respectively:

5574126@mcimail.com

mfraase@mcimail.com

michael_fraase@mcimail.com

Note that when you use the **idnumber@mcimail.com** *format, the dash separating the numbers is eliminated.* Also, spaces—like those between first and last names—are translated to the underscore (_) character.

There is no limit on the size of e-mail messages that pass through the MCI Mail Internet gateway.

MCI Mail subscribers send e-mail to the Internet with the following steps:

1. At the **Command**: prompt, type **create** and press Return.
2. At the **TO**: prompt, type the full name of the recipient followed by **(EMS)** and press Return.
3. At the **EMS**: prompt, type **Internet** and press Return.
4. At the **MBX**: prompt, type the recipient's Internet domain name address in the format **user@domain.top-domain** and press Return.

For example, MCI Mail subscribers address e-mail to my Internet address as follows:

1. At the **Command**: prompt, type **create** and press Return.
2. At the **TO**: prompt, type **Michael Fraase (EMS)** and press Return.
3. At the **EMS**: prompt, type **Internet** and press Return.
4. At the **MBX**: prompt, type **mfraase@farces.com** and press Return.

Internet to America Online & Back

America Online is a commercial information service that maintains an e-mail gateway to the Internet. Each America Online subscriber has a unique "screen name" as a user name, at least three and no more than ten characters long.

To send e-mail to an America Online subscriber, use the format:

screenname@aol.com

For example, to send e-mail to Peter Piper (PetePiper) use the address format:

petepiper@aol.com

Note that there is a 27,000-character limit on e-mail messages that pass through America Online's Internet gateway.

America Online subscribers send e-mail to the Internet using the standard domain name addressing:

user@domain.top-domain

For example, America Online subscribers address e-mail to my Internet address as:

mfraase@farces.com

Internet to AT&T Mail & Back

AT&T Mail is a commercial electronic mail service that opened an e-mail gateway to the Internet in June 1990. Each AT&T Mail subscriber is assigned a unique user name.

To send e-mail to an AT&T Mail subscriber, use the format:

username@attmail.com

For example, to send e-mail to Peter Piper (ppiper) use the address format:

ppiper@attmail.com

AT&T Mail subscribers send e-mail to the Internet using the standard domain name addressing:

user@domain.top-domain

For example, AT&T Mail subscribers address e-mail to my Internet address as:

mfraase@farces.com

Internet to AppleLink & Back

AppleLink is a commercial information service that Apple Computer initially provided for developers, dealers and employees, but Apple now offer accounts to the general public as well. Each AppleLink subscriber is assigned a unique user name.

Note that AppleLink subscribers have to specifically enable the Internet gateway for their account (see below). By default, all AppleLink accounts have the Internet gateway turned off. This means that if you send e-mail to an AppleLink subscriber who has not enabled the Internet gateway for his or her account, your e-mail will be re-turned as undeliverable. *The AppleLink service also carries a fifty-cent surcharge for each message either entering or leaving the AppleLink e-mail gateway to the Internet.*

To send e-mail to an AppleLink subscriber, use the format:

username@applelink.apple.com

For example, to send e-mail to Peter Piper (piper1) use the address format:

piper1@applelink.apple.com

Note that there is a 32,000-character limit on e-mail messages that pass through AppleLink's Internet gateway.

Before an AppleLink subscriber can send e-mail to the Internet, he or she has to enable the Internet gateway for his or her account by sending an empty e-mail message to the address:

TurnOn@Internet#

AppleLink subscribers send e-mail to the Internet using the format:

usernname@domain.top-domain@internet#

The entire address (not counting the "@internet#" portion) must be less than a total of 35 characters or the e-mail will be returned as unde-liverable.

For example, AppleLink subscribers address e-mail to my Internet address as:

mfraase@farces.com@internet#

"Dear Sysadmin, Punish your user for what he said!" Revisited.

In mid-April 1993, Carl Kadie asked a variety of system administrators how they respond to the above request from Internet users. Here's one of the responses he received:

"I believe you need a short lesson in the operation of free speech. I have no particular opinions on the subject of this newsgroup, but I took the trouble to read some of the 'belligerent and harassing' postings of which you speak, and, frankly, they weren't."

"It seems to me that your attempt to characterize them as such stems from a desire to stifle ideas with which you disagree. I have no intention of cooperating with you in this. The remedy for speech with which you disagree is more speech, not a silencing (the rather low signal-to-noise ratio on USENET notwithstanding)."

"If these postings offend you, I suggest you find out how 'kill files' work, rather than wasting the time of overworked system administrators who aren't being underpaid to deal with this sort of childishness."

Cross-Network E-Mail Addressing Quick Reference

The addressing information presented in the previous six sections is distilled for quick reference in the table in Figure 4-1.

Figure 4-1: Cross-network e-mail addressing at a glance.

Service	From Internet	To Internet
UUCP [1]	user@host.uucp user%host.uucp@gateway …!gateway!host!user	user@domain.top-domain [1]
CompuServe	user.number@compuserve.com [2]	>Internet:user@domain.top-domain
MCI Mail	idnumber@mcimail.com [3] idname@mcimail.com full_user_name@mcimail.com	TO: recipient's full name (EMS) EMS: Internet MBX: user@domain.top-domain
America Online	screenname@aol.com [4]	user@domain.top-domain
AT&T Mail	username@attmail.com	user@domain.top-domain
AppleLink [5]	username@applelink.apple.com [6]	usernname@domain.top-domain@internet# [7]

[1] Requires access to a gateway.

[2] The comma in the recipient's user identification number is translated to a period. There is a 50,000-character limit on e-mail messages that pass through CompuServe's Internet gateway.

[3] The dash separating the numbers is eliminated.

[4] There is a 27,000-character limit on e-mail messages that pass through America Online's Internet gateway.

[5] Before an AppleLink subscriber can send or receive Internet e-mail, he or she has to enable the Internet gateway for his or her account.

[6] There is a 32,000-character limit on e-mail messages that pass through AppleLink's Internet gateway.

[7] The entire address (not counting the "@internet#" portion) must be less than a total of 35 characters or the e-mail will be returned as undeliverable.

Quick Guide to Using Eudora

Eudora is an electronic mail program for the Macintosh that is fully compatible with the POP3 mail server offered by most Internet service providers. (If you're not sure whether Eudora is compatible with your mail server, ask your network administrator.) Originally written by Steve Dorner at the Urbana campus of the University of Illinois, Eudora is now supported by Qualcomm, Inc. and will likely become a commercial product in the near future.

The current release of the freeware version of Eudora is provided on the *Macintosh Internet Tour Guide's* companion disk. The Eudora program is packaged in a self-extracting archive file on the disk and must be decompressed before you can use it. For information on how to decompress the archive file, see the instructions in the "Double-Click Me First" file on the companion disk.

To install Eudora, you'll need about 320k of free disk space (plus an additional 100k or so if you want to store e-mail in a folder within Eudora's folder structure). You'll also need at least 276k of RAM to run Eudora.

Eudora is distributed via the express written permission of Steve Dorner and Qualcomm, Inc. It's a freeware product, and you are free to distribute it to others so long as the program is distributed in its entirety. For more information, please see the Read Me documents that accompany Eudora on the companion disk.

Qualcomm representatives have assured the Internet community that a free version of Eudora will remain available and will be updated from time to time. The company has stated that a reasonably priced commercial version will include enhancements ranging from MIME (Multipurpose Internet Mail Extensions—a new e-mail standard that supports graphics, styled text, audio, video and binary file transfers) to PEM (Privacy-Enhanced Electronic Mail—a standard for e-mail encryption and authentication).

Configuring Eudora

Eudora must be properly configured before you can begin using it to send e-mail. To use Eudora, you must have an account on a computer that runs a POP3 (Post Office Protocol version 3) mail server. Use these steps to configure Eudora for use with your mail server.

1. Launch Eudora by double-clicking on its icon.

2. Select the Configuration... command from the Special menu. The Configuration dialog box will be displayed, as shown in Figure 4-2.

Figure 4-2: Eudora
Configuration
dialog box.

POP account:	
Real Name:	
Connection Method:	⦿ MacTCP ◯ Communications Toolbox

SMTP Server:

Return Address:

Check For Mail Every _____ Minute(s)

Ph Server:

Dialup Username:

Message Window Width: _____

Message Window Height: _____

Screen Font: Mishawaka

Size: 9

Print Font: Courier

Size: _____

Application TEXT files belong to:

TeachText

☐ Automatically save attachments to:

[Cancel] [OK]

3. Enter your user name in the POP account box in the format:
   user@domain.top-domain.

   ▇ For example, my login name is mfraase and the name of the
   computer that provides my e-mail service is mr.net. I would
   enter **mfraase@mr.net** in the POP account box.

4. Enter your full name in the Real Name box.

5. Click the **MacTCP Connection Method** radio button.

6. Enter the name of your mail server in the SMTP Server box, using
   the format: **domain.top-domain**.

7. Enter your e-mail address in the Return Address box in the format: **user@domain.top-domain**. This will likely be the same
   domain name address you entered in the POP account box, but
   not necessarily.

8. Click the **OK** button. You've completed the basic configuration
   process for Eudora.

> **TeX.**
>
> It's pronounced "tech," and if you're an academician, you probably already know about it. TeX is a very specialized typesetting software program. It's notoriously difficult to learn and painful to use, but for some things—like typesetting mathematical equations—it's indispensable. CMacTeX is a shareware port of the UNIX version of TeX 3.14 and METAFONT 2.7. It's available by anonymous FTP at math.tamu.edu and is located in the /pub/CMacTeX/ directory.

There are several other convenient features Eudora offers that you might want to take advantage of. Or you can begin using Eudora to compose and send e-mail messages. If you want to begin using Eudora without configuring Eudora for your own personal preferences, you can skip the rest of this section and advance to "Using Eudora."

Follow these steps to further customize Eudora to your own personal preferences.

1. Select the Configuration… command from the Special menu. The Configuration dialog box will be displayed, as shown in Figure 4-2.

2. Enter how often (in minutes) you want Eudora to look in your mailbox for new mail in the Check For Mail Every box. If you want to check for mail manually, leave this box empty.

3. Enter the name of your e-mail address lookup server in the Ph Server box. Leave this box empty if your mail server doesn't provide a Ph server. (For more information on the Ph protocol and Ph servers, see the Ph Server Sidebar.)

4. Leave the Dialup username box empty.

5. Enter the number of characters to display on each line of e-mail messages in the Message Window Width box. Leave the box empty to use the default value of 80 characters.

6. Enter the number of lines of each message you want Eudora to display at a time in the Message Window Height box. Leave the box empty to use the default value of 20 lines.

7. Select a font to use to display e-mail messages from the Screen Font pop-up menu.

8. Specify a font size to use to display e-mail messages in the Screen Font Size box.

9. Select a font to use to print e-mail messages from the Print Font pop-up menu.

10. Specify a font size to use to print e-mail messages in the Print Font Size box.

11. Click the button labelled **TeachText** to assign a new software program to open text files. A standard file dialog box will appear, from which you can make your choice.

12. Click the **Automatically save attachments to** checkbox if you want to save to a standard location any files that are attached to e-mail messages you receive.

13. Click the **empty** button to specify a drive or folder in which to save the attached files. A standard file dialog box will appear, from which you can make your choice.

14. Click the **OK** button. You've completed the basic configuration process for Eudora.

A sample Eudora configuration is shown in Figure 4-3.

Figure 4-3:
Completed Eudora
Configuration
dialog box.

POP account:	mfraase@mr.net
Real Name:	Michael Fraase
Connection Method:	● MacTCP ○ Communications Toolbox

SMTP Server:	mr.net
Return Address:	mfraase@farces.com
Check For Mail Every	[ ] Minute(s)
Ph Server:	
Dialup Username:	

Message Window Width:	80	Application TEXT files belong to:
Message Window Height:	100	**FrameMaker**
Screen Font:	Monaco	☒ Automatically save attachments to:
Size:	9	**Dropƒ**
Print Font:	Courier	
Size:	9	Cancel OK

At this point, you can further tweak Eudora's preferences to suit your individual needs, or you can simply start using it. If you want to use Eudora without further configurations, skip the rest of this section and advance to "Using Eudora."

The table below details the function of each option in the Switches dialog box. Use the information in the following table and execute these steps to finish configuring Eudora.

1. Select the Switches… command from the Special menu. The Switches dialog box will be displayed, as shown in Figure 4-4.

Figure 4-4: Eudora Switches dialog box.

Composition:
☒ Icon Bar
☒ Live Nicknames
☒ Word Wrap
☒ Tabs In Body
☒ Use Signature
☐ BinHex 'TEXT'
☐ Immediate Send
☒ Keep Copies
☐ Reply to All
☐ Include Self

Save As:
☒ Guess Paragraphs
☒ Include Headers

Transport:
☒ Show Progress
☒ Send On Check
☒ Save Password
☐ Leave Mail On Server
☐ Auto-Ok
☐ Skip big messages

Get Attention By:
☐ Alert
☒ Sound
☒ Flash Menu Icon
☒ Open "In" Mailbox
   (Mail arrival only)

Switch Messages With:
☒ Plain Arrows
☒ Cmd-Arrows

Miscellany:
☒ Show All Headers
☐ Zoom Windows
☒ Easy Delete
☒ Mailbox Superclose
☒ Empty Trash on Quit
☒ Easy Open

[Cancel] [OK]

2. Based on the information presented in the table in Figure 4-5, check or uncheck the available boxes to suit your personal preferences.

Figure 4-5: Eudora Switches settings.

Checkbox	Function When Enabled
Icon Bar	Icon bar will be displayed in window of all outgoing messages.
Live Nicknames	Reflects closest match to typed text in open Nicknames window.
Word Wrap	Automatically wraps line endings in outgoing messages.
Tabs in Body	Inserts eight space characters each time Tab key is pressed.
Use Signature	Signature file will be automatically attached to outgoing messages.
BinHex 'TEXT'	Attached text files will be encoded in BinHex format.
Immediate Send	Sends outgoing messages immediately, rather than queuing them.

Checkbox	Function When Enabled
Keep Copies	Leaves copies of outgoing messages in Out mailbox.
Reply to All	Reply message addressed to sender and all recipients.
Include Self	Reply message includes your address.
Guess Paragraphs	Removes non-paragraph-ending returns from saved messages.
Include Headers	Includes header information in saved messages.
Show Progress	Displays Progress window during network connections.
Send on Check	Sends any queued messages when checking for new mail.
Save Password	Saves login password between sessions.
Leave Mail on Server	Retains copies of mail messages on mail server after they have been received.
Auto-OK	Network problem dialog boxes are automatically dismissed.
Skip Big Messages	Downloads only first few lines of very large messages.
Alert	Uses dialog boxes to get attention.
Sound	Uses sound to get attention.
Flash Menu Icon	Flashes icon in menu bar to get attention.
Open "In" Mailbox	Opens In mailbox when new e-mail is received.
Plain Arrows	Arrow keys can be used to navigate messages.
Cmd-Arrows	Command-Arrow keys can be used to navigate messages.
Show All Headers	Displays entire header, including routing information.
Zoom Windows	New mailbox and message windows open to zoomed size.
Easy Delete	Deletes messages without warning dialog box.
Mail Superclose	Closing mailbox window also closes messages from that mailbox.
Empty Trash on Quit	Empties trash mailbox when you quit Eudora.
Easy Open	Deleting or transferring topmost message opens next message.

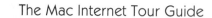

3. Click the **OK** button. The Switches settings will be saved.

4. Select the Signature command from the Special menu. An empty Signature window will be displayed.

5. Enter your *signature* in the Signature window.

   ■ A signature is a three- or four-line text file containing your contact information. An example is shown in Figure 4-6. (For more on signatures, see the sidebar later in this chapter.)

Figure 4-6: Example Eudora Signature window.

```
Signature

--
Michael Fraase, proprietor    |  Voice/Fax: 612/698-0741
Arts & Farces                 |  Internet: mfraase@farces.com
2285 Stewart Avenue           |-------------------------------------
Suite 1315                    |  Nothing to tell, let the words be yours,
St. Paul, MN 55116            |  I am done with mine. (Weir/Barlow)
```

6. Click the Signature window's close box. You'll be asked if you want to save the changes you made to your signature.

7. Click the **Save** button.

You have now completely configured Eudora and are ready to use it to send and receive e-mail.

Internet/NREN Business Journal.

The *Internet/NREN Business Journal* is a new hardcopy newsletter from Michael Strangelove. Internet/Bitnet/NREN topics will include case studies of business ventures, legislation news, advertising strategy and ethics, Net-based public relations, university-industry activity, resource directories and emerging opportunities. Bimonthly, plus six annual special supplements, $75–$149. For information, contact 441495@acadvm1.uottawa.ca

Using Eudora

Eudora is a full-featured e-mail program comparable to many commercial products. In fact, by the time you read this, a reasonably priced commercial version of Eudora will probably be available. The following sections provide instructions for using Eudora's basic features.

Eudora's complete electronic documentation files would not fit on the *Mac Internet Tour Guide* companion disk. You can download complete documentation—in Microsoft Word format—from Qualcomm's server, or you can order a printed manual and distribution disk from the company for $30.

Qualcomm, Inc.
10555 Sorrento Valley Rd.
San Diego, CA 92121
FTP server: ftp.qualcomm.com (192.35.156.5) in the
mac/eudora/ directory

You can always get the latest information about Eudora by sending e-mail to eudora-info@qualcomm.com

Retrieving and Reading E-Mail With Eudora

Use these steps to login to your mail server and automatically retrieve any waiting e-mail.

1. Launch Eudora by double-clicking on its icon.

   ▦ If you have configured Eudora to automatically check for mail, the program will automatically login to the server and download any e-mail addressed to you. The rest of this section assumes that you will be checking for e-mail manually.

2. Select the Check Mail command from the File menu. The Password dialog box will be displayed.

3. Enter your e-mail password and click the **OK** button. The Progress window will be displayed at the top of your screen, providing feedback about the status of your e-mail retrieval.

   ▦ If your password is rejected you'll have to reselect the Check Mail command from the File menu and then reenter your password in the Password dialog box.

   ▦ If there is a problem connecting to the mail server, a dialog box will inform you of the problem. Try selecting the Check Mail command from the File menu again; if Eudora still has problems establishing a connection, see your network administrator.

■ If you have no e-mail waiting on the server, the Progress window will disappear, and Eudora will return to its previous state. If you have waiting e-mail, it will be downloaded and the status will be updated in the Progress window. When all your waiting e-mail has been retrieved, you will be notified (based on the configuration settings you specified), and the In Mailbox window will automatically be displayed. Your new messages will be listed as shown in Figure 4-7.

Figure 4-7: Eudora In Mailbox window.

●	Rick Watson	10:32 PM 3/22/9...	2	re: 1.01b57 script problem
●	TELECOM Moderator	10:46 PM 3/22/9...	25	TELECOM Digest V13 #197
●	The Moderators	6:39 PM 3/22/9...	24	Info-Mac Digest V11 #63 1/5
●	The Moderators	6:39 PM 3/22/9...	24	Info-Mac Digest V11 #63 2/5
●	The Moderators	6:39 PM 3/22/9...	24	Info-Mac Digest V11 #63 3/5
●	The Moderators	6:39 PM 3/22/9...	24	Info-Mac Digest V11 #63 4/5
●	The Moderators	6:39 PM 3/22/9...	22	Info-Mac Digest V11 #63 5/5
●	TELECOM Moderator	11:25 PM 3/22/9...	19	TELECOM Digest V13 #198
●	andy	11:30 PM 3/22/9...	17	FutureCulture Digest #314
●	TELECOM Moderator	12:01 AM 3/23/9...	24	TELECOM Digest V13 #199 1/2
●	TELECOM Moderator	12:01 AM 3/23/9...	1	TELECOM Digest V13 #199 2/2
●	TELECOM Moderator	1:32 AM 3/23/9...	19	TELECOM Digest V13 #200
●	Cu-Digest (tkOjut2...	12:12 AM 3/23/9...	24	Cu Digest, #5.21 1/2
●	Cu-Digest (tkOjut2...	12:12 AM 3/23/9...	14	Cu Digest, #5.21 2/2
●	Adam C. Engst	9:54 PM 3/22/9...	24	TidBITS#169/22-Mar-93 1/2
●	Adam C. Engst	9:54 PM 3/22/9...	8	TidBITS#169/22-Mar-93 2/2
●	TELECOM Moderator	2:40 AM 3/23/9...	24	TELECOM Digest V13 #201
●	TELECOM Moderator	3:23 AM 3/23/9...	20	TELECOM Digest V13 #202
●	TELECOM Moderator	4:01 AM 3/23/9...	19	TELECOM Digest V13 #203
●	adam fast	3:17 AM 3/23/9...	5	Re: Squatters R Us
●	"Focus on 3 things...	8:45 AM 3/23/9...	2	Re: STC'S Electronic Bulletin Board
●	Peggy Thompson	8:58 AM 3/23/9...	2	Re: hyphenation breaks
●	Peggy Thompson	9:23 AM 3/23/9...	2	RE: More bloopers
●	Chet_Cady@OCLC.ORG	9:31 AM 3/23/9...	3	Reply to: Writing Across the Curr
●	aba@OC.COM	6:44 AM 3/23/9...	5	STC on the INTERNET (was STC's Electro
●	lpraderio	9:52 AM 3/23/9...	5	Re: Writing Across the Curriculum
●	Bruce B. Harper	10:05 AM 3/23/9...	7	RE: More bloopers
●	Eric Weiss-Altaner	10:16 AM 3/23/9...	2	Numeric keypads: Kensington or PlusWar
●	Joseph T Chew	7:31 AM 3/23/9...	2	Bitnet vs. Internet
●	Marc Posner	10:34 AM 3/23/9...	2	ExpressModem Software 1.0.1
●	Brian R Bezanson	9:40 AM 3/23/9...	2	Re: ExpressModem Software 1.0.1

31/380K/OK

4. Double-click on the subject line of the message you want to read. The full message will be displayed, as shown in the example in Figure 4-8.

Figure 4-8: Eudora
e-mail message.

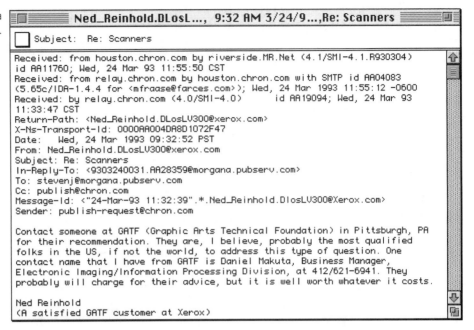

5. Close the message window by clicking in the close box.

6. Repeat steps 4–5 for each additional message you want to read.

E-mail messages are stored in the In mailbox until they are deleted or transferred to another mailbox. See "Managing E-Mail With Eudora" for more information.

Creating an E-Mail Message With Eudora

Use these steps to create an e-mail message with Eudora.

1. Launch Eudora by double-clicking on its icon.

2. Go to the Message menu and select the New Message command. A new Message Composition window will be displayed, as shown in Figure 4-9.

Figure 4-9: Eudora
Message
Composition
window.

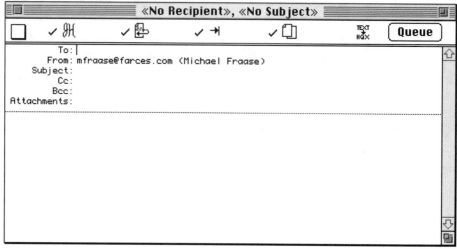

3. Enter the e-mail address of the recipient in the To: field and press the Tab key.

4. Enter a short subject for the message in the Subject: field and press the Tab key.

5. Enter the e-mail addresses of any recipients to whom you want to send a courtesy copy in the Cc: field and press the Tab key. Tab through the field if you don't want to include any courtesy copies.

   ▓ Courtesy copies are copies of your message sent to third parties *with* a notification to the addressee.

6. Enter the e-mail address of any recipients to whom you want to send a *blind* courtesy copy in the Bcc: field and press the Tab key. Tab through the field if you don't want to include any blind courtesy copies.

   ▓ Blind courtesy copies are copies of your message sent to third parties *without* a notification to the addressee.

Blind Courtesy Copies.

Courtesy copies used to be called carbon copies. But since we don't use carbon paper anymore, they're now called courtesy copies by the high-tech, in-the-know crowd. They're useful for distributing identical messages to a number of people.

Most people don't consider *blind* courtesy copies very nice, because they're secretive. They're generally used either by someone who is trying to cover a mistake or by someone who has something to hide. Privacy is a good thing. Secrecy isn't.

Blind courtesy copies are useful for large mailing lists because sending letters using the blind courtesy copy addressing feature prevents the names of all the recipients from appearing in the message header and overwhelming the actual message.

The distribution list for the electronic updates for this book is handled with blind courtesy copies. I could be altruistic and say that I do it that way to keep the header short, but that would not be completely true. If I used courtesy copies instead of blind courtesy copies, anyone on the list would have access to the entire list. That's not a good thing for your privacy. Nor is it a good thing for my bank account. I'm not sure how to balance the tension between privacy and secrecy. Let me know if you've figured it out.

7. Press the Tab key to advance through the Attachment: field.

8. Enter the body of your message. You can type or paste text into this field.

9. Click the **Queue** button. Your message will be stored on your hard drive and sent to the mail server when you select the Send Queued Messages command from the File menu.

   ▪ If you have set Eudora's preferences to send mail immediately, there will be a **Send** button at the far right end of the Icon Bar instead of the **Queue** button.

Replying to E-Mail Messages With Eudora

Replying to an e-mail message is similar to creating a new message. Here's how to do it:

1. Double-click on the subject line of the message you want to read. The message will be displayed.

2. Go to the Message menu and select the Reply command. A new
Message Composition window will be displayed with the original
sender's e-mail address in the To: field. In addition, all of the text
from the original message will also be included, with a ">" preceding each line, as shown in Figure 4-10.

Figure 4-10:
Replying to an
e-mail message
with Eudora.

Figure 4-10:
Replying to an
e-mail message
with Eudora.

Chip Clofine, Re: character tags and table text problem

Queue

To: framers@drd.com
From: mfraase@farces.com (Michael Fraase)
Subject: Re: character tags and table text problem
Cc:
Bcc:
Attachments:

```
>I've been experiencing a little problem when updating my documents
>from a template. I have been using character formats in table text
>and when I Use Formats From my template file (updating all formats),
>the selections of text that have character tags assigned to them
>loose the attributes of the character tag and take on the attributes
>of the paragraph. If I highlight the text, the status bar still
>indicates that the selection has a character tag associated with it
>(it just doesn't look that way).
>
>The only way to fix this is to do another Use Formats From updating
>only character formats. Since I have large books, and the Use Formats
>when I have to do it twice.
```

Internet Quoting Conventions.
The ">" that precedes each line of a message is the Internet convention for quoted text. There are
several variations, but ">" is the most common.

Second-hand quotes—quoted replies to quotes—are shown with a ">>" preceding each line.

This can soon get ridiculous. I've seen heated *flame wars* (vitriolic online debates) erupt into
five or six levels of ">"s. It's not a pretty sight, and it's impossible to figure out who said what
to whom.

A good rule of thumb when replying to e-mail or responding to a message posting is to quote
only material that is necessary to further the understanding of the letter or message thread. Don't,
for instance, quote a 300-line message in its entirety and add only "I agree" at the end.

3. Enter the body of your message. You can type or paste text into
this field.

4. Click the **Queue** button. Your message will be stored on your
hard drive and sent to the mail server when you select the Send
Queued Messages command from the File menu.

▨ If you have set Eudora's preferences to send mail immediately, there will be a **Send** button (instead of the **Queue** button) at the far right end of the Icon Bar.

Sending E-Mail Messages With Eudora

Based on how you've configured Eudora, you can either send messages immediately or queue them to your hard drive for batch sending when you connect to the mail server. In general, it's a more efficient use of network resources to queue your e-mail messages for batch sending unless you maintain a constant connection to the Internet.

To send your queued e-mail messages

1. Launch Eudora by double-clicking on its icon.

2. Select the Send Queued Messages command from the File menu. The Password dialog box will be displayed (unless you have configured Eudora to remember your password between sessions).

3. Enter your e-mail password and click the **OK** button. The Progress window will appear at the top of your screen, providing feedback about the status of your e-mail being sent.

   ▨ If your password is rejected, you'll have to reselect the Send Queued Messages command from the File menu and then reenter your password in the Password dialog box.

   ▨ If there is a problem connecting to the mail server, a dialog box will inform you of the problem. Try selecting the Send Queued Messages command from the File menu again; if Eudora still has problems establishing a connection, see your network administrator.

   ▨ When the last e-mail message has been sent to the mail server, the Progress window will disappear, and Eudora will return to its previous state.

Managing E-Mail With Eudora

Eudora lets you organize your incoming e-mail by creating new mail-boxes for storing and moving messages.

To create new mailboxes

1. Launch Eudora by double-clicking on its icon.

2. Select the New… command from the Transfer menu. The New Mailbox dialog box will appear, as shown in Figure 4-11.

3. Enter a name for the new mailbox.

4. Click the **OK** button. A new mailbox will be created with the name you specified in step 3.

   ▪ Check the **Make it a folder** checkbox if you want to create a new folder within an existing mailbox.

   ▪ Check the **Don't transfer**, just create mailbox checkbox if you want to create the new mailbox without transferring the selected message.

5. Repeat steps 2–4 to create any additional mailboxes you may need.

Mailbox Strategies.

You can create mailboxes for any number of filing and organization strategies. Some people like to create mailboxes for each month or week, filing their messages by date. Others like to create a mailbox for each person they regularly correspond with, organizing messages based on contact.

The strategy that works best for me is to create mailboxes for various topics or projects I'm working on. When new e-mail messages come in, I sort them by content. As much as I like Eudora, I use TCP/Connect II (a commercial Mac Internet program) for most of my e-mail. It has intelligent *filters* that I can use to automatically sort my incoming e-mail based on a wide range of criteria I have set up. For more information on this technique, see "Managing E-Mail With TCP/Connect II."

To move e-mail messages between your mailboxes

1. Launch Eudora by double-clicking on its icon.

2. Open the mailbox containing the message you want to move. You do this by selecting its entry from the lower portion of the Mailbox menu.

3. Select the subject line of the message you want to move. The subject line will be highlighted.

   ▪ You can select a continuous range of messages by clicking on the first message and Shift-clicking on the last message. You can make multiple discontinuous selections by Command-clicking on the messages you want to select.

4. Select from the Transfer menu the new mailbox where you want to move the selected message, as shown in Figure 4-12.

Figure 4-12: Eudora Transfer menu with custom mailboxes.

Transfer

-> In
-> Trash

New...
-> FrameMaker
-> Information Politics
-> Internet Resources
-> Telecommunications

E-mail messages are stored in the In mailbox until they are deleted or transferred to another mailbox. To delete existing e-mail from any of your mailboxes

1. Launch Eudora by double-clicking on its icon.

2. Open the mailbox containing the message you want to delete. You do this by selecting its entry from the lower portion of the Mailbox menu.

3. Select the subject line of the message you want to delete. The subject line will be highlighted.

   ▪ As with transferring messages, you can select a continuous range of messages by clicking on the first message and

Shift-clicking on the last message. You can make multiple discontinuous selections by Command-clicking on the messages you want to select.

4. From the Message menu, select the Delete command.

■ "Deleted" messages aren't actually erased; they're simply moved to a special Trash mailbox. Any message that has been "deleted" can be recovered by moving it out of the Trash mailbox before the Empty Trash command is chosen.

5. Select the Empty Trash command from the Special menu. (Don't confuse these Eudora commands and menus with those of the same names in the Mac's Finder.) The messages you "deleted" in step 4 will be erased when you quit Eudora.

Quick Guide to Using TCP/Connect II

TCP/Connect II is a commercial product (marketed by InterCon Systems Corporation) that integrates electronic mail, USENET News (also known as newsgroups), FTP (transferring or downloading files from remote sites) and TELNET services (those services that require terminal emulation) in a single program. TCP/Connect II's e-mail module is extremely useful. The integrated nature of TCP/Connect II makes it easy to perform some tasks on the Internet that might not be possible with other programs, like forwarding (or responding to) USENET News articles by e-mail. I find that managing the various Internet resources I use most frequently is easier if all the tools I use are in a single program.

You can order TCP/Connect II from most of the Macintosh software mail order houses. The product carries a suggested retail price of $495.

> InterCon Systems Corporation
> 950 Herndon Parkway
> Herndon, VA 22070
> 703/709-9890
> 703/709-5555 (Fax)
> info@intercon.com

Configuring TCP/Connect II Mail Module

TCP/Connect II must be properly configured before you can begin
using it to send e-mail. To use TCP/Connect II, you must have an
account on a computer that runs a POP2 or POP3 (Post Office Protocol version 2 or 3; most sites use version 3) mail server. To configure
TCP/Connect II for use with your network connection

1. Launch TCP/Connect II by double-clicking on its icon. The
   Registration dialog box will be displayed, prompting you for
   name, organization and registration key information.

2. Enter the appropriate information in the Registration dialog
   box and click the **Validate** button. TCP/Connect II will automatically scan for the type of network connection you have
   installed. The Network Configuration panel will appear, as
   shown in Figure 4-13.

Figure 4-13:
TCP/Connect II
Configuration
dialog box's
Network panel.

TCP/Connect II Configuration
General
Host Name of this Macintosh:
Default Remote Host Name:
Network
Type of Hardware Connection:
MacTCP® Ethernet AppleTalk Serial None
File Transfer
Hosts

3. Enter the host name of your Macintosh using the domain name
   format, for instance, **deeper.farces.com**

   ▓ If you're not sure of the appropriate host name of your Macintosh, see your network administrator or service provider.

4. Enter the name of the default remote host using the domain name
   format.

■ If you don't know the name of your remote host, see your network administrator or service provider.

5. Click on the Hosts icon in the scrolling list of configuration items. The Hosts Configuration panel will be displayed, as shown in Figure 4-14.

Figure 4-14: TCP/Connect II Configuration dialog box's Hosts panel.

Compressing space and time.

Ralph Brandi uses the Internet to compress space and time and to meet people that he would otherwise never encounter. Here is his story of how he uses the Internet:

"The Net demolishes the barriers of time and location. If you've got some kind of fairly obscure interest, you can be pretty sure there is someone else on the Net who shares it. The fact that they don't live in your neighborhood doesn't prevent you from carrying on an extended conversation. They can even live on the other side of the world and you don't have to worry about waking them up.

The best thing about the Net that I've encountered in my six or so years connected has nothing to do with computers: it's the people. By communicating with people I share interests with, I've made a number of good friends.

I had a Net.friend from New Zealand visit me for a week last year, after a couple of years of corresponding over the Net. I had a great time showing him New York City and the east coast, and he brought some books and records for me from New Zealand that I couldn't find for love nor money here in the U.S. I'm going to be visiting him in London—where he lives now— this summer.

Some months ago, I was receiving a couple of low-powered radio stations from Australia on my shortwave radio. I had been trying to receive these stations literally for years, and they're highly sought-after targets among shortwave listeners. I posted a note to the rec.radio.shortwave newsgroup. The following morning, I had e-mail from a couple of people in Boston who had followed up on that tip and been rewarded with their first receptions of the stations. I later met them at a convention of shortwave enthusiasts and had a very enjoyable lunch with them and some of their friends.

The common thread here is the interactions with *people*, not computers."

6. Click the **New** button. A dialog box will appear prompting you to enter the name of the host.

7. Enter the name of your mail server and click the **OK** button. A new entry will be created in the Hosts scrolling list.

8. Enter the IP Address of your mail server in the IP Addresses box. Alternatively, enter the domain name of your mail server in the Full Domain Name box.

   ▪ For instance, the IP Address of my mail server is 137.192.2.5 and its domain name is mr.net.

9. Close the Configuration dialog box by clicking the close box.

To configure TCP/Connect II for use with your mail server

1. Launch TCP/Connect II by double-clicking on its icon.

2. Select the Configure… command from the Edit menu. The Configuration dialog box will appear.

3. Click on the **Mail** icon in the scrolling list of configuration items. The Mail Configuration panel will appear, as shown in Figure 4-15.

Figure 4-15:
TCP/Connect II
Configuration
dialog box's Mail
panel.

TCP/Connect II Configuration

Tektronix

IBM 327x

Sessions

Mail

Return Address:

Full Name:

Mail User ID:

Mail Server:

Connect to Server ● Upon Request ○ Every [   ] minutes

Maximum Message Size: [50000] bytes

POP Method: ○ POP2 ● POP3   ○ ACKS ● ACKD

Folder For Mail Files: [Further :Telecom∫ :TCP/Connect II∫]

Mail notification sound: [*Default system beep*]

Message Font: [Monaco]   Size [9]

Lookup Server:

4. Enter your e-mail address—using the format username@domain.top-domain—in the Return Address box.

5. Enter your real name (first and last) in the Full Name box.

6. Enter your e-mail account—using the format username@domain.top-domain—in the Mail User ID box. In most cases this is the same as your e-mail address, but not always.

7. Select your mail server from the Mail Server pop-up menu.

8. Click the appropriate **POP Method** radio button, representing the version of the Post Office Protocol used by your mail server. If you aren't sure which version your system uses, check with your network administrator.

9. Click the appropriate **ACK** radio button, depending on your needs:

   ▦ Click the **ACKS** radio button if you want to keep copies of your received e-mail on the mail server. This is useful for testing, but most system administrators prefer that you delete mail from the server once you have received and read it.

   ▦ Click the **ACKD** radio button to delete your e-mail messages on the server after they have been delivered and saved to your local hard drive.

10. Select the name of your e-mail address lookup server from the Lookup Server pop-up menu. Leave this box empty if your mail server doesn't provide a Ph server (see the Ph Servers sidebar for details).

11. Close the Configuration dialog box by clicking the close box.

Ph Servers.

The Ph protocol was developed by Steve Dorner—author of the Eudora e-mail program—while he was at the Urbana-Champaign campus of the University of Illinois. Ph provides a way to look up e-mail addresses for colleagues and associates, usually at a single location.

In order for you to use the Ph lookup capabilities of either Eudora or TCP/Connect II, your mail server must also have a Ph server installed and properly configured.

Unfortunately, Ph servers are provided only for single locations—a large corporate site or a university, for example. Ph is useful only if you know the organization with which the person you want to contact is affiliated.

There are other methods—some relatively simple, others mind-numbingly sophisticated—to find e-mail addresses, and a few are covered elsewhere in this book. But the easiest way to find out someone's e-mail address is to call him or her on the telephone and ask. Sometimes the simplest methods are the best.

Using TCP/Connect II Mail Module

The mail module of TCP/Connect II uses the Post Office Protocol (POP) to retrieve e-mail and the Simple Mail Transfer Protocol (SMTP) to send mail. All e-mail you send and receive with TCP/Connect II is handled automatically.

You can always get the latest information about TCP/Connect II by sending e-mail to info@intercon.com.

Retrieving & Reading E-Mail With TCP/Connect II

To login to your mail server and automatically retrieve any waiting e-mail

1. Launch TCP/Connect II by double-clicking on its icon.

   ▪ If you have configured TCP/Connect II to automatically check for mail, the program will automatically login to the server and download any e-mail addressed to you. The rest of this section assumes that you will be checking for e-mail manually.

2. From the Mail menu, select the Check Mailbox... command. The Password dialog box will appear.

3. Enter your e-mail password and click the **OK** button. The Mail Status window will appear at the top of your screen, providing feedback about the status of your e-mail retrieval and any outgoing messages waiting in the queue.

   ▪ If your password is rejected, you'll have to reselect the Check Mailbox... command from the Mail menu and then reenter your password in the Password dialog box.

   ▪ If there is a problem connecting to the mail server, a dialog box will inform you of the problem. Try selecting the Check Mailbox... command from the Mail menu again; if TCP/Connect II still has problems establishing a connection, see your network administrator.

   ▪ If you have no e-mail waiting on the server, the Mail Status window will disappear, and TCP/Connect II will return to its previous state. If you have waiting e-mail, it will be downloaded and the progress will be updated in the Mail Status window. When all your waiting e-mail has been retrieved, you will be notified based on the configuration settings you specified, and your In Box window will automatically be displayed, with your new messages listed as shown in Figure 4-16.

Figure 4-16:
TCP/Connect II In
Box window.

From	Subject	Date
lpraderio	Re[2]: What is Information Mapping	Tue, 23 Mar
Rick Watson	MacSLIP beta 58	Tue, 23 Mar
Berthold K.P. Horn	Xerox document system info wanted	Wed, 24 Ma
Roger Smith -- IAS	PS Draft	Wed, 24 Ma
Frame Technical Support Mail	FrameMaker for Windows --Maintenance Re	Wed, 24 Ma
Sergiu S. Simmel	PS Draft	Thu, 25 Mar
Owen Rees	Re: character tags and table text problem	Thu, 25 Mar
Roger Smith -- IAS	PS Draft	Thu, 25 Mar
ventana500@aol.com	**writing/design strategies**	**Thu, 25 M**

mfraase's in box

New Msg   Reme   Reply   Forward   Rerens

4. Double-click on the subject line of the message you want to read. The message appears, as shown in the example in Figure 4-17.

Figure 4-17: TCP/Connect II e-mail message.

5. Close the message window by clicking in the close box.

6. Repeat steps 4 and 5 for each additional message you want to read.

7. Incoming e-mail messages are stored in the In Box until they are deleted or transferred to another mailbox. See "Managing E-Mail With TCP/Connect II" for more information.

Note: The only way to move mail between mailboxes is to use the menus or keyboard commands. There is no way to move it between mailboxes as you might move files from one folder to another from the Finder.

Creating an E-Mail Message With TCP/Connect II

To create an e-mail message with TCP/Connect II

1. Launch TCP/Connect II by double-clicking on its icon.

2. Select the Create New Message... command from the Mail menu. Alternatively, you can click the **New Msg** button in the upper left portion of the In Box window. A new Untitled Message window will appear, as shown in Figure 4-18.

Figure 4-18:
TCP/Connect II
Untitled Mes-
sage window.

3. Enter the body of your e-mail message. You can type or paste text into this field.

4. Click the **Send** button. The TCP/Connect II Send window will appear, as shown in Figure 4-19.

Figure 4-19:
TCP/Connect II
Send window.

5. Enter a short subject for the message in the Subject: box.

6. Click and drag the name of the recipient or recipients from the scrolling Addresses list to the To: box. Alternatively, you can enter the e-mail addresses of the recipients—in the username@domain.top-domain format—directly in the To: box.

7. Click and drag the names of any courtesy copy recipients from the scrolling Addresses list to the Cc: box. Alternatively, you can enter the e-mail addresses of the Cc recipients—in the username@domain.top-domain format—directly in the Cc: box.

   ▪ Courtesy copies are copies of your message sent to third parties *with* a notification to the addressee.

8. Click and drag the names of any *blind* courtesy copy recipients from the scrolling Addresses list to the Bcc: box. Alternatively, you can enter the e-mail addresses of the Bcc recipients—in the username@domain.top-domain format—directly in the Bcc: box.

   ▪ Blind courtesy copies are copies of your message sent to third parties *without* a notification to the addressee.

   ▪ For more information on courtesy copies and blind courtesy copies, see the Blind Courtesy Copy sidebar.

9. If you want to archive a copy of the e-mail message you're sending, select an Archive mailbox from the Archive pop-up menu. You can archive mail in any of your existing mailboxes, or you can create a new mailbox.

   ▪ You can define a default archive mailbox by holding down the Option key while you select a mailbox from the Archive pop-up menu.

   ▪ You can obtain the same result by sending a Cc of the message to yourself. Using an archive is more efficient, however, because a Cc is delivered to you as a new (unread) e-mail message. Another nice touch of TCP/Connect II's mail feature is that the archive message isn't actually filed in the target mailbox until the actual message has been sent successfully.

10. Click the **Send** button. If you have an active network connection, your e-mail message will be sent to the specified recipients. If your network connection is inactive, the e-mail message will be saved in your Mail folder and automatically sent the next time you login to your mail server.

Replying to E-Mail Messages With TCP/Connect II

Replying to an e-mail message is similar to creating a new message, although it's partially automated. To use the e-mail module of TCP/Connect II to reply to an e-mail message

1. Double-click on the subject line of the message you want to read. The message then appears.

2. Click the **Reply** button in the upper portion of the Message window. The Reply dialog box will appear, as shown in Figure 4-20.

Figure 4-20: TCP/Connect II e-mail Reply dialog box.

3. Select the recipients of your reply from the Reply To: radio buttons.

4. Click the **Quote Original Message** checkbox if you want to include quoted text from the original sender with a ">" preceding each line.

5. Click the **Reformat Quote** checkbox if you want to reformat the line endings of the quote to match SMTP's hard carriage returns, which occur after about every 78 characters.

6. Click the **OK** button. A new Message window will be displayed with the original sender's message, with a ">" preceding each line, as shown in Figure 4-21.

BBEdit.

BBEdit is a high-quality text editor that allows you to use the UNIX grep command to search for patterns of text across multiple files. The Claris XTND file translation system is supported, as are various plug-in modules (several are included with the distribution package and more are available in various FTP archives). The program is available by FTP from mac.archive.umich.edu in the /mac/util/editor/ directory.

Figure 4-21: Replying to an e-mail message with TCP/Connect II.

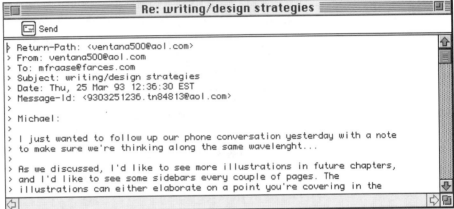

■ For more information on quoting existing messages, see the Internet Quoting Conventions sidebar.

7. Enter the body of your message. You can type or paste text into this field.

8. Click the **Send** button in the upper left portion of the Message window. The TCP/Connect II Send window will appear. Note that the Subject: and To: boxes have already been filled with the correct information.

9. Click the **Send** button in the Send window. If you have an active network connection, your e-mail reply will be sent to the specified recipients. If your network connection is inactive, the e-mail reply will be saved in your Mail folder and automatically sent the next time you login to your mail server.

Managing E-Mail With TCP/Connect II

TCP/Connect II lets you organize your incoming e-mail by creating new mailboxes for storing and moving messages. And TCP/Connect II is the only Macintosh e-mail product I'm aware of that you can use to set up *filters* to automatically sort your e-mail into the appropriate mailboxes. If you're a heavy e-mail user, this feature greatly streamlines your e-mail activities.

To create new mailboxes

1. Launch TCP/Connect II by double-clicking on its icon.

2. From the Mail menu, select the Mailboxes... command. The Mailboxes window will be displayed, like the example (with several mailboxes already created) shown in Figure 4-22.

Figure 4-22: TCP/Connect II Mailboxes window.

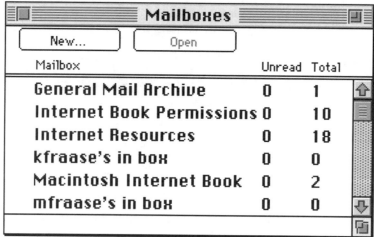

3. Click the **New...** button in the Mailboxes window. A standard Save File dialog box will appear, prompting you to enter a name for the new mailbox.

4. Enter the name for the new mailbox.

5. Click the **Save** button. The new mailbox will be created and its name and status will be added to the Mailboxes window.

For more information on managing your e-mail with different mailboxes, see the Mailbox Strategies sidebar.

Working With E-Mail Filters

Filing important e-mail messages after you've read them is a good way to manage incoming e-mail. But wouldn't it be wonderful if you could file incoming e-mail messages *before* you read them? Well, if you use TCP/Connect II, you can. TCP/Connect II's e-mail *filter rules* allow you to automatically manage your e-mail in a number of ways, including routing e-mail to specific mailboxes.

Filters can be thought of as "almost-intelligent processors" that look at all incoming e-mail messages and manipulate those messages based on a set of rules you have defined. If you don't want to use TCP/Connect II's filters, or if you want to experiment with e-mail a little before setting up filters, feel free to skip this section.

TCP/Connect II provides both local and global e-mail filter actions. Global filter actions apply to all mailboxes; local filter actions apply only to an individual mailbox. It's best to use local filters whenever possible, because global filters cause the program to run more slowly. I have noticed no performance degradation when I use quite a few local filters on my single incoming mailbox.

To create local filter actions to automatically highlight and route e-mail messages to appropriate mailboxes

1. Launch TCP/Connect II by double-clicking on its icon.

2. From the Mail menu, Select the Open Mailbox... command. A standard Open File dialog box will appear.

3. Double-click on your incoming mailbox in the Open File dialog box. The mailbox will be opened on your desktop.

4. Click within the mailbox to make it the active window.

5. Select the Mailbox's Local Actions... command from the Mail menu. Note that this menu command will change to reflect the currently active mailbox window, as shown in the example in Figure 4-23.

Figure 4-23:
TCP/Connect II
Mail menu.

Mail	
Open Mailbox...	⌘⇧O
Check Mailbox...	⌘M
Mailboxes...	⌘⇧P
Create New Message...	⌘⇧M
Send...	⌘⇧U
Send File...	⌘⇧E
Forward...	⌘⇧Y
Reply...	⌘⇧T
Resend...	⌘⇧I
Refile...	⌘⇧R
Select Messages...	
Global Mail Actions...	⌘⇧]
mfraase's in box's Mail Actions	⌘]
Address Book...	⌘⇧B
Lookup...	
Show Mail Status	

■ The Mail Actions dialog box for the currently active mailbox
will appear, as shown in the example in Figure 4-24.

Figure 4-24:
TCP/Connect II
Mail Actions
dialog box.

mfraase's in box's Mail Actions

[New Action]   [Edit Action]   [Remove Action]

6. Click the **New Action** button in the Mail Actions dialog box. The Edit Action dialog box will appear, as shown in Figure 4-25.

Figure 4-25:
TCP/Connect II
Edit Action
dialog box.

Edit Action

Action Rule:

Look In: Message Header ▼

For something that: Contains ▼

☐ Case-sensitive comparisons   ☐ Use * and ? wildcards
☐ Disregard following actions

Highlighting for existing and new messages:

☐ Bold   ☐ Underline   Foreground
☐ Italic   ☐ Outline   Background

Operations performed on new messages only:

◉ No marking, deleting, refiling, or copying
◯ Mark As Read   ◯ Refile To: Archive: No Archive ▼
◯ Delete   ◯ Copy To:

Cancel   OK

7. Select the Message Header item from the Look In: pop-up menu. This is the default selection and should appear automatically.

   ▪ The items on the Look In: pop-up menu instruct TCP/Connect II where to search within e-mail messages for the word or phrase that you supply in the next field.

8. Select the Contains item from the For something that: pop-up menu. This is the default selection and should appear automatically.

9. In the empty search box, enter the word or phrase for which you want the program to search.

10. Click the **Case-sensitive comparisons** checkbox if you want the search to be case-sensitive. Checking this box will match identically the capitalization of the search word or phrase.

   ▪ If this box is checked and you entered Internet in the search box, Internet would be matched, but internet or InterNet would not.

11. Click the **Use * and ? wildcards** checkbox if you want the search to use simple pattern matching.

   ▪ An asterisk (*) represents any string of characters, and a question mark (?) represents a single character.

   ▪ For instance, if you want to find every e-mail message that pertains to the word "writing," you could enter **writ*** in the search box. This would result in write, writer, writing and written all being matched.

   ▪ If you want to really get fancy, you could enter **wr?t*** in the search box. This would result in write, writer, writing, written and wrote all being matched.

12. Click the **Disregard following actions** checkbox if you want to ignore all of the following action items in the Edit Action dialog box.

13. Click any of the **Highlighting for existing and new messages** checkboxes if you want the e-mail messages that meet the search criteria to be highlighted.

   ▪ If you have a black-and-white monitor, your highlighting options are any combination of Bold, Italic, Underline and Outline. If you have a color monitor, you can also select foreground and background colors.

14. Specify an action for those e-mail messages that meet the specified criteria by clicking one of the **Operations are performed on new messages only** radio buttons.

   ▪ Click the **No marking, deleting, refiling or copying** radio button to take no additional action on messages that match the criteria.

   ▪ Click the **Mark As Read** radio button to display an opened envelope icon next to messages that match the criteria, even though you have not read them.

   ▪ Click the **Delete** radio button to automatically delete messages that match the criteria.

   ▪ Click the **Refile To:** radio button to automatically route messages that match the criteria to the mailbox you specify in the Archive pop-up menu.

- Click the **Copy To:** radio button to automatically place a *copy* of all messages that match the criteria to the mailbox you specify in the Archive pop-up menu.

15. Click the **OK** button. The filter action will be added to the Mail Actions dialog box.

Filter Action Ideas.

TCP/Connect II's filter actions are invaluable to me, and I find it hard to justify ever using an e-mail product that doesn't have them. Here are a few ideas for putting filter actions to use.

Most of the employees at Ventana Press, the publisher of this book, use e-mail (you'd be amazed at the number of computer book publishing houses that don't). I created filter actions for various groups at Ventana. Messages from the marketing people got blue highlighting. Mail from the sales people was highlighted in green. E-mail from my editor got an orange highlight with bold type. Messages from the publisher were highlighted in red with bold and italic type attributes. All of the messages from the Ventana folks were refiled to a special mailbox.

I subscribe to a lot of electronic mailing lists—for more information on mailing lists, see "Electronic Mailing Lists." All messages from a mailing list originate from the same e-mail address, even though they are written by lots of different people. I created a mailbox for each mailing list and created a filter action to refile each mailing list message to the appropriate mailbox.

Your requests for the electronic updates to this book (and any correspondence you send about the updates) are similarly routed to appropriate mailboxes.

The biggest problem with mailing lists is that some people insist on sending administrative requests (subscribe, unsubscribe, etc.) to the mailing list address rather than the *administrative* address. It's a simple matter to filter out these bozo messages with TCP/Connect II. Just search for subscribe, unsubscribe, signoff and the like in the message headers and click the **Delete** radio button.

One thing that I'd really like to see added to TCP/Connect II's e-mail module is the ability to automatically send out a message or file based on the results of the specifications of a filter.

Finding Addresses

If you work within a large corporation or university, finding the e-mail addresses of your colleagues is usually simple enough, because your site will probably have a Ph server. The problem is that the Ph server will probably only have addresses for people at your site or within your organization, which doesn't help you if you're trying to send e-mail to someone across the country or around the world.

The easiest way to find the e-mail address of someone is to call him or her on the telephone and ask for the e-mail address. It's a low-tech solution to a high-tech problem. Because of security and privacy concerns, and because there is no unifying standard for e-mail directories on disparate systems, there is no central directory for Internet e-mail addresses.

But even though no central Internet directory exists, there are a few tools you can use to try to find e-mail addresses.

Using Finger

Finger is a software utility that looks at the user login file on a UNIX system. Since most computers on the Internet run some variation of UNIX, Finger is probably the best place to start.

You can FTP (or transfer to your computer) a Macintosh version of Finger from the Sumex Info-Mac archive or the University of Michigan's Macintosh archive. For more information on using FTP to transfer files, see Chapter 6, "Transferring Files." Unfortunately, Finger requires you to know the name of the host machine where the person you are trying to locate has an account.

To use the Macintosh version of the Finger utility

1. Launch Finger by double-clicking on its icon.

2. Select the Finger... command from the File menu. The Finger dialog box will be displayed, as shown in Figure 4-26.

Figure 4-26: Finger
dialog box.

Finger

User

Machine

☐ **Whois Server ⌘S**

[**Cancel**]   [**Set Default**]   (Finger)

3. Enter the name of the person you are trying to locate and the name of the host machine using the domain name format—username@domain.top-domain—in the User box. Alternatively, you can enter a valid IP address (the address that uses numbers instead of domain names) in the Machine box.

4. Click the **Finger** button. The results will be displayed in a window like the example shown in Figure 4-27. If the search is unsuccessful, a dialog box will appear, notifying you of the failure.

Figure 4-27: Finger
Results window.

leonardr@netcom.com (192.100.81.100)

```
Login name: leonardr     In real life: Leonard Rosenthol
Directory: /u23/leonardr          Shell: /bin/csh
Last login Wed Mar 24 00:05 on ttyr7 from leonardr.slip.ne
New mail received Mon Mar 29 14:25:36 1993;
  unread since Sun Mar 28 07:18:35 1993
No Plan.
```

Using MIT's USENET User List

If the person you are trying to locate has ever posted a message to any of the USENET newsgroups, you may be able to locate him or her by using a specialized mail server at the Massachusetts Institute of Technology (MIT). The MIT server constantly monitors incoming USENET postings and extracts each poster's name and e-mail address.

To use MIT's USENET User List service

1. Launch Eudora (or TCP/Connect II) by double-clicking on its icon.

2. Send an e-mail message consisting only of the single line: send usenet-addresses/*name* where *name* is the name of the person you are trying to locate. For example, to search for my e-mail address, the line would be: send usenet-addresses/fraase.

3. Address the e-mail message to mail-server@pit-manager.mit.edu

4. Send the e-mail message. You'll soon receive a responding message from the MIT mail server that looks something like the one shown in Figure 4-28.

Figure 4-28: MIT USENET User List example.

Using Whois

Whois is a directory that is maintained by the DDN Network Information Center. Unfortunately, it contains listings only for people who are responsible for the actual working of the Internet and is useless for most people in the real world.

You can use the Macintosh Finger utility mentioned in the previous section to access a Whois server with these steps.

1. Launch Finger by double-clicking on its icon.

2. Select the Finger… command from the File menu. The Finger dialog box will be displayed, as shown in Figure 4-26.

3. Enter the name of the person you are trying to locate in the User box.

4. Check the **Whois Server** checkbox. The Finger button will change into a Whois button.

5. Click the **Whois** button. The results will be displayed in a window similar to the one shown in Figure 4-27.

Using the PSI White Pages

Performance Systems International (PSI)—an Internet service provider—offers a directory service that is accessible to Mac users with the PSIWP software program. You can FTP the software directly from the PSI archive at the address ftp.psi.com. Unfortunately, most of the listings seem to be for PSI clients or employees.

To access PSI's white pages service

1. Launch the PSIWP program by double-clicking on its icon. The program's Watch window will be displayed. This window is used to translate your menu selections and dialog box actions into command lines that the server can understand.

2. Select the Find… command from the White Pages menu. The program's Find dialog box will be displayed.

3. Enter the name of the person you want to locate in the box. Alternatively, you can enter a partial domain name so long as it is preceded with the "@" symbol.

4. Click the **OK** button. The program will perform the search and display the results in a separate window, as shown in the example in Figure 4-29.

Figure 4-29: PSI
White Pages
search results
window.

Future Directory Services

By the time you read this, AT&T should be providing an Internet
Yellow Pages. Look for specific information about this new service in
your first electronic update. For more information on *The Macintosh
Internet Tour Guide*'s electronic updates, see Appendix A.

E-Mail Address Starter Kit

Lots of Macintosh-related companies and luminaries are accessible by
Internet e-mail. A starter kit of some e-mail addresses is provided in
the table in Figure 4-30.

Figure 4-30:
Macintosh-related
e-mail addresses.

Company/Person	E-Mail Address
Apple Computer, Inc.	info@apple.com
Apple Developer Support	devsupport@applelink.apple.com
John Perry Barlow	barlow@well.sf.ca.us
Jerry Berman	jberman@eff.org
Steve Bobker	72511.45@compuserve.com
Stewart Brand	sbb@well.sf.ca.us

Company/Person	E-Mail Address
CPSR	cpsr-staff@csli.stanford.edu
Steve Dorner	sdorner@qualcom.qualcomm.com
Dan Farber	72511.124@compuserve.com
Ric Ford	72511.44@compuserve.com
Frame Technology	comments@frame.com
Hyde Park Software	info@hydepark.com
Andy Ihnatko	andyi@world.std.com
InterCon Systems, Inc.	info@intercon.com
Mitch Kapor	mkapor@eff.org
Guy Kawasaki	76703.3031@compuserve.com
Bob LeVitus	76004.2076@compuserve.com
Henry Norr	76117.1770@compuserve.com
Ruffin Prevost	ventana500@aol.com
Mitch Ratcliffe	coyote@well.sf.ca.us
Howard Rheingold	hlr@well.sf.ca.us
Kathleen Tinkel	76702.750@compuserve.com
Whole Earth Review	wer@well.sf.ca.us

And don't worry that you might be annoying these people by sending them mail—they've all published their e-mail addresses.

Electronic Mailing Lists

Electronic mailing lists have very little in common with their paper mail counterparts, even though they work in much the same manner.

- Electronic mailing lists actually serve a useful purpose.
- You have to specifically request to join an electronic mailing list.
- Electronic mailing lists don't overflow landfills.

Electronic mailing lists exist either as a forum for group discussions or as distribution lists. Currently, there are close to 3,000 publicly accessible mailing lists on the Internet. They cover a wide variety of subjects, and the number grows daily. You can find a mailing list for just about any subject of interest. If not, you can always start your own.

You can join a mailing list by sending e-mail to the list administrator. Once your name has been added to the list, you'll begin receiving messages from other members of the list, and you can read and respond to any of those messages. Your responses will automatically be forwarded to all the other subscribers on the list.

The quality of mailing lists is generally higher than in USENET newsgroups, because the "signal to noise ratio" is higher—there are generally more worthwhile messages in a day's mailing list message traffic than there are in a day's newsgroup message traffic. It's pretty rare to find an Ivy League freshman wanting to sell a microwave oven in a cyberpunk mailing list, but that's a pretty common happening in most any newsgroup (especially in the early autumn).

You can download a list of current mailing lists from ftp.nisc.sri.com in the directory /netinfo/interest-groups/.

Subscribing to Mailing Lists

Most mailing lists are set up to automatically forward any message sent to the list to all members of the mailing list. You subscribe to an electronic mailing list by sending an e-mail request to the list's administrative address. The list's *administrative address* is almost always different from the list's *submission address*. Many mailing list administrative addresses can be recognized by the word "request" in the list address. Make sure you use the right address for the job.

In general, to subscribe to a mailing list you send a short message requesting a subscription to the mailing list's administrative address. Some mailing lists are automated and have specific subscription requirements.

For example, to subscribe to the Info-Mac Digest mailing list

1. Launch Eudora (or TCP/Connect II) by double-clicking on its icon.

2. Send a message consisting only of the single line: subscribe info-mac *your name* where *your name* is your first and last name. For example, for my subscription, the line would be subscribe info-mac michael fraase

3. Address the e-mail message to listserv@ricevm1.rice.edu

4. Send the e-mail message. You'll receive a response introducing you to the mailing list and instructions on how to use it.

The Info-Mac Digest is run by a *Listserv* automated mail server. A Listserv mail server is simply a computer program that accepts and responds to the commands you send it.

Use these steps to subscribe to a manual mailing list, like the Electronic Frontier Foundation's mailing list.

1. Launch Eudora (or TCP/Connect II) by double-clicking on its icon.

2. Send a brief message requesting to be added to the mailing list. Just a simple message like "please add me to the EFF mailing list, thanks" is enough.

3. Address the message to eff-request@eff.org

4. Send the e-mail message. You'll receive a response from the list owner or the person administrating the mailing list.

The table in Figure 4-31 provides a general overview for some of the popular mailing lists.

Figure 4-31: Electronic mailing list subscription information
Note: Addresses in this chart are too long to fit on a single line, but they should be entered as a single address, with no spaces or breaks.

Mailing List	Administrative Address	Subscription Instructions	Submission Address
EFF	eff-request@eff.org	send brief request	eff@eff.org
Eudora	listserv@vmd.cso.uiuc.edu	subscribe eudora your name in message	eudora@vmd.cso.uiuc.edu
FrameMaker	framers-request@drd.com	send brief request	framers@drd.com
Grateful Dead	dead-flames-request@fuggles.acc.virginia.edu	send brief request acc.virginia.edu	dead-flames@fuggles.acc.virginia.edu
Info-Mac	listserv@ricevm1.rice.edu	subscribe info-mac your name in message	info-mac@ricevm1.rice.edu

Mailing List	Administrative Address	Subscription Instructions	Submission Address
New Lists	listserv@vm1.nodak.edu	subscribe new-list your name in message	new-list@vm1. nodak.edu
PowerBook	listserv@yalevm.ycc.yale. edu	subscribe macpb-l your name in message	macpb-l@yalevm. ycc.yale.edu
TidBITS	listserv@ricevm1.rice.edu	subscribe tidbits your name in message	tidbits@ricevm1. rice.edu
University of Michigan Recent Files	mac-recent-request@mac. archive.umich.edu	Send brief request	mac-recent@mac. archive.umich.edu

Cancelling Subscriptions to Mailing Lists

In general, to cancel your subscription to a mailing list you send a short message requesting to be removed from the list to the mailing list's administrative address. Some mailing lists are automated and have specific subscription cancellation requirements.

For example, use these instructions to cancel your subscription to the automated Info-Mac Digest mailing list.

1. Launch Eudora (or TCP/Connect II) by double-clicking on its icon.

2. Send a message consisting only of the single line: signoff info-mac *your name* where *your name* is your first and last name. For example, for my subscription, the line would be signoff info-mac michael fraase

3. Address the e-mail message to listserv@ricevm1.rice.edu

Send the e-mail message. You'll receive a response acknowledging your subscription cancellation and removal from the mailing list.

Use these steps to cancel your subscription to a manual mailing list, like the Electronic Frontier Foundation's mailing list.

1. Launch Eudora (or TCP/Connect II) by double-clicking on its icon.

2. Send a brief message requesting to be removed from the mailing list. Just a simple message like "please remove me from the EFF mailing list, thanks" is enough.

3. Address the message to eff-request@eff.org

Send the e-mail message. You'll receive a response from the list owner or the person administrating the mailing list acknowledging your subscription cancellation and removal from the mailing list.

E-Mail & Attached Files

In addition to sending *messages*, you can also use e-mail to send any sort of *file* through the Internet. Actually, most Macintosh files have to first be converted to a text document before you can send them through the Internet, but the good news is that the process is automatic and transparent. Both Eudora (which is included on *The Mac Internet Tour Guide* companion disk) and TCP/Connect II automatically convert any Macintosh file for transmission over the network.

The two programs take different approaches to sending files through e-mail, however. Eudora's implementation is more elegant, allowing you to *attach* a file to an e-mail message. This lets you describe the file for your recipient by providing a brief text note at the top of the e-mail message. TCP/Connect II's approach is to simply send the file without any notation.

Sending Files in E-Mail Messages

To attach a file to an e-mail message in Eudora

1. Create an e-mail message as you ordinarily would, following steps 1–8 in "Creating an E-Mail Message With Eudora."

2. Select the Attach Document… command from the Message menu. A standard Open File dialog box will be displayed.

3. Select the file you want to attach to the e-mail message by double-clicking on its name in the Open File dialog box. The attached file's name and location will be added to the Attachments line in the message header, as shown in Figure 4-32.

Figure 4-32:
Eudora message
header with
attached file.

4. Click the **Send** button in the Message Composition window. The message will be sent immediately.

   ▓ If you have set Eudora's preferences to queue mail, there will be a **Queue** button in far right end of the Icon Bar instead of the **Send** button.

To send a file through e-mail with TCP/Connect II

1. Launch TCP/Connect II by double-clicking on its icon.

2. Select the Send File... command from the Mail menu. A standard Open File dialog box will be displayed.

3. Select the file you want to send by double-clicking on its name in the Open File dialog box. TCP/Connect II's Send window will be displayed.

4. Address your file as you would any other e-mail message, using steps 5–9 in "Creating an E-Mail Message With TCP/Connect II."

5. Click the **Send** button. Your file will be sent to the specified recipients if you have an active network connection. If your network connection is inactive, the file will be saved in your Mail folder and automatically sent the next time you login to your mail server.

Receiving Files in E-Mail Messages

Receiving files attached to e-mail messages is automatic in Eudora. The attached files of any e-mail message are automatically converted and saved in the folder you specified for received files when you configured Eudora.

If you're using TCP/Connect II, you have to manually save files that you receive by e-mail. The only exception to this is if the sender used TCP/Connect II to mail the file to you. In either case, the file is automatically converted into its original Macintosh file format.

To save files you receive by e-mail with TCP/Connect II

1. Launch TCP/Connect II by double-clicking on its icon.

2. Retrieve your mail as you ordinarily would, following steps 2–7 in "Retrieving & Reading E-Mail With TCP/Connect II."

3. Files sent to you by another TCP/Connect II user will appear in your In Box window with a document icon (instead of the regular envelope icon), as shown in Figure 4-33.

Figure 4-33: TCP/Connect II In Box window with received file.

4. Double-click on the subject line of the received file. A standard Save File dialog box will appear.

5. Navigate to the folder where you want to save the received file and click the **Save** button. The file will be saved in the location you selected.

6. Drag the file over the StuffIt Expander icon and drop it onto the icon once it is highlighted. The file will be automatically decompressed.

Note that files sent to you by someone using any other e-mail program will appear as standard e-mail messages (with the familiar envelope icon) in your TCP/Connect II In Box window.

To save these files to your hard disk drive

1. Double-click on the subject line of the message you want to read. The message will be displayed, as shown in the example in Figure 4-34.

Figure 4-34:
TCP/Connect II
Message window
with received file.

2. Select the Save As… command from the File menu. A standard Save File dialog box will be displayed.

3. Navigate to the folder where you want to save the received file and click the **Save** button. The file will be saved in the location you selected.

4. Drag the file over the StuffIt Expander icon and drop it onto the icon once it is highlighted. The file will be automatically decompressed.

Files in E-Mail Caveats

From time to time, you may receive non-Macintosh files by e-mail. One of the hottest trends in cross-platform software is something called "binary compatibility." That's a software program that runs on different kinds of computer hardware and saves its documents in a format that is common to all the different kinds of computers. FrameMaker documents, for example, are binary compatible, regardless of the kind of computer used to create them. I can open NeXT, Windows or UNIX FrameMaker files on my Macintosh without converting them.

But since people often compress binary files before sending them, and there are different compression utilities for each kind of computer, you can imagine the problems that can arise. What do you do with UNIX files you receive that have been "tarred and compressed?" Or what about those goofy DOS files that have been "zipped?" This dilemma is covered in "A Primer on File Types," in Chapter 6, "Transferring Files."

Be careful with the size of the files you send by e-mail. Most of the e-mail gateways provided by the commercial information services like CompuServe and America Online have severe file-size limitations, as indicated in Figure 4-1. TCP/Connect II allows you to specify a maximum size for e-mail messages and files, and it will automatically split the file into separate messages, as shown in Figure 4-35.

Figure 4-35:
TCP/Connect II In
Box window with
file received in
split segments.

You can use TCP/Connect II to save a multi-part file by double-clicking on the first segment, specifying the folder where you want to save the complete file, and clicking the **Save** button. TCP/Connect II will automatically convert and reconstitute the file segments into the image of the original file.

Moving On

This chapter has given you a thorough overview of electronic mail, from the nuts and bolts of how to send and receive it to the subtleties of e-mail courtesy and etiquette. Look for more in-depth information about using e-mail (plus evaluations of new e-mail products) in this book's electronic updates.

E-mail is most useful for communicating with individuals or small groups of people. But what if you want to exchange information with large groups of people, all over the world? That's what Network News is for, the topic of the next chapter. So let's stop the tour bus at that newsstand just ahead and take a break to learn about reading and posting USENET news articles.

CHAPTER 5

NETWORK NEWS & NEWSGROUPS
Broadsheets of the Broadband

the text around the outside reads:
"When reality is contained, we all are biblical. Just believe."

As our tour through the Internet continues, it's easy to become overwhelmed with the size and scope of all that it offers. But one of the most important resources on the Net is easy to overlook: people. Network news and newsgroups are valuable because of the insights and information that people bring to them.

For instance, wouldn't it be great if you could poll all the most knowledgeable folks on the Internet for answers to technical questions, or advice on everything from buying the best VCR to cooking the perfect pot roast? While electronic mail is useful for communicating with another individual or small workgroup, you can't send e-mail to thousands of people you don't know, asking questions about topics that don't interest them. (Well, I suppose you *could*, but it probably wouldn't be very productive. And if you think it sounds like it might be a good idea, put this book down and go outside for a walk. A long walk.) But with network news, there's a better way.

What Is Network News & What Are Newsgroups?

Think of network news as a worldwide collection of automatically updated electronic bulletin boards. Except these aren't bulletin boards like the single-line systems set up by thousands of hobbyists in small towns across America. Network news messages are seen by millions of people who generate as much as 40mb of network news information every day.

Electronic bulletin boards are like the cork bulletin boards you see at your local grocery store. You know, where you can find a great deal on a 1955 Buick or a litter of prize poodle puppies. Network news on the Internet is the same concept, only it's all electronic and much more extensive. Imagine the electronic equivalent of 4,000 different grocery store cork bulletin boards, and you've got a pretty good grasp of the thousands of newsgroups that make up network news.

If you've used CompuServe or America Online, you're probably familiar with the concept of forums or bulletin boards. Each newsgroup is roughly equivalent to a message area on America Online or Compu-Serve, except that network news newsgroups are seen by many more people, and on the Internet, highly specialized newsgroups are available for just about any topic.

You'll see everything from announcements for new software products to in-depth technical discussions to candid—and sometimes heated—conversations. These super-heated discussions are called *flame wars*; each individual message in a flame war is called a *flame*. Flames are considered to be in bad taste (except in newsgroups set up just for flames), and starting a flame war will win you lots of enemies with long memories. Each message within an individual newsgroup is called a *post* or an *article*. Articles can be cross-posted to several newsgroups, but this practice is considered bad form unless the article is especially relevant to several newsgroups.

Articles within each newsgroup are arranged in *topics*. Topics within a newsgroup about laptop computers, for instance, may include battery conservation tips, problems with a specific model's keyboard or comparisons between different available configurations. Initial queries or informational articles will likely generate several responses. This patchwork of queries and responses forms a *message thread* within a specific topic. The software you use to read network news will automatically piece together the various queries and responses in logical order. The original article will appear first, followed by any available *followup* (response) articles in the message thread.

E-mail blind courtesy copies that aren't.
There is a troublesome fluke with most mail servers on the Internet that could prove to be as embarrassing for you as it was for me. If you send an e-mail message to a group of people, with each recipient sent a blind courtesy copy, make sure you also e-mail a copy to at least one address in the To: field. If you send an e-mail message with the To: field empty, most mail servers will insert "Apparently-To:" addresses, neatly listing every recipient of your blind courtesy copies.

Network news is actually not even part of the Internet—although, to the uninitiated, it is probably perceived as being the most easily recognizable part of the Internet. Network news is transmitted on USENET, a network of about 3 million people (mostly UNIX users). USENET is even more disjointed and anarchic than the Internet. Just about the only thing USENET sites have in common is that they communicate using the UNIX to UNIX Copy Protocol (UUCP). Some USENET sites have connections to the Internet, which is how network news—and other USENET traffic—gets to the Internet.

Internet sites that provide a network news server use the Network News Transfer Protocol (NNTP) to provide a database for local news clients and to transfer news between servers. In order to read network news on the Internet, you must use NNTP client software or use the archaic UNIX commands for navigating and reading newsgroups.

Network news is divided into *newsgroups*. Each newsgroup is devoted to a single topic (at least hypothetically; most newsgroups sort of cross-pollinate one another). Each newsgroup article is received and stored on each participating USENET computer. Unlike e-mail, where the messages are actually sent to your computer and stored on your own hard drive, newsgroup articles are stored on a *news server*, at the site that services your account. The newsgroup articles you read are stored on the news server, not on your own computer.

The network news—or USENET—newsgroups are organized in a hierarchy. Each newsgroup has a name with periods in it, similar to the Internet domain name system. The periods (read as "dots") separate the various hierarchical levels. For example, comp.sys.mac.system is read as "comp-dot-sys-dot-mac-dot-system" or "comp-sys-mac-system" and reflects the hierarchy shown in Figure 5-1.

Figure 5-1:
Network news
newsgroups
hierarchy.

comp.sys.mac.system

translates in the newsgroup hierarchy to:

Computers

Systems

Macintosh

System Software

There are several top-level newsgroup categories in the hierarchy, as shown in Figure 5-2.

Figure 5-2:
Network news
newsgroups top-
level categories.

Category	Topic Explanation
alt	Alternative discussions; not carried by all sites. The newsgroups found here range from the bizarre to the useful. The most useful "alt" newsgroups were created in this top-level hierarchy to avoid going through the bureaucratic hassle of forming a certified newsgroup.
bionet	Biology discussions.
bit	Discussions that originate from Bitnet Listserv mailing lists.
biz	Business discussions. Commercial articles are permitted only in this top-level hierarchy.
comp	Computer discussions.
misc	Miscellaneous discussions—topics that don't fit in any of the other top-level hierarchies.
news	Discussions related to network news and the software used to transmit, read and create articles.

Category	Topic Explanation
rec	Recreation discussions and topics related to the arts.
sci	"Hard" science discussions.
soc	Discussions related to social issues.
talk	Argumentative discussions.

An Overview of Newsgroups

There are more than 4,000 active newsgroups covering virtually every conceivable topic. Some network-savvy observers in mainstream media hypothesize that the Internet will eventually replace most sources of news. It simply won't happen—at least not for another 10 years or so. Computer news and Grateful Dead concert dates travel faster on the Net than they do through other news channels, but that's about it.

There was one case of "pseudo-news" on the Internet. In April 1992, an area developed on IRC (Internet Relay Chat—similar to a wide-open international conference call using keyboards instead of phones) that carried news relays of the Los Angeles riots following the first Rodney King verdict. Of course, most of the information came from people who were simply relaying what they had received from local television coverage.

You can always find a regularly updated list of all available newsgroups by reading the news.list newsgroup.

Interesting Newsgroups

Interesting newsgroups exist for just about any topic you can think of. A listing of some is provided in the table in Figure 5-3. Remember, this is just a tiny sample of the thousands of newsgroups you can access via the Internet.

Figure 5-3:
Interesting
newsgroup
descriptions.

Newsgroup	Description
comp.archives	Listings and descriptions of public-access archives (moderated) [1]
comp.dcom.isdn	Discussions related to the Integrated Services Digital Network (ISDN)
comp.dcom.telcom	Telecommunications digest (moderated)
comp.infosystems.gopher	Discussions related to Gopher
comp.newprod	Computer product announcements (moderated)
comp.org.acm	Discussions related to the Association for Computing Machinery (ACM)
comp.org.eff.news	Electronic Frontier Foundation (EFF) news (moderated)
comp.org.eff.talk	Discussions related to the Electronic Frontier Foundation (EFF)
comp.risks	Discussions related to the risks of computers (moderated)
comp.society.cu-digest	Computer Underground Digest (moderated)
comp.society.privacy	Discussions related to computers and privacy in society (moderated)
comp.text.desktop	Discussions related to desktop publishing
misc.consumers	Discussions related to consumer interest
misc.entrepreneurs	Discussions related to running a business
misc.invest	Discussions related to investing
misc.jobs.contract	Postings of work-for-hire contract availability
misc.jobs.offered	Listings of positions available
misc.jobs.offered.entry	Listings of entry-level positions available
misc.jobs.resumes	Listings of resumes and position queries
news.announce.important	Announcements of general interest (moderated)
news.announce.newgroups	Announcements of new newsgroups (moderated)

[1] Moderated newsgroups are best described as read-only newsgroups. Don't send articles directly to the newsgroup; instead, follow the instructions available in each moderated newsgroup. In general, you send articles to the group's moderator, who posts them as appropriate.

Newsgroup	Description
news.announce.newusers	Announcements for new users (moderated)
news.newusers.questions	Questions and answers for new users
rec.arts.movies	Discussions related to film
rec.arts.movies.reviews	Movie reviews (moderated)
rec.mag	Discussions related to magazines
rec.music.bluenote	Discussions related to jazz and blues
rec.music.dylan	Discussions related to Bob Dylan's music
rec.music.gdead	Dead-head discussions
rec.music.reggae	Discussions related to reggae music
rec.sport.baseball	Discussions related to baseball
soc.culture.japan	Discussions related to Japan and Japanese culture
soc.politics	Political discussions (moderated)
soc.rights.human	Discussions related to human rights and activism

Macintosh Newsgroups

Several newsgroups cater specifically to the Macintosh community.
A listing of these newsgroups is provided in the table in Figure 5-4.

Figure 5-4: Macintosh newsgroups descriptions.

Newsgroup	Description
comp.sources.mac	Macintosh software sources (moderated)
comp.sys.mac.advocacy	Macintosh flame wars
comp.sys.mac.announce	Important Macintosh-specific announcements (moderated)
comp.sys.mac.apps	Discussions related to Macintosh software programs
comp.sys.mac.comm	Discussions related to Macintosh communications
comp.sys.mac.databases	Discussions related to Macintosh database software
comp.sys.mac.digest	Discussions related to general Macintosh use; includes listings of additions to major archive sites (moderated)
comp.sys.mac.games	Discussions related to Macintosh game software

Newsgroup	Description
comp.sys.mac.hardware	Discussions related to Macintosh hardware
comp.sys.mac.hypercard	Discussions related to HyperCard
comp.sys.mac.misc	Discussions related to the Macintosh that don't fit in any of the other comp.sys.mac newsgroups
comp.sys.mac.oop	Discussions related to Macintosh object-oriented programming
comp.sys.mac.programmer	Discussions related to programming on the Macintosh
comp.sys.mac.system	Discussions related to the Macintosh system software
comp.sys.mac.wanted	Macintosh-specific for sale (and items wanted) articles
misc.forsale.computers.mac	Macintosh-specific items for sale

A Primer on Newsgroup Etiquette

The USENET news system is a remarkable beast. By nature, it is a wide open terrain with absolutely no restraints on freedom of expression. Each author assumes the responsibility for his or her articles, and the uncensored environment of network news is widely appreciated.

News article posting etiquette is based pretty much on the kind of behavior you'd expect in a college dormitory: don't hit anyone, and clean up your own messes. The sole overriding principle is that just about anything is allowed, as long as it does not put the network itself in jeopardy. While you're pondering what that really means, here are a few tips to get you started:

- I remember asking one of my teachers how long an essay I had been assigned should be; her response simultaneously answered my question and taught me about metaphor. She told me the essay should be like a woman's skirt: short enough to be interesting but long enough to cover the subject. Her advice is appropriate for news articles as well.

- Lots of people on the Internet read hundreds of messages each day. You can't reasonably expect someone to remember what has been said in every previous message. Include appropriate background material that will help the reader understand the context of your message.

■ By the same token, don't provide 50 lines of background about a message if you're only responding to a small part of it. Don't for example, quote a 1000-line article only to add "I agree!"

Evangelizing the Internet.

Paul Jacoby is a consultant with David Mitchell & Associates, on assignment with 3M. He's been working long and hard to introduce 3M employees to the Internet:

"I've been in the process of evangelizing the Internet to the folks I work with here at 3M. The main response I get from people who begin to delve into the depths of the Internet is, 'Wow, I had no idea this existed!' Followed closely by 'You mean it's *free?*'

"People are continually amazed at the concepts of software archives ('... filled with *free* software?') and the near instantaneous access to points across the globe. Most are tickled to death to find associates with Internet addresses, exchanging e-mail with turn-around time in the sub-minute range.

"In presenting a summary of the Internet and trying to describe how it works, I boiled all the technical stuff down to one important phrase: It's *automagic*, i.e., don't worry, be happy, use and learn without worrying about the fine points. Most people are quite happy to operate this way :-)"

■ Limit your lines to lengths of 80 characters or less.

■ Don't use long, rambling signatures or include ASCII graphics— keep it to four lines or less.

■ Don't post "me too!" followup articles unless you have a worth-while comment to add.

■ Use the right newsgroup for the job. Some newsgroups are intended for discussions while others are intended for announcements. Don't engage in discussions in newsgroups intended for announcements.

■ Newsgroups are called newsgroups, not bulletin boards, boards or bboards.

■ Don't post private e-mail correspondence in a network news article without the permission of the author. While it may be technically legal to do so, it's rude and could be a copyright violation in some circumstances. (Besides, would you want someone plastering your private e-mail on a network where 10 million people could read it?)

■ Don't ask what ":-)" means (tilt your head 90 degrees to the left and see the smiley sidebar later in this chapter.)

- Don't post flames outside a newsgroup labeled specifically for flames. (See the section "Flames, Flame-Bait, &Flaming" later in this chapter.)

- Don't end your post with a snooty comment like "Please send e-mail, because I don't read this newsgroup." If you don't read a newsgroup, why would you be posting messages there?

- Don't use excessive CAPITALIZATION & PUNCTUATION!!!!!!!!!!

- Don't cross-post to multiple newsgroups unless it's completely relevant and absolutely necessary.

- If you ask for help with a software program, make sure you state what kind of computer you're using. Not everyone uses a Macintosh. Also, include specific details like which model Mac you have, how much RAM you have, what version of the system software you're using and so on.

- Keep a sense of humor. There's little room for self-righteous stuffed shirts in the world of network news.

- Don't post articles about what kind of computer is better. Similarly, don't respond to articles arguing the issue.

- Before posting a question in a newsgroup, read its Frequently Asked Questions (FAQ) file. These files contain answers to—you guessed it—the most frequently asked questions. Most newsgroups post the FAQ file to the newsgroup on a regular basis. The FAQ files for most newsgroups are available by FTP from pit-manager.mit.edu.

- Understand that you're going to make mistakes, and as sure as grits is groceries, some jerk's going to let you know about it when you do. Try to keep a thick skin about it. See the sidebar about my first network news mistake for an example.

My First Network News Mistake.

Less than a month after I started using the Internet, I asked a stupid question in the comp.sys.mac.misc newsgroup. I had accumulated quite a few PostScript files—mostly documentation—some of them very large.

I didn't want to waste paper by printing these files out if I could view them on the screen. My assumption was that if there were all these wonderful Macintosh-specific Internet software tools, there was probably a PostScript viewer somewhere. I had checked every archive I knew about, but I couldn't find one.

More

Timidity is not usually one of my more defining qualities, but I timidly—*yes timidly*—posted a very short query on comp.sys.mac.misc. Something on the order of "Does anyone know where I can find a PostScript viewer for the Mac? This is for multi-page, raw PostScript files, not EPS documents."

Within hours I received 10 e-mail responses. The more polite of the bunch were to the effect of, "You ignorant *?!)&$. Why don't you read the *$?)#!* FAQ??!!" I didn't have the slightest idea what a FAQ was, and I sure wasn't going to ask.

A day or so later the comp.sys.mac.misc FAQ was posted and, of course, my question was answered:

IS THERE A UTILITY TO VIEW POSTSCRIPT FILES ON THE MAC? (11.1)
Net godhood awaits the first person to write a shareware or freeware solution to this problem. The payware products Canvas 3.0 and TScript allow viewing PostScript files on the Mac, but both are large packages with other purposes and cost over $50 each.

I drew some strange consolation from knowing that the FAQ file is at least partially wrong. I've never heard of TScript, but Canvas can't deal with multi-page, raw PostScript files.

What continues to confound me is that every one of the pinheads that responded to my original question at length could have saved themselves a lot of trouble with a simple, two-letter, one-word response: "No."

I think it's either a network culture thing ("let's jump the newbie") or these guys have canned messages that they automatically send out as one of their few means of entertainment.

Since then, a PostScript viewer for the Macintosh—GhostScript—has been released. It's available in the Info-Mac and Michigan archives, if you're interested, but it's useless for multi-page documents.

Flames, Flame-Bait & Flaming

You'll hear a lot about *flames* while reading network news. A flame is an inflammatory message, usually posted for no other reason than to start an argument. It's pretty common for someone to login to one of the comp.sys.mac newsgroups (a stronghold of Macintosh advocates) and post a message with a title like, "Macs suck, buy a PC!" The best response to this sort of wasted bandwidth is to ignore it. Unfortunately, the message always gets answered and a *flame war* erupts, with vile epithets hurled in all directions.

Emotion is hard to communicate on the network. Irony and sarcasm are easily misinterpreted without verbal cues or body language. Similarly, terseness can come across as rudeness. And until we can add italics and bold type to our messages, things are even worse— we're limited to ASCII text as the lowest common denominator.

In general, use of capital letters is considered shouting, so be careful how you use them. You can show emphasis by setting off a word or phrase with asterisks: That's *not* what I said. This is considered more polite and respectful than: That's NOT what I said.

Another result of the difficulty of communicating with only ASCII text is the *smiley*. Tilt your head 90 degrees counterclockwise and look at this:

:-)

Remember those yellow "Have a Nice Day" smiley faces? Well, a smiley, like the one shown above, is the electronic equivalent. A smiley is used to convey emotion within an electronic message, and you'll find them widely used throughout the Internet. I hate them, and I almost never use them (in fact, I can't think of a single time I've used one). But they are everywhere, and you'd better learn to decode them. For more information, see the smiley sidebar.

Smiley Gallery

Here are a few of the more common smileys you're likely to encounter.

Figure 5-5: Basic smiley decoder.

Smiley	Meaning
:-)	basic smiley; connotes cheer or a grin, sometimes tongue-in-cheek sarcasm
;-)	wink; connotes light sarcasm
:-I	indifference
:->	devilish grin; connotes heavy sarcasm
:-(	frown; connotes anger or displeasure
@:-)	curly hair
8-)	eye-glasses
:-D	shock or surprise
:-/	perplexed
:-P	tongue sticking out

Abbreviation Mysteries

There is a set of abbreviations that are commonly used as shorthand in network communications. Don't worry too much about decoding abbreviations you see. You'll find that they're pretty self-explanatory in context; sort of like reading real-estate listings or personal ads in the newspaper. Here are some of the abbreviations in widest use.

More

Figure 5-6:	**Abbreviation**	**Meaning**
Basic shorthand decoder.	**IMHO**	in my humble opinion (it very rarely is)
	BTW	by the way
	ROTFL	rolling on the floor laughing
	TANSTAAFL	there ain't no such thing as a free lunch
	OBO	or best offer
	RTFM	read the *funny* manual
	FYI	for your information

Now that you know a little about the politics and etiquette of using network news, you can start reading and posting on your own. But first, you'll need a first-class utility for navigating newsgroups and composing and posting articles.

Selecting a News Reader

A news reader is a software program that runs on your Mac that simplifies the process of navigating and reading network news articles. You use this program to select which newsgroups you want to monitor on a regular basis and which articles you want to read. You also use the news reader to post new articles or reply to existing ones. It's important that you choose a news reader that you can live with—one that lets you quickly navigate through the thousands of pages of articles available—to target the information you need.

There are several good news readers available for the Macintosh, and new ones under development. One of the most popular Macintosh news readers is Peter Speck's Nuntius. Nuntius is distributed as *freeware*; you can use it free of charge, but the author reserves copyright. The news reader I prefer is the news module of TCP/Connect II, which is a commercial product.

In this chapter, we'll walk through the steps for configuring and using both of these products for reading network news.

Configuring Nuntius

If you don't already have a news reader and you want to get your hands on a great one for free, you can use Fetch (the navigation and file transfer utility included on this book's companion disk) to download the most recent version of Nuntius. You'll find it in the Macintosh archive at Stanford University. If you'd like to get a copy of Nuntius but you're unfamiliar with how to download files, "Downloading Files With Fetch" in Chapter 6, "Transferring Files," gives you complete instructions on where to find and how to download your very own copy of Nuntius.

Briefly, you can download the latest version of Nuntius from the FTP site at sumex-aim.stanford.edu. Check the /info-mac/comm/ directory. As of early April 1993, the current version of Nuntius is 1.1.1d17. The complete pathname in the Stanford archive is /info-mac/comm/ nuntius-111d17.hqx.

To configure Nuntius for use with your news server

1. Launch Nuntius by double-clicking on its icon. The News server dialog box will appear as shown in Figure 5-7.

Figure 5-7: Nuntius News server dialog box.

2. Enter the domain name or IP address of your news server in the box. (If you don't know the address, check with your network administrator or commercial service provider.)

3. Click the **OK** button.

   ▧ Nuntius will retrieve and build a list of all available newsgroups on your news server. This may take a while. This process occurs only the first time you configure Nuntius, and whenever you manually choose to rebuild the list of all available newsgroups.

■ When Nuntius is finished building the list, two windows will be displayed on your screen—a list of available newsgroups and an empty, untitled group list—as shown in Figure 5-8.

Figure 5-8: Nuntius windows: All Groups (left) and empty Untitled group list (right).

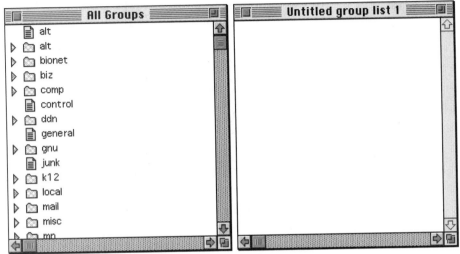

4. Pick a top-level newsgroup category in the All Groups window that interests you, and double-click on its folder icon.

■ The folder will open, displaying a list of available newsgroups, and any subfolders representing subcategories in the newsgroup hierarchy. For example, the comp.sys.mac newsgroups are located inside of the sys folder, which itself is inside the comp folder. Some of the newsgroups are nested deep within multiple subcategories.

5. Click and hold on the newsgroup to which you want to subscribe.

■ Select multiple newsgroups within the same category by shift-clicking on each newsgroup you want to select, just as you choose files or folders in the Finder. Note that you can only use this technique to select newsgroups within the same category.

6. Drag your selection into the empty Untitled group list window, as shown in Figure 5-9.

Figure 5-9:
Nuntius partially
expanded All
Groups hierarchy
(left) and Untitled
group list window
with subscribed
newsgroups
(right).

7. From the File menu, select the Save As... command. A standard Save File dialog box will appear.

8. Enter a name for the group list. Obviously, it helps to choose a name that relates to the subject matter of the newsgroups in that list, so don't name it something like "My Newsgroups."

Meckler Publishing.
Meckler Publishing (Westport, CT) is aggressively developing Internet guides for librarians, researchers and information professionals. Contact meckler@jvnc.net for notification of coming books on Internet basics, electronic scholarship, Internet directories, WAIS and Gopher servers, citation of electronic sources, Internet/NREN policy, etc. Meckler's quarterly *Electronic Networking* will now be *Internet Research: Electronic Networking, Applications, and Policy.*

9. Click the **Save** button. The newsgroup list will be saved to your hard drive at the location you specified.

10. From the Prefs menu, select the Your Name... command. The Your Name Preferences dialog box will appear, as shown in Figure 5-10.

Figure 5-10:
Nuntius Your
Name Preferences
dialog box.

Preferences: Your name

Your real name:

Your e-mail address:

Name of your organization:

[Cancel] [OK]

11. Enter your full name in the name box.

12. Enter your e-mail address (using the username@domain.top-domain format) in the e-mail address box.

13. Enter the name of your organization (if appropriate) in the organization box.

14. Click the **OK** button. You've configured Nuntius appropriately for basic news reading tasks.

Managing network news and newsgroups can quickly become an overwhelming task. A good approach is to begin by selecting only those newsgroups you are especially interested in. Later, if you find you have enough time to read more articles, you can create additional lists or add more newsgroups to existing lists. It's much easier to add newsgroups later than to wade through massive amounts of information you may not be interested in.

Nuntius does not have a built-in editor (a program that you can use to compose and format responses), which is fine if all you want to do is read other people's postings. But who wants to be just a spectator? It's easy to specify an editor using these steps:

1. From the Prefs menu, select the Editing Articles... command. The Editor Preferences dialog box will appear, as shown in Figure 5-11.

Figure 5-11:
Nuntius Editor
Preferences
dialog box.

Preferences: Editor

Editor of choice:

[Select new...]

Articles folder:

[Select new...]

☐ **Use signature as default**
Signature file...

[Select new...]

☐ **Edit signature when editing articles**
☐ **Edit headers (for wizards)**

Auto wrap width: 75

[Cancel]   [OK]

2. Click the **Editor of choice: Select new...** button. A standard Open File dialog box will appear.

3. Locate the text editor or word processor you want to use to write your news articles.

   ▓ Note that you can select any text editor or word processor for use with Nuntius. But you will probably want to choose a small, quick-opening editor, because Nuntius launches the editor automatically whenever you reply to an existing news article or create a new post. TeachText (which Apple includes with every Mac and is used for most Read Me documents) is a good choice if you don't have a text editor you prefer.

4. Click the **Open** button.

5. Click the **Articles folder: Select new...** button. A standard Open File dialog box will be displayed.

6. Navigate to the folder you want to use for your outgoing news articles. This folder will be used to hold temporary copies of the articles you create.

7. Click the **Select Folder** button.

8. Click the **Use signature as default** checkbox if you want your signature to be attached to each article you post. A signature is a three or four line text file containing your contact information. (For more on signatures, see the sidebar later in this chapter.)

9. Click the **Signature file… Select new…** button. A standard Open File dialog box will be displayed.

10. Navigate to the signature file you want to use. (If you don't have a signature file prepared, you can cancel and create one, then select it later when you're working in Nuntius once again.)

11. Click the **Open** button.

12. Click the **OK** button in the Preferences Editor dialog box. You've completely configured Nuntius for all network news tasks.

Configuring TCP/Connect II News Module

I prefer TCP/Connect II's news module for reading and posting network news. Although it's a commercial product, it provides an integrated environment for replying to news articles via e-mail. I especially like its article filtering capabilities—called "bozo filters" in UNIX-speak—which I use to automatically delete postings from certain individuals and automatically highlight postings from people whose opinions I don't want to miss.

Freeware SLIP software.

The programmers at Intercon Systems Corporation have created and released a freeware SLIP driver for the Macintosh. SLIP software allows you to login to the Internet (via a SLIP server) using a high-speed modem and ordinary telephone lines. The early reports are that it works quite well. The software is available by anonymous FTP at ftp.intercon.com in the /intercon/sales /directory.

To configure TCP/Connect II for use with your news server

1. Launch TCP/Connect II by double-clicking on its icon.

2. From the Edit menu select the Configure... command. The TCP/Connect II Configuration dialog box will appear.

3. Click on the News icon in the scrolling list of configuration items. The News Configuration panel will appear, like the configured example shown in Figure 5-12.

Figure 5-12: TCP/Connect II Configuration dialog box's News panel.

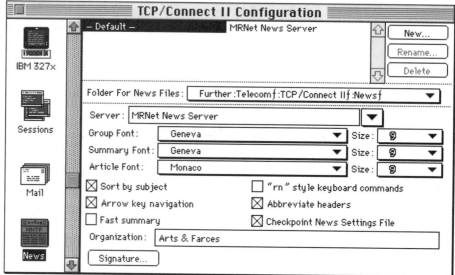

4. Enter the domain name or IP number of your NNTP server in the Server box. Alternatively, if you have already configured the server information for your news server, you can select its entry from the Server pop-up menu.

5. From the Folder For News Files pop-up menu, choose the Select Another Folder... item. This will specify a folder on your hard drive where news settings will be stored.

6. Customize the news display characteristics using the following criteria:

   ▇ From the Group Font pop-up menus, select an available font and size for displaying newsgroups.

■ From the Summary Font pop-up menus, select an available font and size for displaying news article summaries.

■ From the Article Font pop-up menus, select an available font and size for displaying news articles. .

■ Check the **Sort by subject** checkbox if you want news article summaries to be displayed in alphabetical order, rather than the order in which they were received by your news server.

■ Check the **Arrow key navigation** checkbox if you want to navigate through available news articles with the Arrow keys on the keyboard.

■ Check the **Fast summary** checkbox if you want to display only the Subject line of news articles within the news article summaries. This can be useful if you use SLIP or PPP to access the Internet. Note that when using this setting is that you can't use some of the more powerful news article filtering capabilities of TCP/Connect II.

■ Check the **"rn" style keyboard commands** checkbox if you want to torture yourself with the UNIX news reading commands. Actually, many long-time Internet users like the rn (read news) commands. I suspect it's because they got used to using them before there were news readers with a Macintosh interface, and their brains have been permanently imprinted with the appropriate commands. I've never been able to remember the commands, but TCP/Connect II provides them if you want them.

■ Check the **Abbreviate headers** checkbox if you want the header of each article to display only the subject, author, organization, summary, keywords and newsgroup information. This will eliminate a lot of the arcane network addressing information about where the message has been that works its way into article headers.

■ Check the **Checkpoint news settings file** checkbox if you want the current news settings to be saved whenever you switch newsgroups or modify your subscription list. This setting helps preserve the read/unread status of news articles in the event of a network error, software crash or power failure.

7. Enter the name of your organization (if appropriate) in the Organization box.

8. If you want your postings to include a signature, click the **Signature...** button. The Signature dialog box will be displayed.

9. Enter your optional signature in the box. A signature is a three or four line text file containing your contact information.

10. Click the **OK** button.

11. Click the close box of the Configuration dialog box. You've configured TCP/Connect II for network news tasks. All that's left now is to subscribe to the newsgroups you want to read. Subscribing to newsgroups via TCP/Connect II is covered in "Reading News With TCP/Connect II."

Internet Signatures.

Electronic communications—both e-mail and network news postings—are usually much less formal than the typical business letter. Formal salutations are rarely called for and are generally considered something of a waste of bandwidth.

Similarly, formal closings are almost never seen. Instead, most networkers end their messages with a *signature*. A signature is a short—four lines or less—identification tag that includes your full name, organization and contact information.

Signatures range in style from the strictly functional to the almost rococo-like. The function of a signature is to provide identification and contact information in case the address header is incorrect or incomplete.

The best signatures usually include a quote that tells you something about the person writing the message. Quotes are fine, but should be kept short and pithy .

In creating a signature, remember that ASCII text is still the lowest common denominator for Internet communications. Use a monospaced font and keep the length of each line under 80 characters.

Here's the signature I use:

```
—
Michael Fraase, proprietor | Voice: 612/698-0741
Arts & Farces              | Fax:  612/698-5106
2285 Stewart Avenue        | E-mail: mfraase@farces.com
Suite 1315                 |————————————————
St. Paul, MN 55116 USA     | writing and document design
```

You can gather a lot of interesting information from a person's signature. From mine you could assume that I'm self-employed (the top-level domain is a commercial account and the domain name matches part of my company name); I live in Minnesota; and I like the Grateful Dead more than just a little (and you can draw your own conclusions from that).

Sometimes, signatures carry a disclaimer stating that the comments represent the views of the individual posting the message, but not necessarily the views of that person's employer, company or organization. Sometimes, these disclaimer lines are even written with a sense of humor:

```
"Opinions this ludicrous are mine. Reasonable opinions will
  cost you."
```

Here are some of the better signature tag lines I've come across lately:

```
"I need some indication that all of this is real now."
"Slipping into madness is good for the sake of comparison."
"Tens of thousands of messages, hundreds of points of view. It was
  not called the Net of a Million Lies for nothing." -Vernor Vinge
"Spread peanut butter, not AIDS."
"Fear is a little darkroom where negatives are developed."
"Stop yawning. Start yearning."
"Bandwidth expands to fit the waste available."
"Practice random kindness and senseless acts of beauty."
"I stand behind all of my misstatements." — Dan Quayle
```

How to Read, Post & Reply to Articles

In a graphical environment like the Macintosh, each news article is represented by an individual icon, regardless of the news reader you use. You read an article by clicking on its icon. You can reply to an article by selecting the range of text to which you want to respond and using your news reader's Reply command. Sometimes you'll want to create a completely new topic within a newsgroup. To do this, simply create a new message using the appropriate Create New Message command in your news reader. This section shows you how to read, post and reply to network news articles using two popular Mac news readers, Nuntius and TCP/Connect II.

Using Nuntius

Nuntius is one of the most popular newsreaders in the Macintosh community, probably because it's free and offers an intuitive interface. Newsgroups are represented as folders in windows, and articles are represented as documents. This is similar to how you already sort files on your Macintosh using the Finder, so using Nuntius will probably be second nature to experienced Mac users.

Reading News With Nuntius

Use the following steps to read network news articles with Nuntius. This section assumes that you have already properly configured Nuntius and selected the newsgroups you want to monitor. The examples provided here use the comp.sys.mac series of newsgroups, but Nuntius works the same for all available newsgroups.

1. Launch Nuntius by double-clicking on its icon. The All Groups window and the newsgroup set window you previously configured will be displayed, as shown in Figure 5-9.

2. Double-click on the newsgroup within the Group List window that you want to read. A window for the selected newsgroup will appear, with a list of all message *threads* in the newsgroup, as shown in Figure 5-13.

Figure 5-13:
Nuntius
newsgroup
window.

comp.sys.mac.comm	
More PowerPrint Infos?	• Hans Otto Trutmann
need help:building a mutiplatform net	• cvakg001
	• Elizabeth A Seitz
	• Richard Braun
Help on GNU bigotry (was Re: .z files)	• eric larson
	• Ted Lemon
	• Greg Trimper
[?] Macintosh BBS w/uucp or Internet features?	• Peter Stone
Re: Mud Client help :)	• Peter N Lewis
Re: Mud Client help :)	• Bob Snyder
Re: Mud Client help :)	• Kevin Saunders
LineShare (commercial version)?	• Rob Trevor
Zterm 0.9	• Tom Spence
Where can I get software demo...	• Tom Spence
Re: 14.4K Modems	• Neil_MacDonald
	• John Werner
Re: Modem Recommendation	• Neil_MacDonald
	• Guy B. Purcell

■ A message *thread* is a collection of a group of articles that are all related to the same topic. They sometimes—but not always—evolve around an original question and a collection of responses and discussions. Often, the message threads evolve far afield of their original topic.

3. Double-click on the message thread that interests you. A window for the selected thread will appear, showing a list of all news articles contained in the thread, as shown in Figure 5-14.

Figure 5-14:
Nuntius message
thread window.

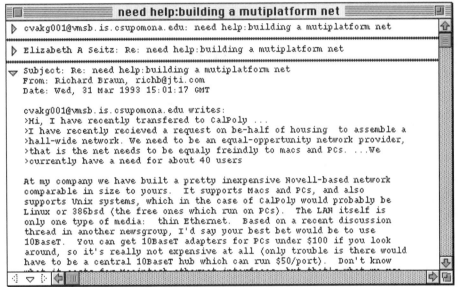

```
need help:building a mutiplatform net
▷ cvakg001@vmsb.is.csupomona.edu: need help:building a mutiplatform net

▷ Elizabeth A Seitz: Re: need help:building a mutiplatform net

▽ Subject: Re: need help:building a mutiplatform net
   From: Richard Braun, richb@jti.com
   Date: Wed, 31 Mar 1993 15:01:17 GMT

   cvakg001@vmsb.is.csupomona.edu writes:
   >Hi, I have recently transfered to CalPoly ...
   >I have recently recieved a request on be-half of housing  to assemble a
   >hall-wide network. We need to be an equal-oppertunity network provider,
   >that is the net needs to be equaly freindly to macs and PCs. ...We
   >currently have a need for about 40 users

   At my company we have built a pretty inexpensive Novell-based network
   comparable in size to yours.  It supports Macs and PCs, and also
   supports Unix systems, which in the case of CalPoly would probably be
   Linux or 386bsd (the free ones which run on PCs).  The LAN itself is
   only one type of media:  thin Ethernet.  Based on a recent discussion
   thread in another newsgroup, I'd say your best bet would be to use
   10BaseT.  You can get 10BaseT adapters for PCs under $100 if you look
   around, so it's really not expensive at all (only trouble is there would
   have to be a central 10BaseT hub which can run $50/port).  Don't know
```

4. Click the **Closed article** button (it's a little triangle) next to the article you want to read. The article button will change to its Open state (the triangle will point down instead of to the right), as shown in Figure 5-14. If you're familiar with using System 7's hierarchical Finder view, this stuff will be nothing new.

5. Click the **Page down** button to scroll the window one full window at a time.

6. Click the **Next thread** button to advance to the next sequential message thread.

7. Click the **Previous thread** button to move to the previous sequential message thread.

8. Repeat steps 3–8 for each newsgroup you are interested in.

▓ Each article in the Nuntius message thread window may have one of two symbols next to the author's name—or the area to the left of the message may be blank—indicating the status of each message. These symbols are illustrated in the table in Figure 5-15.

Figure 5-15:
Nuntius message
thread symbols.

Symbol	Meaning
●	You have not seen the article and the article is a new posting since the last time you browsed this newsgroup.
—	You have not seen the article and the article is not a new posting in this newsgroup.
	You have seen the article.

Posting a News Article With Nuntius

Reading news articles is only half the point of participating in news-groups. To get the most out of your time with network news, you also have to know how to post original articles and responses to existing articles. To post a news article with Nuntius

1. Launch Nuntius by double-clicking on its icon. The All Groups window and the newsgroup set window you previously config-ured will be displayed, as shown in Figure 5-9.

2. From the Threads menu, select the Post article in new thread… command. The Creating Article dialog box will appear, as shown in Figure 5-16.

Figure 5-16:
Nuntius Creating
Article dialog box.

Creating article

Subject:

Newsgroups: comp.sys.mac.comm

Distribution: world

☐ **Add signature**

[Cancel] [**Edit it**]

▣ To reply to an existing news article, select the range of text within the article that you specifically want to reply to, and select the Post follow-up article... from the Article menu.

3. Enter a short subject for your article in the Subject: box. The current newsgroup will be automatically reflected in the Newsgroups: box.

4. Enter the level of distribution for the article in the Distribution: box. The default is world-wide distribution and is indicated by the word "world."

▣ This setting determines how widely your article is distributed, and you should set it with some caution. If you're posting an article that has little or no interest outside of your geographic location, specify a narrower level of distribution. If you're selling a large monitor, for example, you may want to limit your distribution to your local area.

How Fast Can UFOs Go?

There are all sorts of strange newsgroups available on the Internet. Here's a sample exchange—the message title is "How fast can UFOs go?"—from the alt.alien.visitors newsgroup.
(Original post)

"Putting aside the energy requirements for accelerating to c, how far is 'far into space?' Assuming that their solar system is constructed similarly to ours, and the time spent in 'hyper-space' is effectively none, that would imply a 3.5 hour trip to the jump point on each side of the hyper-flight. I vaguely recall my high school astronomy teacher telling me that Pluto is 5 lighthours from the sun. So in order to reach a point at which the light speed drive can be used, our insystem drive needs to reach 1.4c? I'm available to these guys as an efficiency consultant."
(Follow-up post)

"When I think of the problem of needing to get some distance from a gravitational source—Earth, Moon, Sun, whatever—I would not head towards Pluto. I would head straight up the Y-axis. Cartoon analogy: When a truck is headed towards Daffy Duck, he runs away down the road instead of going left or right to get off the road. The solar system is sort of flat, the universe is not."

5. Click the **Edit it** button. The text editor or word processor you specified when you configured Nuntius will launch automatically.

6. Enter your article in your text editor.

7. Save your article.

8. Close the window in your text editor or word processor. The Nuntius Post Article dialog box will appear, as shown in Figure 5-17.

Figure 5-17:
Nuntius Post
Article dialog box.

Article to post

Subject: | SLIP Performance Question

☐ **Add signature**
☐ **Trash disk copy after posting**   (Cancel)   (**Post it**)

9. Check the **Add signature** checkbox if you want to attach your signature file to the end of your article.

   ▓ For more information on signatures, see the signatures sidebar.

10. Check the **Trash disk copy after posting** checkbox if you want the file your text editor saved to disk to be deleted after your article has been posted.

11. Click the **Post it** button. Your article will be posted to the open newsgroup.

12. If you have second thoughts about a posting, click the **Cancel** button. You can always open your saved copy, edit it and post it later.

Using TCP/Connect II News Module

It's hard to beat the bargain you get with a piece of quality freeware like Nuntius, but I generally use TCP/Connect II to read and post network news articles. TCP/Connect II lacks Nuntius's expandable message threading capabilities, but I can navigate between the few newsgroups I read more quickly using TCP/Connect II.

Reading News With TCP/Connect II

Before you can actually use TCP/Connect II to read network news articles, you have to subscribe to the newsgroups you want to monitor on an ongoing basis. The subscription process is as simple as dragging items between panes in a window.

To subscribe to newsgroups with TCP/Connect II

1. Launch TCP/Connect II by double-clicking on its icon.

2. From the News menu, select the Connect... command. The news session dialog box will appear, as shown in Figure 5-18.

The Mac Internet Tour Guide

Figure 5-18:
TCP/Connect II
Open a News
Session dialog
box.

3. Select your news server from the pop-up menu. Alternatively, you can enter the domain name or IP address of any available NNTP server in the box.

4. Click the **OK** button. The News Browser window will appear, as shown in Figure 5-19.

Figure 5-19:
TCP/Connect II
News Browser
window.

- ▓ The first time you login to your news server, only two newsgroups appear in the News Browser window: news.announce.newusers and news.newusers.questions.

5. From the News menu, select the Edit Newsgroups… command. The News Groups dialog box will be displayed, as shown in Figure 5-20.

Figure 5-20: TCP/Connect II News Groups dialog box.

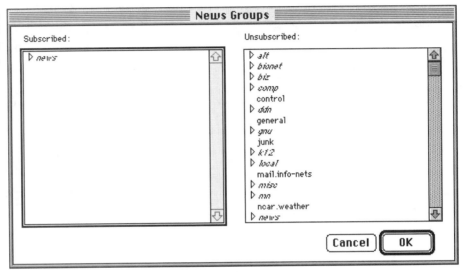

6. In the Unsubscribed panel of the News Groups dialog box, click on the triangle icon next to the top-level newsgroup category that interests you.

- ▓ The newsgroup category will expand, displaying a list of available newsgroups and any subcategories in the newsgroup hierarchy. For example, the comp.sys.mac newsgroups are located under of the sys subcategory, which itself is under the comp category. Some newsgroups are nested deeply within multiple subcategories.

7. Click on the newsgroup to which you want to subscribe.

- ▓ Select multiple newsgroups within the same category by shift-clicking on each newsgroup you want to select. Note that you can only select newsgroups within the same category with this technique.

8. Drag your selection into the Subscribed panel to the left, as shown in the example of several comp.sys.mac newsgroups in Figure 5-21.

Figure 5-21:
TCP/Connect II
News Groups
dialog box with
comp.sys.mac
subscriptions.

9. Repeat steps 6–8 for additional newsgroups to which you want to subscribe.

10. Click the **OK** button. The newly subscribed newsgroups will be added to the News Browser window, as shown in Figure 5-22.

Figure 5-22:
TCP/Connect II
News Browser
window with
subscribed
newsgroups.

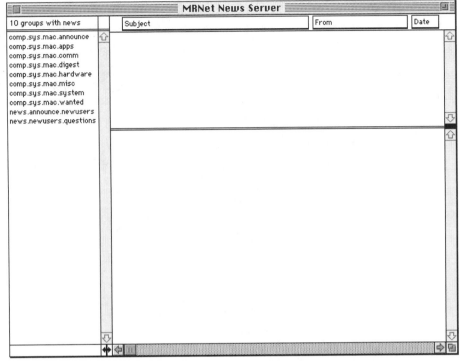

You can add newsgroups to your subscription list at any time. But now that you've got at least a few newsgroups lined up for reading, we'll learn how to read news articles with TCP/Connect II.

1. Launch TCP/Connect II by double-clicking on its icon.

2. From the News menu, select the Connect… command. The news session dialog box will be displayed, as shown in Figure 5-18.

3. Select your news server from the pop-up menu. Alternatively, you can enter the domain name or IP address of any available NNTP server in the box.

4. Click the **OK** button. The News Browser window will be displayed, as shown in Figure 5-19.

5. In the Newsgroups panel of the News Browser window, click the newsgroup containing articles you are interested in reading. A list of messages will appear in the Summary panel of the window.

6. In the News Browser window's Summary panel, click on the message summary you want to read. The text of the news article will appear in the Article panel as shown in Figure 5-23.

Figure 5-23:
TCP/Connect II
News Browser
window with
open news
article.

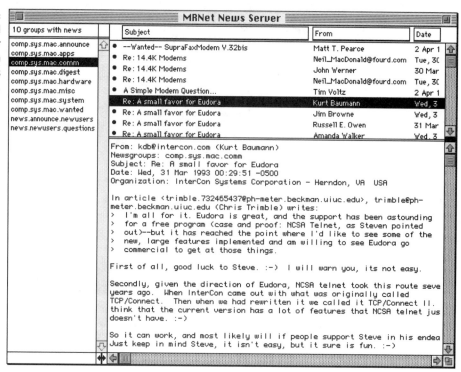

7. Repeat steps 5–6 for each newsgroup containing articles you are interested in reading.

I use TCP/Connect II to read network news because it is the only news reader I've found that offers filtering capabilities. I use TCP/Connect II's filtering capabilities to highlight articles from people whose opinions I value. I also use it as a "bozo-filter," automatically deleting articles posted by individuals whose postings are invariably useless.

The filtering capabilities in TCP/Connect II's news module work almost the same as the mail module's filter actions (with the exception that you can't reroute a message to a specified mailbox).

Posting a News Article With TCP/Connect II

Reading news articles is only half the point of participating in newsgroups. To get the most out of your time with network news, you also have to know how to post original articles and responses to existing articles. To post a news article with TCP/Connect II

1. Launch TCP/Connect II by double-clicking on its icon.

2. From the News menu, select the Connect… command. The news session dialog box will appear, as shown in Figure 5-18.

3. Select your news server from the pop-up menu. Alternatively, you can enter the domain name or IP address of any available NNTP server in the box.

4. Click the **OK** button. The News Browser window will appear, as shown in Figure 5-19.

5. Click the newsgroup where you want to post a new article. A list of messages in that newsgroup will be displayed in the Summary panel of the window.

6. From the News menu, select the Create New Article… command. An empty Article window will appear, as shown in Figure 5-24.

Figure 5-24: TCP/Connect II empty Article window.

7. Enter the text for your article.

8. Click the **Post** button in the Article window. The Post dialog box will appear, as shown in Figure 5-25.

Figure 5-25:
TCP/Connect II
Post dialog box.

Post

Subject:

Newsgroups:
▷ *comp*

▷ *alt*
▷ *biz*
▷ *comp*
ddn.newsletter
local.general
▷ *misc*
mn.general
▷ *news*
rec.music.gdead

Followup-To: ⦿ **Newsgroups** ○ **Poster**

Distribution:

Keywords:

Summary:

References:

Archive: *No Archive*   ▼   (**Mail a copy...**) (**Cancel**) (**Post**)

9. Enter a short subject description for the article in the Subject: box.

10. Click and drag the names of the newsgroups in which you want to post the article from the scrolling list in the right portion of the dialog box. Note that the default newsgroup is the one that is currently open.

MOOGopher.
MOOGopher is an object-oriented, multi-user dimension that uses an integrated Gopher client. Objects in the environment can contain Gopher items, and you navigate the Gopherspace as if you're exploring a game. You can try it by pointing your TurboGopher program at theory.cs.mankato.msus.edu port 1709. (For more on Gopher and TurboGopher, see chapter 7, "Using Gopher.")

11. Click the **Follow-up To: Newsgroups** radio button.

12. Select the level of distribution for the article from the Distribution: pop-up menu. The default is world-wide distribution.

   ▪ This setting determines how widely your article is distributed, and you should set it with some caution. If you're posting an article that has little or no interest outside your geographic location, specify a narrower level of distribution. If you're selling a large monitor, for example, you may want to limit your distribution to your local area.

13. Optionally, enter any keywords for your article in the Keywords: box.

14. Optionally, enter a very short summary of your article in the Summary: box.

15. Leave the References: box empty. This box is filled in automatically when you are posting a reply, or follow-up, to an existing article within the newsgroup.

16. Select a mailbox from the Archive: pop-up menu if you want to e-mail a copy to yourself for archival purposes.

17. Click the **Mail a copy...** button if you want to send a copy of your article to someone by e-mail. The standard e-mail Send dialog box will be displayed. (For more information, see "Creating an E-Mail Message With TCP/Connect II," in Chapter 4, "Electronic Mail.")

18. Click the **Post** button. Your article will be posted to the newsgroup.

Moving On

Now you're ready to venture into the thousands of newsgroups on the Internet. But be careful, you can waste a lot of time trolling through network news looking for nuggets of useful information. Unfortunately, there are no proven secrets to tracking down worthwhile articles. I've found that the best information tends to cluster within the smaller newsgroups and those that are moderated. Also, it's usually a better idea to carefully read a few newsgroups than to try to skim scores of them. There are more newsgroups available than anyone can possibly read, so pick your targets wisely.

If hunting for truly informative newsgroups can be a challenge, then finding great Mac shareware files is a cakewalk. As our tour bus cruises through the next chapter, you'll learn how to effectively use the Internet's File Transfer Protocol (FTP) and two of the most popular Macintosh FTP clients (software that simplifies transferring files) to mine these information-rich resources.

CHAPTER 6

TRANSFERRING FILES
The Mother Downlode

Part of the fun of visiting any distant place is taking snapshots and collecting souvenirs to take back home. Our tour through the Internet is no exception. There are plenty of strange and wonderous curios—as well as practical items you'll use every day—nestled throughout the Net. And you don't have to hop a steamer or board a plane to collect them all. Thanks to the Internet's File Transfer Protocol (FTP), it takes only a few mouse clicks to download a shareware program or text file from a computer halfway around the world. But perhaps the most satisfying thing about using the Internet's FTP to download files is that you get exactly the information you want without wading through a lot of stuff you don't want.

Depending on how relevant it is to you as an individual, information has a level of density. E-mail is usually information-dense on one level, because it is of unique concern to you. Network news, on the other hand, is comparatively information-sparse, because there are a lot of useless messages you must plow through to get to the information that's important to you. Files that you download and use on your Macintosh are information-dense, perhaps more than anything else you will encounter on the Internet.

In this chapter, we'll cover the basics of the File Transfer Protocol itself, and we'll also go over the details of using two popular software programs that let you transfer files across the Internet: Fetch, by Jim Matthews of Dartmouth College and InterCon's TCP/Connect II. So sit back, get your cameras ready and fish out those traveler's checks—we're going souvenir hunting.

What is FTP?

FTP is an acronym for File Transfer Protocol, but nobody says File Transfer Protocol; everyone says FTP, as in "you can FTP that file from the Sumex archive" or "that file is available by FTP from the Michigan archive."

People use FTP as a noun when they refer to the actual File Transfer Protocol, but they also use it as a verb when describing the process of transferring files on the Internet. Technically, FTP is a full-fledged data-transfer protocol, like Z-Modem or Kermit. It allows files to be transferred between different kinds of computers, without regard to the operating system used by the computers, or even how they are connected.

As you explore this chapter, keep in mind that while different examples are used for Fetch and TCP/Connect II, you can use either program to access any FTP archive on the Internet.

Why Would You Want to Transfer Files?

You can use Macintosh applications (like Fetch and TCP/Connect II) that employ FTP to send and receive files between your Macintosh and any other computer on the Internet that supports FTP. There is a wealth of software available through the Internet by *anonymous FTP*. Anonymous FTP is an Internet service that allows anyone to enter publicly accessible file archives, practically anywhere in the world, without having an account on that archive. If an FTP server accepts anonymous logins (and there are thousands that do), you login with the username *anonymous* and any text as a password. It is a generally accepted convention that anonymous FTP users enter their e-mail address—in the username@domain.top-domain format—as their password.

Hot News on the Net.

Savvy folks in public relations and publicity departments know that news travels fast along the Net. That's why you can count on the Internet to be one of the first places to offer news releases from all kinds of sources, ranging from the White House to Apple Computer. In short, you can see it on the Net today, or read about it in the paper tomorrow.

"SAN JOSE, California—May 10, 1993—Apple Computer, Inc., announced today at its Worldwide Developers Conference that significant progress has been made in developing the first PowerPC-based Apple Macintosh personal computers. Apple plans to incorporate the powerful RISC-based microprocessor, designed in conjunction with IBM and Motorola, into its line of personal computers beginning in the first half of 1994.

"Apple demonstrated at the conference that Macintosh on PowerPC has passed several significant development milestones since IBM delivered the first PowerPC 601 sample chips in September 1992. The update on the PowerPC program included the following:

"—Demonstration of a prototype Macintosh computer running on an 80 MHz PowerPC 601 microprocessor, achieving a new performance level in the personal computer industry.

"—Demonstration of compatibility with existing Macintosh applications software, running without modification.

"—Preview of new third-party applications exploiting the native power of the PowerPC chip.

"—Announcement of support from 11 leading software developers who are writing new versions of their applications for the platform. (See accompanying release.)

"—Commitment to an upgrade path for current Macintosh customers.

"Apple announced that it intends to offer upgrades to PowerPC for the Macintosh Centris 610 and 650 computers, Macintosh IIvx and IIvi, Performa 600 and Quadra 800 systems. Apple and third-party developers are working to create upgrade paths for other Macintosh models as well."

Resources available from anonymous FTP archives include fully-functional software programs (spreadsheets, text editors, telecommunications programs, databases, graphics programs, utilities and more) as well as graphic images, sounds, QuickTime movies and texts ranging from President Bill Clinton's speeches to *Macbeth*. Some of the most valuable software resources available on the Internet are updaters and bug fixes for commercially distributed software. Software companies distribute the updaters to the general public via the Internet and various online services. People who own a program that may not be compatible with a new hardware or software release can download the updater and run it on their outdated program to upgrade it to the newest version. It's a classic win-win situation: users get quick updates and the vendor gets inexpensive distribution and loads of good will within the community while at the same time keeping its installed base of users current and up-to-date.

Other valuable resources—information resources—are available by FTP. Developer notes, technical reports, technical support documents, electronic magazines, journals, templates and tutorials are all available. And then there are the thousands of "miscellaneous" resources that seem to find their way to FTP sites: things like musical notation and lyric sheets for just about any piece of music from the last 30 years, or full-text copies of classic literature ranging from *Alice in Wonderland* and *Peter Pan* to the complete works of Shakespeare.

A Primer on Software Resources

For the time being, there are three general types of software resources you can find on the Internet: information resources, software programs, and program-specific files for use with those software programs (templates and samples). Information resources—documents that were distributed as ink (or toner) on paper in the past—are widely available from numerous sources on the Internet. Software programs and files for use with those programs are generally less widely available, but plentiful nonetheless.

Dial "S" for Software.
Just about the only kind of software resource you won't find on the Internet is commercially distributed software. And even that may change in the relatively near future. Imagine the benefit MondoCorp can reap if it can distribute within seconds a new version of its MondoWriter software to anyone on the Internet. Users could simply type in a credit card number and instantly download the software and documentation right to their hard drives. Look for this to happen soon, and look to see who the initial players are. Chances are, the first companies to distribute their software across the Internet will be the most forward-thinking in the industry.

There are three classifications for the software resources you will find on the Internet: public domain, freeware and shareware. Let's take a look at the differences between these three distribution methods.

Public Domain

Public domain resources are those that carry no copyright. The author or developer has created the resource for the good of the community and has released it for any and every use. There is no limit on redistribution or sale of public domain resources, and it can be modified or transformed by anyone.

Freeware

Freeware resources are those that carry the author's copyright. The author retains copyright but allows you to use the resource free of charge. There are generally some restrictions on freeware resources, most often regarding distribution and modification. The usual case with freeware is that you can give it away, but you can't sell it. Eudora—the e-mail program included on the *Mac Internet Tour Guide* companion disk—is an example of freeware. You can use it free of charge, but you can't sell it, and the author retains copyright.

Shareware

Shareware resources are those that are distributed on a "try-before-you-buy" basis. The author retains copyright and allows you to use the resource on a trial basis for a short evaluation period. At the end of the evaluation period, you must either pay the author for the resource or destroy all the copies of the resource in your possession. You are encouraged to make copies for your friends, but you can't charge for them. Shareware resources carry a relatively low price because the author doesn't have to pay distribution or advertising costs. The author cuts out the middlemen like distributors and resellers, dealing with you—the user—directly.

Fetch—the FTP program included on the companion disk—is an example of shareware. Actually, it's a freeware-shareware hybrid. If you're a non-commercial Internet user, you can use Fetch free of charge; it's freeware. But if you're a commercial Internet user, Fetch is distributed as shareware, and you must pay a $25 fee to the author.

Freeware PPP software.

PPP software allows you to login to the Internet using a high-speed modem and ordinary telephone lines. SLIP is more common right now (Summer 1993) than PPP, but PPP will probably surpass SLIP in the near future because it offers more features and better throughput during interactive sessions where small bits of information are passed in both directions. MacPPP is available by anonymous FTP at merit.edu in the /pub/ppp/ directory.

Making Shareware Work

If shareware is to remain a viable way to distribute and sell software, people who use it must pay the shareware authors. If you regularly use a piece of shareware, it's in your own best interest to pay the shareware fee. Some of the programs included on the companion disk are shareware products and are included for evaluation purposes only. If you continue to use these programs, you must pay the software authors directly. See the documentation for each program for details.

A Primer on File Types

Files on the Internet are usually going to have names that look different than what you're used to seeing. Most Macintosh files that you find will be listed in this filename format:

filename.ext.hqx.

The "ext" part of a file's name represents the compression tool used to create the file. The most common options are: sit, cpt and sea. The "hqx" extension indicates that the file has been placed on the FTP server in BinHex format. BinHex is a standard format that allows files to be accessed by virtually any computer, regardless of the hardware or software it uses.

You'll also probably find a lot of files that end with a "txt" or "ps" extension. These are ASCII text and PostScript files respectively and are intended for use on all kinds of computers. ASCII text can be read by any word processor and PostScript files can be printed—fully formatted—by any PostScript-capable output device.

Fetch will automatically determine the transfer mode to use based on the type of file you download. TCP/Connect II can also automatically determine the transfer mode to use, but it's not as reliable as Fetch.

Aladdin's StuffIt Expander utility—included on the companion disk—will automatically decode (convert from BinHex format) and decompress files created with the most popular Macintosh compression programs: StuffIt Lite (and previous versions of the shareware StuffIt program), StuffIt Deluxe and Compact Pro. To use StuffIt Expander, simply drag and drop the files you download onto the StuffIt Expander icon. StuffIt Expander will automatically launch, decode and decompress the file and quit.

Note that StuffIt Expander will not work with compressed files that have been split into multiple segments. You must have whatever program was used to create the compressed file segments to decompress and join the files.

Figure 6-1 lists the file extensions and file types handled by StuffIt Expander.

Figure 6-1:
StuffIt Expander
file handling
capabilities.

Extension	Compression Program Used
bin	Native file formats created by various software programs (these files aren't actually processed by StuffIt Expander but are usually in BinHex format with an hqx extension)
hqx	BinHex 4.0
sit	StuffIt, StuffIt Lite or StuffIt Deluxe
cpt	Compact Pro
sea	Self-extracting archives created with StuffIt, Compact Pro, DiskDoubler or another program

If you stick to the major Macintosh FTP servers, you'll probably never see any other filename extensions. But then you'd be missing out on most of the software resources available on the Internet. (For a list of the most popular Macintosh FTP sites on the Internet, see the "Famous Macintosh FTP Archives" sidebar later in this chapter.)

Aladdin's StuffIt Deluxe is currently the best program for decompressing files created by computers other than the Macintosh. StuffIt Deluxe is also the best tool for compressing files you want to upload. Figure 6-2 lists the file extensions and types handled by StuffIt Deluxe.

Figure 6-2:
StuffIt Deluxe
file-handling
capabilities.

Extension	Compression Program Used
hqx	BinHex 4.0
sit	StuffIt, StuffIt Lite or StuffIt Deluxe
cpt	Compact Pro
sea	Self-extracting archives created with either StuffIt or Compact Pro
seg	Compressed files saved in multiple segments with either StuffIt or Compact Pro
pit	PackIt (the original Macintosh compression software)
dd	DiskDoubler (Macintosh)
zip	PKZip (DOS)
lzh	LHarc (DOS)
arc	ARC (DOS)
z	Compress (UNIX)
tar	Tar (UNIX)

If you download files almost exclusively from the most popular Macintosh archives, you'll probably be able to decompress them with the free StuffIt Expander utility included on the companion disk. But if you're planning to wander the Net, sampling files from all over, you may need a compression utility that's a little more versatile. StuffIt Deluxe is a commercial product available from Aladdin Systems, Inc., 165 Westridge Drive, Watsonville, California 95073, 408/761-6200. Other programs, including the shareware StuffIt Lite, are available from most large Macintosh archives.

A Disinfectant for Viruses

If you're going to download files from any FTP archive on the Internet, you run the risk of having your system infected with a *virus*. A virus (and similar files like trojan horses or worms) is actually a computer program imbedded within another file you download. It "infects" your computer in one of a number of different ways. Some viruses are merely annoying, but others can cause severe damage by erasing files on your hard disk, scrambling your disk's file catalog or a number of other malicious tricks.

Your computer can't get infected by a text file—only by binary files—but it's generally a good policy to consider any file you download to be a potential source of viruses. While viruses are relatively rare, the Internet is a fertile breeding ground for them. So many files are uploaded and transferred every day, it's impossible to check them all, especially since there's no single system for checking for viruses.

The best way to protect yourself is to download the current version of John Norstad's Disinfectant anti-virus program. You can always find the latest version of Disinfectant at ftp.acns.nwu.edu in the /pub/disinfectant/ directory.

University of Michigan Macintosh archive.

The Macintosh archive maintained by the University of Michigan is one of the most popular archives on the Internet. Just about any public domain, freeware or shareware software for the Macintosh is available here. It's accessible with TurboGopher (as well as the traditional methods). Point your TurboGopher at gopher.archive.merit.net port 7055.

Alternatively, all files are available by anonymous FTP at mac.archive.umich.edu. You can download an index of descriptions of all available files in the /mac/00help/ directory.

Using Disinfectant

Disinfectant is probably the most frequently updated and widely used anti-virus utility for the Macintosh. With it, you can periodically scan your hard drive for viruses, install an extension that detects viruses as soon as they appear, and eradicate most any virus you might find. To scan your hard drive for any known virus and disinfect the drive if a virus is found

1. Launch the Disinfectant program by double-clicking on its icon. The Disinfectant window will be displayed, as shown in Figure 6-3.

Figure 6-3:
Disinfectant
window.

```
═══════════════ Disinfectant ═══════════════

  Disinfectant 3.0                          ☐─[ Further ▼]

  Please read the "Quick Start" section of the manual    ☐
  before running Disinfectant for the first time. It will
  tell you how to use this program to check your system    ☐
  for viruses, remove any viruses which you may have on
  your system, and protect your system against future    ┌──────────────┐
  infections. To read the manual, select the "Disinfectant └──────────────┘
  Help" command in the Apple menu.
                                            Files scanned: 0
          IMPORTANT NOTE                    Infected files: 0    [ Reset ]
                                            Errors: 0
  Version 2.7 introduced an important change to the way
  the Disinfectant protection INIT works. Please read the    ┌──────────┐   ┌──────────┐
  "Version History" section of the manual for details.       │  Drive   │   │  Eject   │
                                                             └──────────┘   └──────────┘
                                                             ┌──────────┐   ┌──────────┐
                                                             │   Scan   │   │ Disinfect│
                                                             └──────────┘   └──────────┘
                                                             ┌──────────┐   ┌──────────┐
                                                             │  Cancel  │   │   Quit   │
                                                             └──────────┘   └──────────┘
```

2. Select the disk you want to work with from the Disk pop-up menu. (You can scan and disinfect external drives as well as floppy disks.)

3. Click the **Disinfect** button. The program will scan the selected volume for viruses and attempt to remove any viruses it finds. The number of files scanned, the number of infected files and the number of errors will all be reported in the Disinfectant window during the process.

4. When the process is complete, click the **Quit** button.

Disinfectant contains extensive online help (select the Disinfectant Help command from the Apple menu). Refer to the Help file for further instructions on using Disinfectant, including installing the protective extension.

Using Fetch to Transfer Files

Fetch is a Macintosh File Transfer Protocol (FTP) program written by Jim Matthews of Dartmouth College. With Fetch, you can quickly and easily download (get) files from or upload (put) files to a remote host on the Internet. The file transfer speed will vary, based on the type of Internet connection you have. I use a Serial Line Internet Protocol

(SLIP) connection and a V.32bis modem with error correction and data compression. I almost always get throughput of about 1300 characters per second on compressed data files and significantly faster results on text files. Using a V.32bis modem with error correction and data compression, you can expect to download a 500k file in about five or six minutes. Of course, if you're fortunate enough to enjoy a direct connection to the Internet, you can transfer a 500k file in a few seconds (just a little bit longer than it takes to transfer the same amount of data from your local file server).

Fetch is an excellent, full-featured FTP program—in fact, it's the FTP tool I use most often. It is simple to use, providing an intuitive Macintosh interface for the FTP process. It automatically translates standard Macintosh file conventions into the required FTP commands.

A Real Internet Power User.

You thought being able to send e-mail to Australia made you a power user? Think again! There are people doing work on the Internet that boggles the mind of even the most arrogant Net gurus. One true power user writes:

"I'm an employee of the University of California and the US Department of Energy at Lawrence Livermore National Laboratory in California.

"The most interesting Internet usage I've ever participated in has been at the Supercomputing '92 conference in Minneapolis.

"We typically take one or more Macs with dual 16-inch monitors to the meeting and connect them to the show Net. Then, by way of MacX, we are able to open windows onto machines back at our home site in California, as well as at the vendor displays on the show floor, and even at the home sites of the vendors involved.

"For instance, at the Albuquerque conference in 1991, it wasn't unusual for us to have windows open on a Sun and a Cray at Livermore, an SGI machine on the show floor, and a Cray in Egan, Minnesota, all displayed and accessed from a Mac in Albuquerque."

A copy of Fetch is included on the *Mac Internet Tour Guide* companion disk that came with this book. If you're on the Internet as a commercial user, the program is provided for evaluation purposes only. If you decide to continue to use Fetch, you must pay a $25 fee to the author. If you're a non-commercial user, you may use Fetch at no charge.

Fetch is licensed free of charge for use in educational and non-profit organizations. Users in for-profit enterprises may obtain an individual license by sending $25 to

Software Sales
Dartmouth College
6028 Kiewit Computation Center
Hanover, NH 03755-3523 USA

Site licenses are also available; please send inquiries to the above address, or e-mail to Fetch@dartmouth.edu

Configuring Fetch

To configure Fetch to connect as an anonymous user to those FTP sites that allow connections without accounts

1. Double-click on the **Fetch icon** to launch the program. The Connection dialog box containing the default connection information will appear.

2. Click the **Cancel** button in the Connection dialog box.

3. Select the Preferences... command from the Customize menu. The Fetch Preferences dialog box will appear, as shown in Figure 6-4.

Figure 6-4: Fetch Preferences dialog box.

Fetch Preferences

Topic: [General ▼]

Default password (i.e. your e-mail address):
[user@host]

☒ Display server messages.
☐ Keep connection active.
☒ Show file sizes and dates (if possible).

[Cancel] [OK]

4. Enter the password to use as a default in the Default password box.

   ▓ Note that it is common Internet convention and courtesy to use your full e-mail address—in the username@domain.top-domain format—as your password when you log into an FTP server as an anonymous user.

   ▓ If you were logging into an FTP server on which you had an account, you would enter your login name and your password for that account in the appropriate boxes.

5. Select the other items from the Topic pop-up menu in the Preferences dialog box, and customize the Fetch settings to suit your purposes.

   ▓ These additional settings are usually best left in their default state until you have more experience using Fetch and FTP.

6. Click the **OK** button. Your customized settings will be saved in the Fetch Preferences file on your hard disk drive.

You have successfully configured Fetch for use with those FTP servers that are pre-configured in Fetch. Included in the group of Fetch's pre-configured servers are: the Dartmouth College archive, the Stanford University Mac archive (Info-Mac), the University of Texas archive, the University of Michigan archive, Apple's general file archive, the NCSA archive and the Washington University archive (which includes mirrors of the most popular archives). If you are anxious to begin downloading files, you can skip to the next section. The remainder of this section covers how to add additional FTP server connection information to Fetch.

Locating FTP servers.

Can't get enough of downloading files via FTP? Don't worry, it's not likely you'll run out of files or FTP sites.

A list of publicly accessible FTP sites is available by FTP from pilot.njin.net in the /pub/ftp-list/ directory.

Any FTP site listed allows anonymous logins. It's Internet courtesy to supply your e-mail address—in the username@domain.top-domain format—as your login password.

Use these steps to configure Fetch for use with additional FTP servers. This tutorial provides information on configuring access to the University of Minnesota software distribution FTP server. This Fetch configuration will be used later in this chapter in another example.

1. Launch Fetch by double-clicking on its icon. The Connection dialog box containing the default connection information will be displayed.

2. Click the **Cancel** button in the Connection dialog box.

3. From the Customize menu, select the Edit Shortcuts... command. The Shortcuts dialog box will appear, as shown in Figure 6-5.

Figure 6-5:
Fetch Shortcuts
dialog box.

4. Click the **New** button to create a new FTP server entry. The New Server Entry dialog box will appear, as shown in Figure 6-6.

Figure 6-6: Fetch
New Server Entry
dialog box.

Shortcut: |

Host:

User ID:

Password:

Directory:

[Cancel]   [**OK**]

5. Enter **U of M (Boombox)** in the Shortcut box. This entry is used only as a display reference; it has no effect on the server address.

6. Enter **boombox.micro.umn.edu** in the Host box.

7. Enter **anonymous** in the User ID box.

   �ધ Note that if you were configuring Fetch for use with an FTP server on which you have an account, you would enter your login name *at the remote host* in the User ID box. Most public FTP servers will accept anonymous users.

8. Leave the Password box empty. The e-mail address you entered when you initially configured Fetch will be used as a password.

   ▧ Note that if you were configuring Fetch for use with an FTP server on which you have an account, you would enter your password *at the remote host* in the Password box. Most public FTP servers will accept (some even require) an e-mail address for anonymous users.

9. Leave the Directory box empty. The New Entry Server dialog box for the U of M (Boombox) entry should look like the example shown in Figure 6-7.

The Mac Internet Tour Guide

Figure 6-7: Fetch
New Entry Server
dialog box for
the U of M (Boom-
box) entry.

Shortcut: U of M (Boombox)

Host: boombox.micro.umn.edu

User ID: anonymous

Password:

Directory:

[Cancel] [OK]

▥ Note that you can add a default directory—in the format
/directory/subdirectory/sub-sub-directory—if you want to
login to a specific directory. Most publicly accessible FTP
servers that accept anonymous logins restrict anonymous
access to the /pub/ directory.

10. Click the **OK** button in the New Server Entry dialog box.

11. Repeat steps 4–10 to add additional FTP server entries. All you
    need to know to add an additional FTP server to the Shortcuts list
    is the domain name or IP address of the site and whether the site
    will allow anonymous logins.

12. Click the **OK** button in the Shortcuts dialog box to save your FTP
    server entries to the Fetch Preferences file.

You can further customize Fetch to automatically process files
compressed with the most popular Macintosh compression utilities,
including Compact Pro, StuffIt Lite and StuffIt Deluxe. To configure
Fetch to automatically expand certain compressed files

1. Make sure you have copied the StuffIt Expander program to your
   hard drive.

2. Launch Fetch by double-clicking on its icon. The Connection
   dialog box containing the default connection information
   will appear.

3. Click the **Cancel** button in the Connection dialog box.

4. Select the Post-Processing… command from the Customize menu. The Post-Processing Configuration dialog box will appear, as shown in Figure 6-8.

Figure 6-8: Fetch Post-Processing Configuration dialog box.

File Type	Opening Application	
GIF Files	Giffer	**Add**
Compact Pro Archives	Compact Pro	**Change**
StuffIt Archives	StuffIt Expander	**Remove**
StuffIt SEAs		**Enable**
		Disable
		Cancel
		OK

NOTE: Automatic file-opening requires System 7.0.

Pass the Popcorn.

Popcorn is a freeware QuickTime viewer developed by Leonard Rosenthal at Aladdin Systems. It's a simple, no-nonsense player that offers a clean interface. Multiple QuickTime movies can be displayed and edited. It's available by FTP from mac.archive.umich.edu in the /mac/graphics/quicktime/ directory.

5. Click on the grayed-out Compact Pro Archives item in the scrolling list.

6. Click the **Change** button. The Post-Processing Program Selection dialog box will appear, as shown in Figure 6-9.

Figure 6-9: Fetch
Post-Processing
Program Selection
dialog box.

Automatically open a type of file with the specified application:

File Description: `Compact Pro Archives`

Type: `PACT`   Creator: `CPCT`   [Choose Example...]

Application: `Compact Pro`

Signature: `CPCT`   [Choose Application...]

[Cancel]   [OK]

7. Click the **Choose Application...** button. A standard Open File dialog box will appear.

8. Navigate to the folder containing the StuffIt Expander program, and double-click on its name in the scrolling list. The Post-Processing Program Selection dialog box will be updated to reflect your change.

9. Click the **OK** button in the Post-Processing Program Selection dialog box.

10. Click the **Enable** button in the Post-Processing Configuration dialog box. The Compact Pro Archives item in the scrolling list will appear as an enabled item, with black type instead of gray.

11. Repeat steps 5–10 for both the StuffIt Archives and StuffIt SEAs items in the Post-Processing Configuration dialog box's list.

12. Click the **OK** button in the Post-Processing Configuration dialog box to save your changes to the Fetch Preferences file.

Downloading Files With Fetch

An important information-browsing tool—TurboGopher—is discussed in the next chapter. TurboGopher brings a simple but very powerful interface to the Internet, and it's a program every Mac Internet user should have. You can use Fetch to download the TurboGopher application files.

1. Launch Fetch by double-clicking on its icon. The Connection dialog box containing the default connection information will appear, as shown in Figure 6-10.

Figure 6-10: Fetch
Connection
dialog box.

**Enter host name, user name, and password
(or choose from the shortcut menu):**

Host:	dartvax.dartmouth.edu
User ID:	anonymous
Password:	
Directory:	/pub
Shortcuts:	▼ (Cancel) **OK**

2. Select the U of M (Boombox) item from the Shortcuts pop-up menu. The Connection dialog box should look like the example in Figure 6-11.

   ▦ Note that this step assumes that you added the University of Minnesota's software distribution FTP server to your Fetch Shortcuts configuration, as explained in the previous section. If you skipped that section, enter **boombox.micro.umn.edu** in the Host: box, and **anonymous** in the User ID: box.

**Enter host name, user name, and password
(or choose from the shortcut menu):**

Host: boombox.micro.umn.edu

User ID: anonymous

Password:

Directory:

Shortcuts: ▼ [Cancel] [OK]

3. Click the **OK** button. Fetch will establish an FTP connection with the University of Minnesota's software distribution FTP server, log you in as an anonymous user, and update the File Browser dialog box to reflect the current directory.

   ▓ In this case, the directory you login to is the *root* directory (called the root directory because it is the lowest level directory), as shown in Figure 6-12.

Fetch: boombox.micro.umn.edu

Fetch Copyright © 1992
Trustees of Dartmouth College

[**Close Connection** ⌘W]

/ ▼

🗀 bin - Oct 6 1992
🗀 etc - Oct 6 1992
🗀 pub - Apr 1 18:17

[Put File...]

[Get File...]

◉ Automatic
○ Text
○ Binary

Status
Connected.

File

Transfer

2.1

4. Navigate through the folder hierarchy on the remote FTP server by double-clicking on the appropriate folder icons within the scrolling list at the left side of the Fetch window.

   ▪ In this example, double-click on the pub folder, then double-click on the gopher folder and finally, double-click on the Macintosh-TurboGopher folder. This hierarchy of folders is known as a *pathname*, and is written like this: /pub/gopher/macintosh-turbogopher/. The root directory is indicated by the first backslash (/).

5. Locate the most recent version of the TurboGopher file. As of early June 1993, the current version was 1.06b5, and the complete pathname is /pub/gopher/macintosh-turbogopher/TurboGopher.1.06b5.hqx. The File Browser dialog box should look like Figure 6-13.

Figure 6-13: Fetch File Browser dialog box with TurboGopher file highlighted.

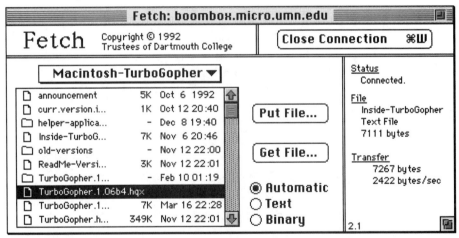

6. Click the **Get File...** button. The file transfer will begin, and its progress will be reported in the lower-right portion of the File Browser dialog box, as shown in Figure 6-14.

Figure 6-14: Fetch File Browser dialog box with file transfer in progress.

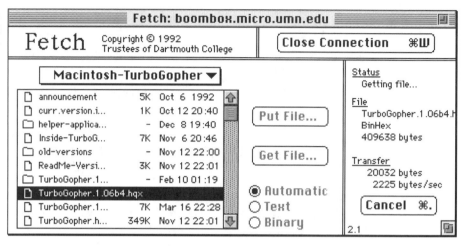

7. When the file transfer is complete, you can download additional files from the same FTP server by repeating steps 4–7 for each file. Feel free to browse the files available at this site and download any that interest you.

8. When you are finished transferring files, click the **Close Connection...** button. Your connection to the remote FTP server will be severed.

File Extensions.

Every file you download from the Internet will probably have at least one—and perhaps several—*filename extensions*. This is a method used to identify the types of files (and the software program used to create the files). Filename extensions have become a veritable alphabet soup and often end up confusing people more than they inform.

The filename extension will give you a clue about which transfer mode (ASCII or Binary) to use in your FTP program. The good news is, if you're using Fetch, all this is automatically handled for you; just click the **Automatic** radio button in the File Browser dialog box.

If you're using another FTP program, such as TCP/Connect II, files that end with hqx, txt or ps extensions are the *only* files that can be downloaded in ASCII mode. All other types of files *must* be downloaded in Binary (also called Image) mode. Chances are that if you get errors during file decompression indicating that your file is corrupt, it's because you used ASCII mode when you should have used Binary mode.

StuffIt Expander will automatically handle most Macintosh-format files you download from the Internet. Unfortunately, most of the files on the Internet aren't Macintosh files.

Uploading Files With Fetch

Downloading files is just one side of the file transfer coin. You can also *upload*, or send files to a remote FTP server using Fetch. If you have a file that you want to share with the rest of the world, consider uploading it (as long as there are no restrictions on its distribution) to your favorite FTP site. To upload files to a remote FTP server with Fetch

1. Launch Fetch by double-clicking on its icon. The Connection dialog box containing the default connection information will be displayed.

2. From the Shortcuts pop-up menu, select the remote FTP server to which you want to upload a file. Alternatively, enter the domain name or IP address for the remote FTP server in the Host: box.

3. Enter **anonymous** in the User ID: box.

   ▓ Alternatively, if you have an account on the remote FTP server, enter your login name *at the remote host* in the User ID box. Most public FTP servers will accept anonymous users.

4. Leave the Password box emtpy. The e-mail address you entered when you initially configured Fetch will be used as a password.

   ▓ Alternatively, if you have an account on the remote FTP server, enter your password *at the remote host* in the Password box.

5. Click the **OK** button. Fetch will establish an FTP connection with the remote FTP server, log you in and update the File Browser dialog box to reflect the current directory.

6. Navigate through the folder hierarchy on the remote FTP server by double-clicking on the appropriate folder icons within the scrolling list.

7. Create a new directory, if necessary, by selecting the Create New Directory… command from the Directories menu. You'll be prompted for a name for the new directory.

   ▓ Note that you must have the appropriate permissions on the remote FTP server in order to create a new directory. It's generally not a good idea to try creating new directories at remote FTP sites without clearing it first with that site's network administrator.

■ Note also that your new directory will be created as a subdirectory within the current directory.

8. Click the **Put File...** button in the File Browser dialog box. A standard Open File dialog box will appear.

9. Double-click on the name of the file you want to upload.

10. The file transfer will begin, and its progress will be reported in the lower right portion of the File Browser dialog box.

11. When the file transfer is complete, you can upload additional files to the same FTP server by repeating steps 6–10 for each file.

12. When you are finished transferring files, click the **Close Connection...** button. Your connection to the remote FTP server will be severed.

Etiquette for Uploaders.

Here's a quick checklist of things to keep in mind when you upload files to remote FTP sites:

■ Make sure you include all relevant documents.

■ Compress your files using either a member of the StuffIt family or Compactor Pro (these are the two "standard" file compression utilities in the Macintosh community).

■ Check your files for viruses before uploading them.

■ Upload your file to the appropriate directory.

■ Provide a brief, but accurate, description for your uploaded file.

Using TCP/Connect II to Transfer Files

TCP/Connect II provides a fully functional FTP module—as well as an FTP server—but I don't find myself using it as much as Fetch. It offers some niceties that Fetch doesn't have (it beeps when file transfers are finished and it automatically lists host selections in alphabetical order), but it's not as intuitive to use on some remote FTP servers. Nonetheless, TCP/Connect II's FTP module is powerful and the product's developer, InterCon Systems, is responsive, so its few shortcomings will almost surely be addressed.

Configuring TCP/Connect II FTP Module

As mentioned in the previous section, TCP/Connect II includes an FTP server implementation. This allows you to provide remote FTP service to other users on the Internet. For example, if you were a shareware author, you could set up a few directories where others on the Net could download your shareware and upload their questions, comments or favorite files of their own. Be careful with this capability; you can easily leave your Macintosh wide open to electronic intruders who will take great pleasure in browsing through your hard drive.

Use these steps to configure TCP/Connect II's FTP module, including the FTP server.

1. Launch TCP/Connect II by double-clicking on its icon.

2. Select the Configure... command from the Edit menu. The Configuration dialog box will appear.

3. Click on the File Transfer icon in the scrolling list of configuration items at the left side of the window. The File Transfer Configuration panel will appear, as shown in Figure 6-15.

Figure 6-15: TCP/Connect II File Transfer Config-uration panel.

4. To define to what extent (if at all) others may connect to your Macintosh as an FTP server, click one of the **Background FTP Server** radio buttons based on the following criteria:

- Click the **Off** radio button to completely deactivate the FTP server options in the program. This will prevent anyone from connecting to your Macintosh via remote FTP.

- Click the **Secure** radio button to allow connections by only those users for whom you have defined access privileges.

Commercial software updates.

The University of Michigan archive (as well as Stanford University's Info-Mac archive) maintains a directory for commercial software updates on its FTP server. Updater programs for AfterDark, Canvas, FileMaker Pro, Now Up-to-Date, Now Utilities, PageMaker additions, QuarkXPress (and XTensions), Photoshop, QuicKeys, SoftPC and StuffIt are only a few of those you can download and use completely free. They're available by FTP from mac.archive.umich.edu in the /mac/misc/update/ directory.

- Click the **Secure + Anonymous** radio button to allow connections by users for whom you have defined access privileges as well as anonymous users. Anonymous users will be restricted to a single folder (and any subfolders it contains) and will be unable to upload or delete files on your Macintosh.

- Click the **Promiscuous** radio button to allow connections from anyone. Be aware that if you select this option, *anyone will be able to login to your Macintosh and upload or download any file without an account or password*. Think at least twice before you choose this option.

5. If you turned **Off** TCP/Connect II's Background FTP Server capabilities, skip this step and advance to step 6. If you're going to allow others to connect to your Macintosh and transfer files, define a set of privileges for each user with this procedure:

- Click on the Users icon in the scrolling list of configuration items. The Users Configuration panel will be displayed, as shown in the preconfigured example in Figure 6-16.

Figure 6-16:
TCP/Connect II
Users Config-
uration panel.

- Click the **New...** button. You'll be prompted to enter a name
  for the user.

- Enter a name for the user. This will be used for display
  reference purposes only, and will have no effect on the user's
  privileges.

- Enter the user's full name in the Full Name: box.

- Click the **FTP Password...** button. You will be prompted to
  enter a password for the user.

- Enter the user's password. Remember that passwords should
  never be someone's first name, and a good password includes both numbers and letters and mixes both upper- and
  lower-case letters.

- Click the **OK** button.

- Specify a default folder for the user with the FTP Folder pop-
  up menu.

- Check the **Restricted** checkbox if you want to restrict the
  user's access to the specified FTP Folder. *If this checkbox is
  unchecked, the remote user could conceivably access any files and
  folders on your hard drive.*

▓ Enter any information you want to be displayed when a remote user on the Internet uses *finger* to contact your Macintosh. Finger is a UNIX command that lets remote users search for someone's login name and e-mail address if they know the name of the computer where that person has an account.

    ▓ Click on the File Transfer icon in the scrolling list of configuration items. The File Transfer Configuration panel will appear.

6. To configure the general preferences of the FTP client portion of the software

    ▓ Check the **Prompt for file names** checkbox if you want to be asked for the destination filenames for all file transfers.

    ▓ Check the **Beep when transfers complete** checkbox if you want the System beep to sound when a file transfer is complete.

    ▓ Check the **Show Invisible Files** checkbox if you want to display in the file transfer window those files that are normally invisible.

    ▓ Select a folder for saving downloaded files from the Default FTP Client Folder: pop-up menu.

    ▓ Check the **Default to MacBinary** checkbox if you want the MacBinary file format to be used when you transfer files in TCP/Connect II's image mode. It's rare to find an FTP archive on the Internet that has native MacBinary files (as opposed to regular Binary files), so this option should usually be left unchecked.

The Beauty of ZTerm.

ZTerm is one of the most popular Macintosh shareware programs. It provides terminal emulation, ANSI support and a built-in phonebook. ZTerm was the first Macintosh communications program that provided the Z-Modem file transfer protocol. X-Modem and Y-Modem protocols are also supported. But the real beauty of ZTerm is its sublime combination of power and simplicity. It's available by FTP from mac.archive.umich.edu in the /mac/util/comm/ directory.

▪ Specify a Creator for files received in image mode. You do this by entering the four-character creator code of the program you want to use to open and edit files received in image mode. This option is useful for specifying a program to use for opening downloaded files that your Mac can't recognize. Again, since it's rare to find an FTP archive on the Internet that has native Macintosh files, it's best to leave this option in its default state of four question marks (????).

▪ Specify a Type for files received in image mode by entering the four-character type code. This option is useful for specifying a file type for downloaded files that your Mac can't recognize. Because it's rare to find an FTP archive on the Internet that has native Macintosh files, it's best to leave this option in its default state of four question marks (????).

7. Click in the Configuration dialog box's close box to close the dialog box and save your changes to the TCP/Connect II preferences file.

You may want to configure a few of your favorite FTP servers before you begin to transfer files with TCP/Connect II. To configure the Info-Mac archive at Stanford University as one of TCP/Connect II's hosts

1. Launch TCP/Connect II by double-clicking on its icon.

2. From the Edit menu, select the Configure… command. The Configuration dialog box will appear.

3. Click on the Hosts icon in the scrolling list of configuration items at the left side of the window. The Hosts Configuration panel will appear, as shown in the pre-configured example in Figure 6-17.

Figure 6-17:
TCP/Connect II
Hosts Config-
uration panel.

TCP/Connect II Configuration

– Default –	Appalachian State CWIS (Telnet)
Apple (A/UX Support)	Apple (Bric-a-Brac)
Apple (Cambridge)	Apple (General Archive)
Baseball Schedules (Telnet)	Biosphere Newsletter
Bucknell (Telnet/Knowbot)	CARL (Telnet)

New...
Rename...
Delete

General

Network

File Transfer

Hosts

IP Addresses:

Full Domain Name:

Operating System: CPU Type:

RWIN:

Paste Style: ○ Full Speed ◉ By Line ○ Blocked to
Paste Delay: 1   ticks (60ths of a second)

FTP Client:
☒ Automatically log in   ☒ Automatically show file list
☒ Use PORT commands   ☐ Transfer unknown file types as ASCII

4. Click the **New** button. A dialog box will appear, prompting you to enter the name of the host.

5. Enter **Macintosh (Info-Mac)** and click the **OK** button. A new entry will be created in the Hosts scrolling list.

6. Enter **sumex-aim.stanford.edu** in the Full Domain Name box. Alternatively, enter **36.44.0.6** in the IP Addresses box. The entry for the Macintosh archive at Stanford University should look like the illustration in Figure 6-18.

Figure 6-18:
TCP/Connect II
host entry for
Stanford Univer-
sity's Macintosh
archive (Info-Mac).

TCP/Connect II Configuration

Macintosh (Info-Mac)	Macintosh (Sounds/Rochester)
Macintosh (Univ. Maryland Archive)	Macintosh (Univ. Maryland)
Macintosh (Univ. Mich.)	Macintosh (Univ. Minn.)
Macintosh (Univ. Texas Rascal)	Macintosh (Univ. Texas)
Mars Hotel (Telnet)	Media Lab

New...
Rename...
Delete

General

Network

File Transfer

Hosts

IP Addresses: 36.44.0.6

Full Domain Name: sumex-aim.stanford.edu

Operating System: CPU Type:

RWIN:

Paste Style: ○ Full Speed ◉ By Line ○ Blocked to
Paste Delay: 1   ticks (60ths of a second)

FTP Client:
☒ Automatically log in   ☒ Automatically show file list
☒ Use PORT commands   ☐ Transfer unknown file types as ASCII

7. Close the Configuration dialog box by clicking the close box.

Downloading Files With TCP/Connect II

The previous chapter described how to configure and use Nuntius to read network news. You can follow these steps to use TCP/Connect II to download the current version of Nuntius from Stanford University's Macintosh archive (Info-Mac).

1. Launch TCP/Connect II by double-clicking on its icon.

2. Hold down the Option key and select the Anonymous Connect… command from the FTP menu. The Open FTP Session dialog box will be displayed, as shown in Figure 6-19.

Figure 6-19:
TCP/Connect II
Open FTP Session
dialog box.

Open FTP session

Host name:	Macintosh (Info-Mac) ▼
User name:	anonymous
Password:	••••••••••••••••••
Host type:	Automatic

[Cancel]　[OK]

3. Select the Macintosh (Info-Mac) item from the Host name: pop-up menu.

▥ Note that this step assumes that you added the Info-Mac FTP server to your Hosts configuration, as explained in the previous section. If you skipped that section, enter **sumex-aim.stanford.edu** in the Host name: box and **anonymous** in the User name: box.

Internet Cruise.
Internet Cruise is an interactive animation that provides an excellent overview of the Internet and the various Internet services. Internet resources are available, including ways to access them listed by state. The software program is available by FTP from mac.archive.umich.edu in the /mac/misc/documentation/ directory.

4. Click the **OK** button. You will be logged in to the root directory and the FTP window will appear, as shown in Figure 6-20.

Figure 6-20:
TCP/Connect II FTP
window.

5. Click on the info-mac directory icon.

6. Click the **Set Directory...** button. The Set directory to: dialog box will appear, with the directory you selected in step 5 (info-mac in this example) shown in the text box, as depicted in Figure 6-21.

Figure 6-21:
TCP/Connect II Set
directory to: dia-
log box with info-
mac directory.

7. Navigate through the folder hierarchy on the remote FTP server by double-clicking on the appropriate folder icons within the scrolling list in the right portion of the window.

   ▓ In this example, double-click on the comm folder. This hierarchy of folders is known as a *pathname* and is written like this: /info-mac/comm/. The root directory is indicated by the first backslash (/) character.

8. Locate the most recent version of the Nuntius file. As of early June 1993, the current version was 1.1.1d17 and the complete pathname is /info-mac/comm/nuntius-111d17.hqx. The FTP window should look like the example shown in Figure 6-22.

Figure 6-22: TCP/Connect II FTP window with Nuntius file highlighted.

9. Click the **<< Copy <<** button. The file transfer will begin and its progress will be reported in the lower portion of the FTP window, as shown in Figure 6-23.

The Mac Internet Tour Guide

10. When the file transfer is complete, you can download additional files from the same FTP server by repeating steps 5–9 for each file. Feel free to browse among the other files available at this site and download any that interest you.

11. When you are finished transferring files, click the FTP window's close box. Your connection to the remote FTP server will be severed.

TCP/Connect II lacks the integrated ability to automatically undecode BinHex files and expand compressed files that makes Fetch so painlessly easy to use. Thanks to the wizards at Aladdin Systems, you can automatically massage the Macintosh files you download using TCP/Connect II by simply dragging their icons over the StuffIt Expander icon until it is highlighted and then dropping them. It's almost painless and certainly easy to use, but not nearly as elegant as Fetch.

Famous Macintosh FTP Archives.
Here are the most popular Macintosh-specific FTP sites. All accept anonymous logins, but be sure to use your full e-mail address—in the username@domain.top-domain format—as a password.

Domain Name	Directory
sumex-aim.stanford.edu	/info-mac/
mac.archive.umich.edu	/mac/
ftp.apple.com	/dts/
microlib.cc.utexas.edu	/microlib/mac/
ftp.funet.fi	/pub/mac/
ftp.lu.se	/pub/mac/
ezinfo.ethz.ch	/mac/

Here are the most popular Macintosh mirror FTP sites. A mirror site is an exact copy of another site. They are designed to relieve the heavy traffic in the major FTP sites. If you find that you can't login to one of the sites in the above listing, try one of these mirror sites.

Domain Name	Directory
archie.au	/micros/mac/
ftp.lth.se	/mac/
minnehaha.rhrk.uni-kl.de	/pub/mac/
utsun.s.u-tokyo.ac.jp	/mac/info-mac/
wuarchive.wustl.edu	/systems/mac/
shark.mel.dit.csiro.au	/info-mac/

More information on these and other FTP sites is provided in Chapter 8, "Other Internet Resources," and the electronic updates for this book.

Uploading Files With TCP/Connect II

Downloading files is just one side of the file transfer coin. You can also *upload*, or send files to a remote FTP server using TCP/Connect II. If you have a file that you want to share with the rest of the world, consider uploading it (as long as there are no restrictions on its distribution) to your favorite FTP site. To upload files to a remote FTP server with TCP/Connect II

1. Launch TCP/Connect II by double-clicking on its icon.

2. Hold down the Option key and select the Anonymous Connect... command from the FTP menu. The Open FTP Session dialog box will be displayed.

3. Select the FTP server where you want to login from the Host name: pop-up menu.

4. Click the **OK** button. You will be logged in to the root directory and the FTP window will be displayed.

5. Navigate through the folder hierarchy on the remote FTP server by double-clicking on the appropriate folder icons within the scrolling list in the right portion of the FTP window.

6. Locate the file you wish to upload by navigating through the folder hierarchy on your Macintosh by double-clicking on the appropriate folder icons within the scrolling list in the left portion of the FTP window.

7. Click on the name of the file you wish to upload in the scrolling list in the left portion of the FTP window.

8. Click the **>> Copy >>** button. The file transfer will begin and its progress will be reported in the lower portion of the FTP window.

9. When the file transfer is complete, you can upload additional files to the same FTP server by repeating steps 5–8 for each file.

10. When you are finished transferring files, click the FTP window's close box. Your connection to the FTP server will be severed.

Moving On

There are huge repositories of very interesting files scattered throughout the thousands of FTP servers available on the Internet. With a little perseverance—and more importantly, knowing where to look—you can use FTP to find files on just about any topic. There is an important Internet resource that can help you navigate many of the available FTP servers—its name is Archie, and you'll learn about it in Chapter 8 "Other Internet Resources." Of course, the electronic updates to this book are another important resource available to you.

One of the best ways to navigate quickly and effectively through the Internet is to use the University of Minnesota's Gopher, covered in the next chapter. When it comes to touring the Net, Gopher is a knowing native, helpful concierge and savvy travel agent, all rolled into one.

CHAPTER 7

USING GOPHER
Burrowing for Information

So far, our tour has covered the many strange languages and customs of the Internet, but we've barely scratched the surface of the vast resources the Net has to offer. And when navigating unexplored territories, even pioneers need all the help they can get. It's always a relief to find an amicable cab driver or savvy concierge who can clue you in to those great out-of-the-way spots where most tourists never venture. In this chapter, we'll explore how to use Gopher—the Internet's most sociable, well-connected pathfinder—to browse aimlessly or search specifically for everything from Russian poetry to local weather reports.

What is Gopher?

Network news, e-mail, and FTP are great tools for specific tasks. As you've seen, it's simple enough to use a program like Eudora to dash off an e-mail message to someone, and it's a snap to use Nuntius to look for Macintosh-specific information in someplace like the comp.sys.mac newsgroups. Even finding and downloading a specific file from an FTP archive is a cinch if you're using Fetch. These programs and Internet resources are all specific tools for specific jobs.

But what if you don't know exactly what you're looking for, or only have a broad idea about a topic of interest? What if you just want to surf through the oceans of information available on the Internet? That's where Gopher comes in.

Gopher is one of the most powerful resources available to Internet users, and TurboGopher for the Macintosh is one of the most powerful implementations. Written by a team of programmers at the University of Minnesota, Gopher puts a menu-based interface on many of the Internet's resources, making moving from spot to spot on the Net as easy as picking options from a numbered list—and often easier.

Whole Earth 'Lectronic Link (WELL) Gopher.
The Whole Earth folks have put some of the best articles from the *Whole Earth Review* in a Gopher server. You'll find articles by Bruce Sterling, Stewart Brand and many others. This is one of the best information resources on the Internet. Access it by pointing your TurboGopher program at nkosi.well.sf.ca.us port 70.

If Gopher had been developed in California, instead of on the far edge of Minnesota, it might have been called Surfer. It's name comes from the University of Minnesota's mascot, the Golden Gopher. Information servers on the Internet that support access with the Gopher software are always called *Gopher sites*, *Gopher servers* or *Gopher holes*. The software's actual communication and database protocol is also referred to as *Gopher*. The program you run on your Mac to browse through Gopher holes is called *TurboGopher*.

What Can I Use Gopher For?

Gopher (the protocol) lets you burrow through information resources using a series of easy-to-navigate menus that appear as numbered lists. TurboGopher (the Mac program) lets you navigate through Gopher information resources using standard Macintosh file folders and icons. You can use TurboGopher on the Macintosh to navigate huge "dataspaces" by simply double-clicking the mouse button.

Gopher is best used as a browsing tool. It doesn't matter where an information resource you find with Gopher is physically located. As long as it is compatible with Gopher, it simply appears as another folder or icon in the hierarchy. You don't have to worry about IP addresses or even domain names with Gopher—when you find a resource you want to browse, just double-click on its folder.

Extensions to the Gopher protocol allow you to browse through different kinds of information resources—pictures, sounds, video, computer files—as well as text. Instead of groping around blindly through a series of interconnected servers, connecting and disconnecting each one in turn, you can use Gopher to wander aimlessly without worrying about the process of connecting and disconnecting. This chapter also explains how you can wander around through *Gopher-spaces* (those areas that support the Gopher protocol) purposefully, as if you had a well-trained research librarian helping out.

Why Should I Use Gopher Instead of FTP?

Gopher is a *stateless* software program, making the most efficient possible use of network resources. Instead of keeping a connection to a remote site continuously open, Gopher opens a connection to initiate your request, closes the connection, and then reopens a connection to receive the host's response. By comparison, FTP maintains a continuous connection while you are browsing directories and transferring files. Many of the best archive sites restrict FTP access, while allowing unrestricted Gopher access. You can be a good Internet citizen by using Gopher whenever you can. Most of the major FTP archives also support Gopher access, and more Gopher servers are continually being added. Some sites support only FTP access, though, so it's important that you use the right tool for the job.

Using TurboGopher

The elegant simplicity of Gopher is that its developers didn't reinvent the wheel. They configured Gopher, and the TurboGopher software you use from your Mac, to take advantage of existing network conventions. When you use the TurboGopher application to login to a Gopher server and double-click on a network resource, TurboGopher automatically determines the right tool for the job. If you're accessing a computer file, it will be sent to you using FTP. If you double-click on an icon that represents a login resource, TurboGopher will automatically open a TELNET session. It's all handled transparently.

Configuring TurboGopher

The latest version of the TurboGopher software is always available from the Visitors Center, as well as a number of FTP sites throughout the Internet. It's also included on the disk that came with this book. Complete instructions for downloading the current version of the program are provided in Chapter 6, "Transferring Files," beginning with the section "Using Fetch to Transfer Files."

A copy of TurboGopher is included in on the *Mac Internet Tour Guide* companion disk that came with this book. The program is provided for evaluation purposes only. If you decide to continue to use Turbo-Gopher, you must pay a $25 fee to the Regents of the University of Minnesota.

International technical support in a flash.

North Americans take technical support for granted because the vast majority of software developers are based in the United States and Canada. International users are faced with a host of problems when they have technical questions. Many use the Internet as their sole avenue of support. Zviki Cohen of Israel is a good example:

"I'm from Israel, and I work and study at the Technion—Israel Institute of Technology. I use the Internet as an important tool to get support for my Macs. Last month, I was interested in buying some products. In America or Europe you can pick up a phone, dial a toll-free number and hear all about it. But here, when you are interested in a product the local salesman hasn't heard of (and there are plenty), you can forget about it.

"Well, not with the Internet. A few e-mail messages to the companies sorted out the problem, and I got a few suggestions for the products I needed. When I found a serious bug in a software program I bought, I didn't wait for the tech support people here to get me the answer. I got it myself the next day from the company's headquarters in the USA."

To configure TurboGopher

1. Launch TurboGopher by double-clicking on its icon. Turbo-Gopher comes pre-configured for use with the University of Minnesota's Gopher server, and the program will automatically login to the "mother" Gopher and display both a Bookmarks window and a Home Gopher Server window, as shown in Figure 7-1.

Figure 7-1:
TurboGopher
initial display.

Bookmarks

Home Gopher Server

Internet Gopher ©1991–1993 University of Minnesota.

☐ Information About Gopher
☐ Computer Information
☐ Discussion Groups
☐ Fun & Games
☐ Internet file server (ftp) sites
☐ Libraries
☐ News
☐ Other Gopher and Information Servers
☐ Phone Books
? Search lots of places at the U of M
☐ University of Minnesota Campus Information

2. From the Setup menu, select the Configure TurboGopher…
command. The TurboGopher Configuration dialog box will be
displayed as shown in Figure 7-2.

Figure 7-2:
TurboGopher
Configuration
dialog box.

TurboGopher Configuration

Server name	Port
gopher.tc.umn.edu	70
gopher2.tc.umn.edu	70

(Cancel)   (OK)

3. If you want to continue to use the University of Minnesota's Gopher server as your Home Gopher server, click the Cancel button, and skip to step 6.

   ▦ There are other Gopher servers you can choose as your home server. Chances are your organization, campus or service provider offers a home server for your use.

   ▦ Some of the other Gopher servers are probably geographically closer to you and are less crowded than the University of Minnesota server.

   ▦ A list of popular Gopher servers is provided in the table in the sidebar on Gopher servers later in this chapter.

4. Enter the domain name of your Home Gopher server in the upper Server Name box, following the format shown in Figure 7-2.

5. Delete the domain name entry in the lower Server Name box.

   ▦ All Gopher servers use Port 70, so you should never need to change the Port settings in the TurboGopher Configuration dialog box.

6. Click the **OK** button. Your settings will be saved in a TurboGopher Settings file in the Preferences folder within your System Folder.

You've configured TurboGopher for use with your Home Gopher server. You can customize some aspects of TurboGopher with these steps.

1. Launch TurboGopher by double-clicking on its icon. The program will automatically login to the Home Gopher server you specified in the previous set of steps, and the Home Gopher server and Bookmarks windows will be displayed.

2. From the Setup menu, select the Options... command. The Options dialog box will appear, as shown in Figure 7-3.

Figure 7-3:
TurboGopher
Options dialog
box.

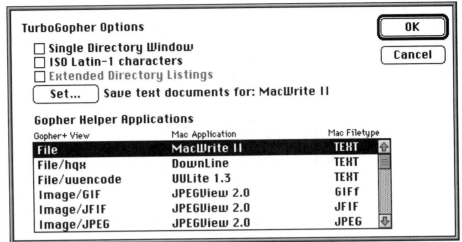

3. Check the **Single Directory Window** checkbox if you want to prevent TurboGopher from using multiple windows. This is usually a good option only for users with very small screens or beginning users who might be confused by multiple windows.

4. If you want to use a text editor or word processor other than MacWrite II, click the **Set...** button. A standard Open File dialog box will be displayed.

5. Double-click on the application file of the text editor or word processor you want to use to open text files downloaded with Gopher.

6. Modify the Gopher Helper Applications to suit your needs by double-clicking on an item in the scrolling list. A modified Open File dialog box will be displayed, like the example for BinHex files shown in Figure 7-4.

Figure 7-4:
TurboGopher
Helper Appli-
cations selection
dialog box.

7. Click on the program you want to use for the type of file you double-clicked. In this example, we double-clicked on the BinHex option, so in the new dialog box, we'll choose the StuffIt Expander icon. (StuffIt Expander is included on *The Mac Internet Tour Guide* companion disk and automatically decodes and decompresses files in BinHex format.)

StuffIt Lite.

StuffIt Lite is the shareware version of Aladdin Systems's commercial StuffIt Deluxe file compression utility. It's much less powerful than its commercial cousin, but it's still quite useful. With StuffIt Lite, you can create self-extracting archive files and segment files that are too large to fit on a single floppy disk. The program is available by FTP from mac.archive.umich.edu in the /mac/util/compression/ directory.

8. From the pop-up menu in the upper-right corner of the dialog box, select a file type for the Gopher Helper application to recognize. In this case, accept the StuffIt Expander default selection.

9. Click the **OK** button.

10. Repeat steps 6–9 for each additional type of Gopher Helper application you want to define.

    ▦ If you don't have a favorite set of programs that you use to display graphics files, view QuickTime movies and read various word processor files, you can download from the "mother" Gopher server at the University of Minnesota some shareware TurboGopher Helper applications that will perform these functions adequately.

11. Click the **OK** button in the Options dialog box. Your settings will be saved in the TurboGopher Settings file in the Preferences folder within your System Folder.

Browsing Information With TurboGopher

If you know how to use a Macintosh, you already know how to use TurboGopher. Navigate Gopherspace—that is, browse through those resources accessible via the Gopher protocol—by double-clicking on anything that looks interesting. It's as simple as that. Really!

▦ Double-clicking on a folder opens that folder and displays its contents.

▦ Double-clicking on a text file's icon displays the text of that document on your screen. If the file is larger than about 32k, you'll be prompted to save the file to disk.

▦ Double-clicking on a disk icon downloads that software resource to your Macintosh; you'll be prompted to save the file to disk.

▦ DOS-specific software resources are displayed with a PC icon.

▦ UNIX-specific software resources are displayed with a UX icon.

▦ Star icons represent graphics files—usually either GIF, JPEG or PICT format. Double-clicking on a star icon downloads the graphic image to your Macintosh and, optionally, launches a graphics program to display the image.

▦ Double-clicking on a terminal icon causes TurboGopher to open a TELNET session using NCSA TELNET.

■ To open a TELNET session via TurboGopher, you must be running System 7 and have NCSA TELNET installed on your hard drive. For more information, see "Using NCSA TELNET" in Chapter 8, "Other Internet Resources."

■ Double-clicking on a question mark allows you to search within a database.

■ Double-clicking on a phone-book icon allows you to search within a phonebook.

The Politics of Gopher.

As the Internet changes from a network of networks dominated by research and education institutions to one populated by a mixture of commercial and academic users, the Internet community itself is experiencing great stress.

Nowhere has this stress been more apparent recently than with Gopher and the University of Minnesota's Gopher development team.

Gopher, like most other Net resources, had always been made available for use by anyone, free of charge. In March 1993, however, the Gopher team decided it was time to recover some of their expenses and issued a policy statement that requires commercial sites to pay an annual license fee for any Gopher servers they operate.

Under the new policy, the Gopher team is charging a first-year license fee of $5,000 per server ($2,500 license fee for succeeding years) to any commercial site accessible from the Internet that offers only free information. For commercial sites that sell their information or charge a fee for access, an additional license fee of 7.5 percent of receipts is required.

Needless to say, a firestorm erupted in the comp.infosystems.gopher newsgroup—the spot on the Net where users discuss Gopher-related issues. Charges of "greed killing Gopher" were fired off by angry Gopher users. People who had contributed to the development of Gopher publicly wondered how they would be compensated for their work. Others wondered how a taxpayer-supported University could attempt to turn a profit on something they had already been compensated for. A few days later, the University of Minnesota's Gopher development team posted an article stating that the Gopher server license fees would be "negotiable."

Within a month, a freeware Gopher-compliant server (software that would allow administrators to set up their own Gopher servers without using the University of Minnesota's software) was available on the Internet, with no license fee for commercial use. It was reportedly somewhat buggy, but it was available. The new software was provided by a consortium of programmers, in the spirit of the free flow of information that characterizes the Internet.

More▷

Should the University of Minnesota be able to charge license fees for what they used to give away free of charge? Sure. Gopher is theirs to do with as they please. That doesn't prohibit someone else from developing a competing product and giving it away. And in fact that's already happening.

Will greed kill Gopher? It's not very likely. Gopher has evolved and developed an identity of its own. Cream rises, and something as useful as Gopher isn't likely to fade away at this point.

But this "problem" isn't going to go away, and the commercialization of the Internet is something the researchers and academics are going to want to accept.

Downloading Files With TurboGopher

Some of the most popular FTP sites (especially archives rich with Mac software) on the Internet offer access to their files via Gopher. This means you can use TurboGopher instead of another program (like Fetch or TCP/Connect II) to download files from those sites.

To download files with TurboGopher

1. Launch TurboGopher by double-clicking on its icon. It will automatically login to the Home Gopher server you specified when you configured the program. The Home Gopher server and Bookmarks windows will be displayed.

2. Navigate through Gopherspace by double-clicking on folder icons until you reach the Gopher server where you want to download files.

   ▣ Stanford University offers Gopher access to its Info-Mac archive, and I'll use that Gopher server as an example for the rest of this section. The Info-Mac Gopher server is shown at the bottom of the window in Figure 7-5.

Figure 7-5:
TurboGopher win-
dow with Info-
Mac Gopher
server selected.

Popular FTP Sites via Gopher

▼ Internet Gopher ©1991–1993 University of Minnesota.

📄 Read Me First
📁 Boombox – Home of Gopher and POPmail
📁 Case Western Reserve University FREENET
📁 Indiana University Mac Gopher Client App (beta)
📁 Interest Group Lists
📁 Internet Resource Guide (tar.Z files)
📁 Latest Disinfectant (ftp.acns.nwu.edu)
📁 Lyrics
📁 NCSA – Home of NCSA Telnet
📁 National Science Foundation Gopher (STIS)
📁 OCF Document Archives
📁 OSS-IS Info Archives (slow)
📁 SUMEX-AIM Archives – (Includes Info-Mac: a large collection of Mac

3. Double-click on the SUMEX-AIM Archives folder. TurboGopher will automatically log you into the Info-Mac Gopher server, and a new TurboGopher window will be opened, as shown in Figure 7-6.

Figure 7-6:
TurboGopher
SUMEX-AIM
Archives window.

Info-Mac Archives (sumex-aim.stanford.edu)

▼ Internet Gopher ©1991–1993 University of Minnesota.

❓ Search SUMEX-AIM archive titles
📄 README.ACCESS
📄 README.POSTING
📁 imap
📁 info-mac
📁 pub
📁 tmycin

- The Info-Mac Gopher server offers a search function, as indicated by the first icon in the window. Not all Gopher servers provide a search function.

4. Double-click on the icon marked: Search SUMEX-AIM archive titles. The Search dialog box will appear, as shown in Figure 7-7.

Figure 7-7:
TurboGopher
Search dialog box.

Find documents containing these words:

[   ]

Cancel   OK

5. Enter a word or series of words contained in the name of the document or file you wish to download.

- In this example, I'll search for a file that will allow me to turn my Macintosh into an FTP server. The name of the program I'm looking for is **FTPd**, so I'll enter that in the search box. (If I didn't know the exact name of the program, I could have entered just FTP, and TurboGopher would have displayed any files with FTP in their name, including FTPd.)

Barney the Dinosaur.
I don't know about you, but I just don't understand this Barney the Dinosaur phenomenon. At the April Fools Day 1993 Grateful Dead concert, Barney appeared on stage. Everyone there except the kids thought it was bassist Phil Lesh in a purple suit. The kids knew it was Barney.

And on the Internet there are dozens of savvy adults, wise to Barney's global conspiracy to brainwash kids into spewing a mindless doctrine of vapid grins and hyperkinetic world-glee. In fact, one guy even started a newsgroup, alt.barney.dinosaur.die.die.die, to help rally opposition against the "Great Evil Purple One."

6. Click the **OK** button. TurboGopher will search within the current Gopher server for documents and files matching the search words you specified. A new TurboGopher window will soon appear, displaying a list of the documents and files matching your search words, as shown in Figure 7-8.

Figure 7-8: TurboGopher window with search results.

7. Double-click on the ftpd-210.hqx icon. Because it's a Macintosh file (indicated by the disk icon), a standard Save File dialog box will appear.

8. Navigate to the folder where you want to save the file, and click the **Save** button. As shown in Figure 7-9, TurboGopher will display a status window showing the progress of the download.

Figure 7-9: TurboGopher download status window.

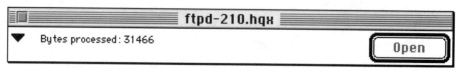

■ The status window will report when the download is complete, and the file will be automatically decoded from BinHex format and decompressed according to the Helper Application you specified when you configured TurboGopher.

9. Select the Quit command from the File menu.

Sometimes you just want to browse through a Gopher server, look-ing for interesting files and documents. This is a great way to keep up with what new software is available, and you'll often discover files and applications you might not have otherwise noticed.

To browse through the Info-Mac Gopher server

1. Launch TurboGopher by double-clicking on its icon. It will auto-matically login to the Home Gopher server you specified in the configuration process. The Home Gopher server and Bookmarks windows will be displayed.

2. Navigate through Gopherspace by double-clicking on folder icons until you reach the Info-Mac Gopher server, as in Figure 7-5.

3. Double-click on the SUMEX-AIM Archives folder. TurboGopher will automatically log you into the Info-Mac Gopher server, and a new TurboGopher window will appear, as shown in Figure 7-6.

4. Double-click on the info-mac folder. A new TurboGopher window will appear, as shown in Figure 7-10: "TurboGopher info-mac Archive window."

Figure 7-10: TurboGopher info-mac Archive window.

```
┌──────────────────────── info-mac ────────────────────────┐
│ ▼     Internet Gopher ©1991-1993 University of Minnesota. │
├───────────────────────────────────────────────────────────┤
│ 📄 00readme.txt                                          ⬆ │
│ 📁 app                                                     │
│ 📁 art                                                     │
│ 📁 card                                                    │
│ 📁 comm                                                    │
│ 📁 cp                                                      │
│ 📁 da                                                      │
│ 📁 demo                                                    │
│ 📁 digest                                                  │
│ 📁 ex                                                      │
│ 📁 fkey                                                    │
│ 📁 font                                                    │
│ 📁 game                                                  ⬇ │
└───────────────────────────────────────────────────────────┘
```

5. Double-click on the folder icon that interests you, such as the comm (communications) folder, as shown in this example. A new TurboGopher window will appear, as shown in Figure 7-11.

Figure 7-11:
TurboGopher
/info-mac/comm
window.

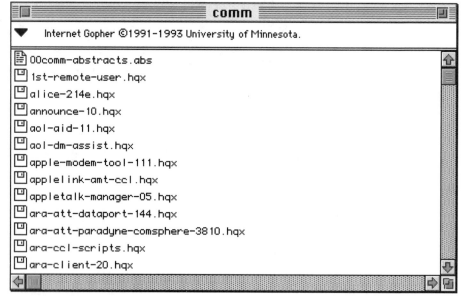

6. Double-click on the icon of any item that interests you. Short text files will be displayed in a window, while larger text files and application files will be transferred to your hard drive. For more information, see "Browsing Information With TurboGopher" earlier in this chapter.

7. Select the Quit command from the File menu.

Using TurboGopher Bookmarks

TurboGopher is great for browsing through lots of different kinds of information resources on the Internet. As you gain more experience prowling these resources, you'll probably start wishing for a way to leave a "crumb trail" to your favorite Gopher servers so you can easily find your way to them again. TurboGopher's Bookmark feature lets you define a trail to your favorite Gopher servers. This allows you to quickly and easily login to your favorite Gopher servers by double-clicking on a single icon.

To set Bookmarks within TurboGopher

1. Launch TurboGopher by double-clicking on its icon. The program will automatically login to the Home Gopher server. The Home Gopher server and Bookmarks windows will appear.

2. Navigate through Gopherspace by double-clicking on folder icons until you reach the resource for which you want to create a Bookmark.

3. Select the resource's icon by clicking on it once. Figure 7-12 shows how you would select the Info-Mac archive before setting a bookmark for it.

Figure 7-12:
TurboGopher
window with
Info-Mac archive
selected.

```
╔══════════════ Popular FTP Sites via Gopher ══════════════╗
║  ▼    Internet Gopher ©1991-1993 University of Minnesota.       ║
╠═══════════════════════════════════════════════════════════╣
║ 📄 Read Me First                                              ⬆ ║
║ 📁 Boombox - Home of Gopher and POPmail                      ║
║ 📁 Case Western Reserve University FREENET                   ║
║ 📁 Indiana University Mac Gopher Client App (beta)           ║
║ 📁 Interest Group Lists                                      ║
║ 📁 Internet Resource Guide (tar.Z files)                     ║
║ 📁 Latest Disinfectant (ftp.acns.nwu.edu)                    ║
║ 📁 Lyrics                                                    ║
║ 📁 NCSA - Home of NCSA Telnet                                ║
║ 📁 National Science Foundation Gopher (STIS)                 ║
║ 📁 OCF Document Archives                                     ║
║ 📁 OSS-IS Info Archives (slow)                               ║
║ 📁 SUMEX-AIM Archives - (Includes Info-Mac: a large collection of Mac ⬇ ║
╚═══════════════════════════════════════════════════════════╝
```

The Mac Internet Tour Guide

Chatting in Real-Time.

Two programs, Ircle and Talk, offer Mac users a couple of handy options for communicating on the Net in real-time.

Ircle is an Internet Relay Chat (IRC) client for the Macintosh that features a familiar Mac interface. Internet Relay Chat allows you to communicate with other individuals (or software agents) that are currently logged into an IRC server. All communication takes place in real-time.

Talk is a Macintosh implementation of the UNIX Talk command. It allows you to communicate with UNIX users on the Internet in real-time. The best part is that they need never know you're using a Macintosh.

Both programs are available by FTP from mac.archive.umich.edu in the /mac/util/comm/ directory.

4. From the Gopher menu, select the Set Bookmark… command. The Save Bookmark dialog box will appear, as shown in Figure 7-13.

Figure 7-13: TurboGopher Save Bookmark dialog box.

5. Enter a name for the Bookmark in the text box.
6. Click the **OK** button. The Bookmark will be added to the Bookmarks window, as shown in Figure 7-14.

Figure 7-14:
TurboGopher
Bookmark
window with
several configured
Bookmarks.

```
┌─────────────────────── Bookmarks ═══════════════════════┐
│ ▼   Internet Gopher ©1991-1993 University of Minnesota.     │
├──────────────────────────────────────────────────────────┤
│ 📁POPmail for Macintosh                                   ⇧│
│ 📁TurboGopher Distribution                                 │
│ 📁Info-Mac Archives (sumex-aim.stanford.edu)               │
│ 📁Weather Maps                                             │
│ 📁MRNet Gopher Server                                      │
│ 📁Univ. of Mich. Mac Archives                              │
│ 📁EFF Gopher Server                                        │
│ 📁ACM SIGGRAPH                                             │
│ 📁O'Reilly & Associates                                    │
│ 📁West Georgia College                                     │
│ 📁Washington University Archive                            │
│ 📁Boombox (Univ. of MN)                                    │
│ 📁Supreme Court Rulings (CWRU)                            ⇩│
├──────────────────────────────────────────────────────────┤
│ ⇦ ▓▓                                                    ⇨ ⤡│
└──────────────────────────────────────────────────────────┘
```

7. Select the Quit command from the File menu.

You can delete any Bookmark by clicking once on the item to select it and choosing the Delete Item command from the Gopher menu.

To use a Bookmark, just double-click on its icon in the Bookmarks window. TurboGopher will immediately login to that resource.

You can set Bookmarks for any resource within Gopherspace. For instance, if you're constantly downloading telecommunications software from the /info-mac/comm/ directory of the Info-Mac archive, you can set a Bookmark specifically for the comm folder. Double-clicking on the comm bookmark will cause TurboGopher to immediately login to Info-Mac's comm folder, rather than forcing you to navigate through the directory hierarchy. You don't even have to be logged into the Info-Mac Gopher server for this to work. Double-clicking on the comm bookmark will automatically login to the Info-Mac server and navigate instantly to the /info-mac/comm/ directory.

Sharing Bookmarks

TurboGopher's Bookmark feature is very useful for navigating Gopherspace efficiently. But the power of Bookmarks is increased by an order of magnitude when you realize you can *share* the Bookmarks you create with friends and associates. In effect, you can give someone else a cookie-crumb trail through enormous amounts of information to a single, specific spot on the Internet.

Be sure to send in your reply card for the electronic updates for this book, because I'll be distributing interesting Bookmarks to subscribers from time to time. Likewise, if you find a really interesting resource, send me a TurboGopher Bookmark at mfraase@farces.com.

To export the Bookmarks you create

1. Launch TurboGopher by double-clicking on its icon. It will automatically login to the Home Gopher server you specified when you configured the program. The Home Gopher server and Bookmarks windows will appear.

2. Click in the Bookmarks window to make it the active window.

3. From the File menu, select the Save as Bookmark File... command. A standard Save File dialog box will appear.

4. Enter a name for the Bookmark file in the text box.

   ▦ The default name of Exported Bookmarks isn't very descriptive. Enter a name for the Bookmark file that is more representative of what it contains.

Locating e-mail addresses.
You can locate the e-mail address of anyone who has posted a network news article by sending this message to mail-server@pit-manager.mit.edu
        send usenet-addresses/*name*
where *name* is the name of the person for whom you want an e-mail address.

5. Click the **Save** button. Your Bookmark file will be saved to your disk at the location you specified.

You can e-mail your Bookmark file to a friend or associate just as you would any other Macintosh file.

It's easy to use Bookmark files created by friends and colleagues. This is a handy way to find files and other resources on the Net that might otherwise take hours of hunting and searching. You launch TurboGopher and open a Bookmark file, which will open that file's Bookmarks only for that TurboGopher session, or you can import a Bookmark file, which will add that file's Bookmarks to your own resident Bookmark file.

To *open* a Bookmark file you have created or received from someone else

1. Launch TurboGopher by double-clicking on its icon. It will automatically login to the Home Gopher server you specified when you configured the program. The Home Gopher server and Bookmarks windows will appear.

2. From the File menu, select the Open Gopher Bookmark File… command. A standard Open File dialog box will appear.

3. Double-click on the Bookmark file you want to open. The Bookmark file will be opened in a new TurboGopher window.

4. Double-click on any icon within the TurboGopher window to access its associated resource.

To *import* a Bookmark file you have created or received from someone else into your TurboGopher resident Bookmark window

1. Launch TurboGopher by double-clicking on its icon. It will automatically login to the Home Gopher server you specified when you configured the program. The Home Gopher server and Bookmarks windows will appear.

2. Select the Import Bookmarks… command from the Gopher menu. A standard Open File dialog box will appear.

3. Double-click on the Bookmark file you want to import. The items contained in the external Bookmark file will be added to the items in your resident Bookmark window.

4. Double-click on any icon within the Bookmark window to access its associated resource.

Items from Bookmark files you import will remain part of your resident Bookmark file the next time you launch TurboGopher. Bookmark files you've opened will remain closed until you manually reopen them.

Remember, you can export and save your own Bookmark files for your own use. You might consider creating a main file that you use most often as your resident Bookmark file, which will be opened whenever you launch TurboGopher. But you can also create Bookmark files for specific areas of interest, like all your favorite Mac archives, or sites of social and political interest, or whatever tickles your fancy. That way, when you launch TurboGopher and you know you're only looking for Mac files, you can open your Mac sites Bookmark file and navigate directly from it, and so on.

Gopher Servers

There are a number of unique and information-rich sites throughout the Internet that support the Gopher protocol. The following table provides a listing of just a few of the more interesting Gopher servers available on the Internet.

Domain Address	Comments
boombox.micro.umn.edu	Gopher/TurboGopher distribution archive
sumex-aim.stanford.edu	Stanford University's Info-Mac archive
gopher.uis.itd.umich.edu	University of Michigan Macintosh archive
ashpool.micro.umn.edu	Washington University (St. Louis) archive
wx.atmos.uiuc.edu	Weather maps
gopher.eff.org	Electronic Frontier Foundation archive
ashpool.micro.umn.edu	Supreme Court rulings
gopher.well.sf.ca.us	Whole Earth 'Lectronic Link (WELL) archive
gopher.bu.edu	Boston metropolitan guide
sunsite.unc.edu	University of North Carolina archives
wiretap.spies.com	White House press release service
siggraph.org	Conference proceedings and materials from the graphics special interest group (SIGGRAPH) of the Association for Computing Machinery

Domain Address	Comments
ashpool.micro.umn.edu	Internet Resource Guide
hunter.cs.unr.edu	Search Gopherspace using Veronica
wcni.cis.umn.edu	Academic Position Network
gopher.cpsr.org	Computer Professionals for Social Responsibility archive
gopher.msen.com	Search for individuals on the Internet
akasha.tic.com	Sample issues of John Quarterman's *Matrix News Internet newsletter*
internic.net	Internet directory services
info.hed.apple.com	Apple's Internet Pilot program

TurboGopher Tips

TurboGopher is at the same time incredibly powerful and deceptively simple. Here are a few tips and tricks for using TurboGopher to its fullest potential:

- Eliminate screen clutter by holding down the Option key while double-clicking on a folder. This will re-use the current window instead of opening a new one.

- TurboGopher list views work the same way as the Mac's standard Open File dialog box: you can quickly type the first couple of letters of an item to automatically scroll to that item in the list.

- Download any file in its native state by holding down the Control key while double-clicking on the file icon. This is especially useful for downloading MS-DOS or UNIX files.

- Close all open TurboGopher windows by holding down the Option key while clicking any window's close box, just as in the Macintosh Finder.

- TurboGopher remembers the last question-mark icon you used to initiate a full text search. Holding down the Option key while double-clicking on a word within a document window results in a search for all documents containing the word on which you double-clicked.

- If you're a keyboard maven, you can speed your navigation through Gopherspace by using the Up and Down arrow keys to move up and down within lists. Pressing the Enter or Return key when an item is selected is equivalent to double-clicking on that item. The Right and Left arrow keys move to previous and next windows, respectively.

The Gopher of the Future.

Although the original Gopher protocol is frozen, a forward-compatible protocol (called Gopher +) is currently in development by the Gopher team at the University of Minnesota.

Gopher is currently the tenth-most-used protocol in terms of number of connections and the ninth-most-used protocol in terms of the number of bytes transferred.

Gopher + will support multiple views of a document, allowing information providers to include Microsoft Word, PostScript, RTF and ASCII text versions of a single document, for example.

Support for forms is also planned for inclusion in Gopher +. This will allow an interface to database back-ends as well as user information ranking, user-created items and directories, and conferencing systems.

Authentication support will be included in Gopher +. This will allow a finer control of information access on Gopher servers. Although it's not designed to replace public-key encryption or Kerberos, Gopher + authentication will allow access to particular information to be granted on an individual basis. Interestingly, the password is never sent across the network, so security will also be enhanced.

Moving On

TurboGopher is the best way to navigate parts of the Internet you aren't familiar with, because it sports a familiar interface of folders and icons. And because Gopher is a *stateless* software program, it makes the most efficient possible use of network resources.

While previous chapters of this book have focused on the most widely used programs and most frequently visited spots on the Internet, the next chapter will take a look at the dozens of other small but important Internet resources. You'll learn about TELNET, another software program widely used to access Internet resources, and we'll visit a few of the more secluded cul-de-sacs on the Net. Our tour bus is making only one more excursion before our trip is over. If there's a program, resource, organization or site on the Internet that you're still wondering about, odds are we'll be visiting it in the next chapter. So now would be a good time to stock up on provisions and get a little rest, because the final leg of our tour promises to be the most exciting one yet.

CHAPTER 8

OTHER INTERNET RESOURCES
Geez, what is all this stuff?

By this point in our tour, you're an old pro at cruising the Internet. You've learned the terrain of the network, the language and customs of its inhabitants and the quickest routes to the information you need. Yet there are still dozens of helpful but lesser-known resources that can make your time online more productive and enjoyable. For this last leg of our tour, we're loading up the bus for a final loop around the outer fringe of the Net. We'll be moving pretty fast, so climb aboard and hang on.

For those who use Macintosh computers on the Internet, electronic mail, network news, FTP and Gopher are four of the most widely used resources. For non-Macintosh users, TELNET is likely the most commonly used Internet resource. Macintosh users enjoy task-specific software programs that make TELNET less necessary on the Internet. But some specialized applications require the use of TELNET. This chapter offers a look at TELNET, as well as some of the many organizations and resources available via the Internet. We'll also cover some of the less commonly used Macintosh software tools available for use on the Internet.

What Is TELNET?

Using TELNET, you can login to other computers on the Internet in an interactive, command-line mode. You use TELNET to access experimental services, library card catalogs, weather reports and various other specialized databases. If you have a UNIX account on another computer on the Internet, you use TELNET to login remotely to your account on that computer.

In the early days of the Internet, TELNET was one of the few tools available to the infonaut. Today, many of the services available by TELNET also provide an alternative method of access, like WAIS or WWW (both discussed later in this chapter) or Gopher (covered in detail in Chapter 7, "Using Gopher"). Although more and more TELNET services are becoming accessible via other methods, some Internet services still require a TELNET connection.

Using NCSA TELNET

NCSA TELNET is a freeware application program for the Macintosh that lets you take full advantage of the TELNET protocol . It is available by anonymous FTP from ftp.ncsa.uiuc.edu in the /mac/ directory. Extensive documentation is also available in the same directory.

Configuring NCSA TELNET

Before you can use NCSA TELNET to login remotely to another computer on the Internet, you must configure the program for use with your domain. NCSA TELNET can be customized in many different ways, but this section provides only the configuration information necessary to establish a remote login connection.

To configure NCSA TELNET for basic use

1. Double-click on the config.tel icon. A dialog box will appear, asking if you want to use TeachText to open the file.

   ▤ Alternatively, you can use any text editing program to open the config.tel file as an ASCII text file.

Vendor e-mail addresses.

One site on the Internet offers a collection of e-mail addresses, BBS numbers and fax numbers for more than 250 Macintosh software and hardware vendors. The list is provided in Microsoft Word, Microsoft Excel, and tab-delimited text formats. It's available by FTP from mac.archive.umich.edu in the /mac/misc/documentation/ directory.

2. Click the **OK** button. The NCSA TELNET configuration file will be opened within an editable TeachText window, as shown in Figure 8-1.

Figure 8-1:
NSCA TELNET
configuration file.

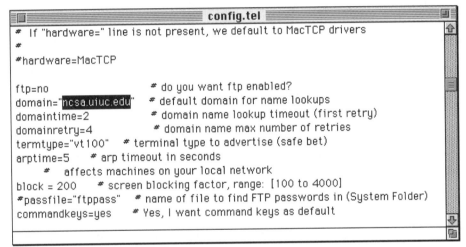

3. Change the default domain (highlighted in Figure 8-1) to reflect your domain, using the domain.top-domain format.

4. Optionally, change the scrollback setting to provide a larger capture buffer. The default setting is 200.

   ▤ The capture buffer allows text that has scrolled off your Macintosh screen to be saved in memory. The scrollback setting determines how many lines of text will be saved in memory once they have scrolled off the screen.

5. Select the Save command from the File menu.

6. Quit TeachText or the text editing program you used to edit the config.tel file. NCSA TELNET is now configured for basic use.

For information on customizing the NCSA TELNET program, see the extensive NCSA TELNET User Guide (available by anonymous FTP from ftp.ncsa.uiuc.edu in the /mac/ directory).

Opening an NCSA TELNET Session

You can use TELNET to access an Internet resource or archive in much the same way you might use Gopher or FTP. To initiate a remote login session with NCSA TELNET

1. Double-click on the NCSA TELNET icon to launch the program.

2. Select the Open Connection... command from the File menu. A Connection dialog box will be displayed, as shown in Figure 8-2.

Figure 8-2: NCSA TELNET Connection dialog box.

Session name	
Window Name	

☐ FTP session (⌘F)
☐ Serial/SLIP (⌘S)

[Configure] [OK] [Cancel]

3. In the Session name box, enter the domain name—in the domain.top-domain format—for the host to which you want to login.

   ▪ This exercise will use the weather information available from the University of Michigan's Weather Underground as an example, so if you're following along, enter **downwind.sprl.umich.edu 3000** in the Session name box. Alternatively, several other TELNET resources—including online library card catalogs, Supreme Court rulings and major league baseball schedules—are mentioned later in this chapter.

4. Optionally, enter a name for the TELNET window to be opened in the Window Name box.

⬛ Window names aren't of much use in a single connection, but they're very useful if you open more than one connection at a time.

5. Click the **OK** button. NCSA TELNET will establish a connection to the host you specified, and a Session window will be opened, as shown in Figure 8-3.

Figure 8-3: NCSA TELNET Session window.

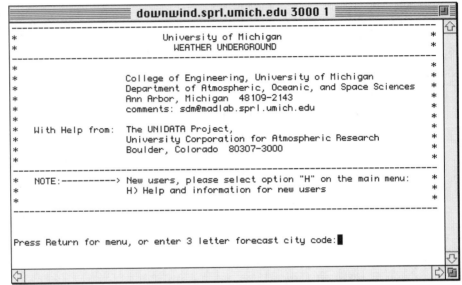

```
================ downwind.sprl.umich.edu 3000 1 ================
---------------------------------------------------------------------
*                         University of Michigan                    *
*                         WEATHER UNDERGROUND                        *
---------------------------------------------------------------------
*                                                                    *
*              College of Engineering, University of Michigan        *
*              Department of Atmospheric, Oceanic, and Space Sciences *
*              Ann Arbor, Michigan  48109-2143                       *
*              comments: sdm@madlab.sprl.umich.edu                   *
*                                                                    *
*   With Help from:  The UNIDATA Project,                            *
*                    University Corporation for Atmospheric Research *
*                    Boulder, Colorado  80307-3000                   *
*                                                                    *
---------------------------------------------------------------------
*   NOTE:---------> New users, please select option "H" on the main menu: *
*                   H) Help and information for new users            *
*                                                                    *
---------------------------------------------------------------------

Press Return for menu, or enter 3 letter forecast city code:█
```

⬛ Note that some hosts may prompt you for a terminal type (The University of Michigan's Weather Underground service doesn't). Sometimes, there is a menu selection available, but many times, there is simply a TERMINAL: prompt. NSCA TELNET emulates a VT102 terminal by default, so you can enter **VT100** (or VT102) at the prompt. Almost every host will support a VT102 terminal.

⬛ Note that if you are logging into a remote host on which you have an account, you may have to set the terminal type yourself. For a UNIX host, using the C shell, enter **set term=vt100;tset** at the command prompt. For a VAX/VMS host, enter **set term /inq** at the command prompt.

6. You can navigate through the choices and information on the host by entering commands and menu selections at the command prompt.

   ▥ Menu selections are usually self-explanatory. The commands available to you vary from host to host; refer to each specific host's documentation for an explanation of the commands that may be available.

7. Enter **exit** or **logout** at the command prompt to logout, ending the remote session. Alternatively, select the Close Connection command from the File menu. The Session window will disappear when the connection is closed.

Using TCP/Connect II's TELNET Module

InterCon's popular commercial Mac Internet software, TCP/Connect II, includes a TELNET module that provides more terminal emulations than NCSA TELNET. Use TCP/Connect II's TELNET module to login to other computers on the Internet in an interactive, command-line mode.

Configuring TCP/Connect II's TELNET Module

Like NCSA TELNET, TCP/Connect II can be customized in many different ways. This section provides only the configuration information necessary to establish a basic remote login connection.

To configure TCP/Connect II's TELNET module for basic use

1. Launch TCP/Connect II by double-clicking on its icon.

2. From the Edit menu, select the Configure... command. The Configuration dialog box will appear.

3. Click on the Hosts icon in the scrolling list of configuration items at the left side of the window. The Hosts Configuration panel will be displayed, as shown in Figure 8-4.

Figure 8-4:
TCP/Connect II
Hosts Config-
uration panel.

```
┌─────────────────────────────────────────────────────────────────┐
│ ▓▓▓▓▓▓        TCP/Connect II Configuration        ▓▓▓▓▓▓          │
│ ┌──┐ ┌─────────────────────────────────────────┐   ┌─────────┐   │
│ │▓▓│ │ – Default –          Appalachian State CWIS (Telnet)│ New... │
│ └──┘ │ Apple (A/UX Support) Apple (Bric-a-Brac)  │ Rename...│      │
│ ┌──┐ │ Apple (Cambridge)    Apple (General Archive)│ Delete │      │
│ │▓▓│ │ Baseball Schedules (Telnet) Biosphere Newsletter     │      │
│General│ Bucknell (Telnet/Knowbot)   CARL (Telnet)  │        │      │
│      ├─────────────────────────────────────────────────────┤      │
│ ┌──┐ │ IP Addresses: [                              ]       │      │
│ │▓▓│ │ Full Domain Name: [                          ]       │      │
│Network│ Operating System: [      ]  CPU Type: [          ]  │      │
│      │                                    RWIN: [          ] │      │
│      ├─────────────────────────────────────────────────────┤      │
│ ┌──┐ │ Paste Style: ○ Full Speed ◉ By Line ○ Blocked to    │      │
│ │▓▓│ │ Paste Delay: [1      ]  ticks (60ths of a second)    │      │
│File Transfer│                                                │      │
│      ├─────────────────────────────────────────────────────┤      │
│ ┌──┐ │ FTP Client:                                          │      │
│ │▓▓│ │ ☒ Automatically log in    ☒ Automatically show file list│   │
│Hosts │ ☒ Use PORT commands       ☐ Transfer unknown file types as ASCII│
└─────────────────────────────────────────────────────────────────┘
```

4. Click the **New** button. A dialog box will appear, prompting you to enter the name of the host.

NotePad++.

NotePad++ is a replacement for Apple's standard Notepad desk accessory. This desk accessory has up to 35 pages for notes, multiple notepad files, a Find command, a ruler and handles styled text. It's available by FTP from mac.archive.umich.edu in the /mac/extensions/da/ directory.

5. Enter a reference name for the host and click the **OK** button. A new entry will be created in the Hosts scrolling list.

   ▨ This example in the next section will use a specific host to login remotely to the Library of Congress card catalog. Again, you can choose another TELNET site from the list of resources at the end of this chapter.

6. Enter **dra.com** in the Full Domain Name box. Alternatively, enter **192.65.218.43** in the IP Addresses box. The entry to login remotely to the Library of Congress card catalog should look like the example in Figure 8-5.

Figure 8-5:
TCP/Connect II host
entry for Library of
Congress card
catalog.

TCP/Connect II Configuration

General

Grateful Dead Archive II | Internet Mail Guide
Internet Services | InterNIC (Directory)
Law Library (Telnet) | Libraries (Telnet)
Library of Congress (Telnet) | Lyrics Archive
Macintosh (Info-Mac) | Macintosh (Sounds/Rochester)

New...
Rename...
Delete

Network

IP Addresses: 192.65.218.43
Full Domain Name: dra.com
Operating System: [ ] CPU Type: [ ]
RWIN: [ ]

File Transfer

Paste Style: ○ Full Speed ● By Line ○ Blocked to
Paste Delay: 1 ticks (60ths of a second)

FTP Client:
☒ Automatically log in ☒ Automatically show file list
☒ Use PORT commands ☐ Transfer unknown file types as ASCII

Hosts

7. Click on the Sessions icon in the scrolling list of configuration
items. The Sessions Configuration panel will appear, as shown in
Figure 8-6.

Figure 8-6:
TCP/Connect II
Sessions Config-
uration panel.

TCP/Connect II Configuration

Tektronix

– Default – | Appalachian State CWIS
Baseball Schedules | Bucknell
CARL | Chicago/NWU Information
Cleveland Free-Net | InterNIC Directory Searches
Law Library | Libraries

New...
Rename...
Delete

IBM 327x

Host: [ ]
DEC Emulation [Default ▼] Tek Emulation [Default ▼]
IBM Emulation [Default ▼]

Sessions

Telnet Terminal type:
● DEC-VT240 ○ IBM-3278-2
○ Other:

☐ 4.2BSD CR-NUL required
☒ Backspace sends DEL
☐ Alternate Telnet port

☐ Show control characters
in local edit mode
☒ Map characters to Telnet controls
Abort output: [^O] Interrupt: [^C]
☒ Local Flow Control
Stop output: [^S] Start: [^Q]

Telnet Options...

Mail

8. Click the **New** button. A dialog box will appear, prompting you to
enter the name of the host.

9. Enter a reference name for the host (something that describes the contents of that resource, for instance) and click the **OK** button. A new entry will be created in the Hosts scrolling list.

   ▪ The example in the next section will use a specific host to login remotely to the Library of Congress card catalog.

10. From the Host: pop-up menu, select the host you defined in step 6.

11. Close the Configuration dialog box by clicking the close box.

Opening a TCP/Connect II TELNET Session

Once you've configured TCP/Connect II, you can use it to access TELNET sites via remote login just as you do with NCSA TELNET. To initiate a remote login session with TCP/Connect II

1. Launch TCP/Connect II by double-clicking on its icon.

2. From the Terminal menu, select the Connect... command. The Terminal Connect dialog box will appear, as shown in Figure 8-7.

Figure 8-7: TCP/
Connect II Terminal
Connect dialog box.

Terminal Connect

Session Name `entropy.farces.com` ▼

Window Name

Cancel   OK

3. Select the Library of Congress session you created in the "Configuring TCP/Connect II's TELNET Module" section from the Session Name pop-up menu.

4. Optionally, enter a name for the TELNET window to be opened in the Window Name box.

   ▪ Window names aren't of much use in a single connection, but they're very useful if you open more than one connection at a time.

5. Click the **OK** button. TCP/Connect II will establish a connection to the host and a new TELNET Session window will be opened, as shown in Figure 8-8.

Figure 8-8:
TCP/Connect II
TELNET Session
window.

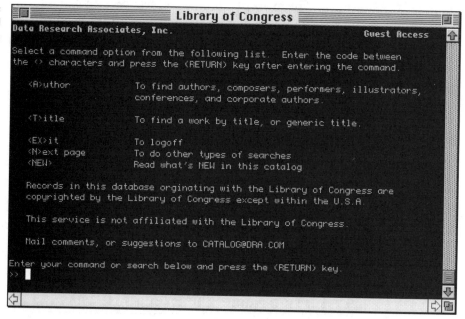

■ Note that some hosts may prompt you for a terminal type (The Library of Congress card catalog doesn't). Sometimes there is a menu selection available, but many times there is simply a TERMINAL: prompt. TCP/Connect II emulates a VT102 terminal by default, so you can enter **VT100** (or VT102) at the prompt. Almost every host will support a VT102 terminal.

■ Note that if you are logging into a remote host on which you have an account, you may have to set the terminal type yourself. For a UNIX host, using the C shell, enter **set term=vt100;tset** at the command prompt. For a VAX/VMS host, enter **set term /inq** at the command prompt.

6. You can navigate through the choices and information by entering commands and menu selections at the command prompt.

■ Menu selections are usually self-explanatory. The commands available to you vary from host to host; refer to each specific host's documentation for an explanation of the commands that may be available.

7. Enter **exit** or **logout** at the command prompt to logout, ending the remote session. Alternatively, click the TELNET Session window's close box to end the remote session. The TELNET Session window will disappear when the connection is closed.

Knowbots

Knowbots are knowledge robots—or at least that's the theory behind them. Think of them as electronic librarians that can help you find what you're looking for when you don't know where to look. Currently, Knowbots are used mostly for looking up Internet addresses, but the potential for using Knowbots for other uses is very exciting. Theoretically, you should be able to send a Knowbot into the Internet with a set of search criteria. When it finds sources for the information you're looking for, the Knowbot would return with the information it finds.

CTerm.

CTerm is an IBM 3270 terminal emulator—Macintosh software that mimics the functions and commands of a particular piece of hardware. Some Internet services require IBM 3270 terminal emulation. CTerm requires System 7 or the Communications Toolbox with System 6. The program is available by FTP from mac.archive.umich.edu in the /mac/util/comm/ directory.

Unfortunately, I've never been able to login to a site where the Knowbots live, and the general consensus of those on the Net is that Knowbots aren't quite ready for prime time. Look for more information about Knowbots in one of the electronic updates to this book.

Netfind

Netfind is a program that searches certain databases to help you find an e-mail address. It's not very easy to use, and requires that you login remotely using TELNET, but Netfind can be useful when other options prove fruitless.

To use Netfind to locate someone's e-mail address

1. Use NCSA TELNET or TCP/Connect II to login to bruno.cs.colorado.edu.

2. At the login: prompt, enter **netfind** and press Return.

3. Select the Search item from the menu.

4. At the prompt, enter the name and general location (called "keys") for the person you're looking for.

   ▧ For example, let's say you're trying to find the e-mail address of your pal, Wanda Caldwell, at the University of Georgia. You think she might have "wanda" as part of her address, but it's a pretty good bet that she'll have "caldwell" in her address, so you would enter **caldwell uga edu** at the prompt. A list of people named Caldwell at the University of Georgia will be displayed, and you can select the entry that matches the person you're looking for.

5. Select the Exit item from the menu.

The key to working with Netfind is to learn how to conduct searches that are neither too vague nor too specific. If you enter a search that is too vague—like Caldwell Georgia—the search will return too many possible choices. Conversely, if you enter a search that is too specific—like W_Caldwell peachnet uga edu—the search will yield no results.

Finger

Finger is a useful program for searching the user log on a computer connected to the Internet. This allows you to find someone's e-mail address, provided you know the name of the computer he or she uses.

Peter Lewis has written a shareware Finger program for the Macintosh. You can download it by FTP from the Info-Mac archive at Stanford University (sumex-aim.stanford.edu) in the /info-mac/comm/ directory. The file name is finger1.35.sit.hqx.

The word "Finger"—like many of the other Internet terms including "FTP" and "TELNET"—is used as both a noun and a verb. You use the word "Finger" to refer to the program you use to "finger" (the process of obtaining information with the Finger program) a person or resource on the Net.

To locate someone using Finger

1. Double-click on the Mac Finger application's icon to launch the program. The Finger dialog box will appear, as shown in Figure 8-9.

Figure 8-9: Finger
dialog box.

```
┌──────────────────────────────────────────────┐
│ ▣ ═══════════════ Finger ═══════════════════ │
│                                                │
│  User      ┌──────────────────────────────┐  │
│            └──────────────────────────────┘  │
│                                                │
│  Machine   ┌──────────────────────────────┐  │
│            └──────────────────────────────┘  │
│                                                │
│  ☐ Whois Server ⌘S                            │
│                                                │
│  ( Cancel )      ( Set Default )   (( Finger )) │
└──────────────────────────────────────────────┘
```

2. In the User box, enter the name of the person you're looking for and the name of the host computer—in the username@domain.top-domain format.

3. Click the **Finger** button. The results will be displayed in a new window, as shown in Figure 8-10.

Figure 8-10: Finger
search results.

```
┌──────────────────────────────────────────────┐
│ ▣ ══════════ mfraase@mr.net (137.192.2.5) ═══ │
│ finger: /usr/adm/lastlog open error          │
│ Login name: mfraase      In real life: Michael Fraase │
│ Directory: /home/mfraase        Shell: /bin/csh │
│ Never logged in.                               │
│ New mail received Fri Apr 16 15:38:11 1993;   │
│   unread since Fri Apr 16 15:24:33 1993        │
│ No Plan.                                       │
└──────────────────────────────────────────────┘
```

4. Select the Quit command from the File menu.

You can also use Finger to get a list of everyone currently logged into a computer on the Internet. The basic steps are the same as those you use for searching for an individual, except you enter the name of the computer—using the @domain.top-domain format—in the Machine box (note the "@" symbol). The results will be displayed in a new window, as shown in Figure 8-11.

Figure 8-11: Finger machine search results.

```
                    @riverside.mr.net (137.192.2.5)
finger: /usr/adm/lastlog open error
Login      Name             TTY Idle    When      Where
root       Operator         co 5:17 Mon 14:49
dfazio     Dennis Fazio     p0    5 Fri 14:58     Mac.MR.Net
bergum     Dave Bergum      p4      Fri 15:05     NIC.MR.Net
```

You can also use Finger as a sort of general information server. Finger has the ability to display a text file (named .plan if you're curious) to any Finger query. You can find all sorts of interesting information on the Internet by using Finger. For example, if you Finger jtchern@ocf.berkeley.edu, a list of today's baseball scores will be displayed.

Making the world a smaller place.

Sheldon Smith forwarded news of a project undertaken by his wife's 5–6 grade class in San Luis Obispo, Calif.

"This is an example of how the Internet brings the world into the classroom. We, as educators, cannot take the kids out into the world, but the Internet can bring the world to the kids.

"Last October, about the time Ross Perot re-announced his candidacy, an American ship accidentally shot a Turkish ship during a NATO exercise, killing the Captain and three crew members. Because of the Presidential election, there was not much about it in the news.

"My wife's students heard about the accident and felt the U.S. should apologize. The kids wrote notes of apology, which were compiled into a class letter.

"I sent their letter to the Turkish newsgroup, and I forwarded it to my sister, who moderates a Middle Eastern conference on PeaceNet. She works for AWAIR, which is a non-profit group that produces curriculum materials on the Middle East. In any case, after posting their letter, my wife and I received about 30 replies over a two week period."

Here are excerpts from two students' letters:

"Hi my name is Jesse Cutburth. I do not understand why we shot your ship. I think we should apologize, and this is what I am doing. I don't understand how we shot your ship on accident. I think we should replace your ship with one of ours, but we can't replace four people."

"Hi, my name is Brianne Reimer. As an American, I am very sorry about what we did. I don't know what we were doing there. But I am only a child. Someday, I hope I will go to Turkey. And if I do go, I will surely apologize to you face to face. Sorry."

If you Finger buckmr@rpi.edu, a list of this week's top popular music recordings in the United States will be displayed.

Perhaps the strangest Finger resources are the cold-drink vending machines that some universities have connected to the Internet. When Fingered, these machines report which bins in the vending machine are empty and which bins hold the coldest drinks, as shown in Figure 8-12.

Figure 8-12: Finger cold-drink vending machine.

```
┌──────────────────────────────────────────────────────────┐
│  ▣           drink@csh.rit.edu (129.21.60.4)            ▣ │
├──────────────────────────────────────────────────────────┤
│ Login: drink          Name: Drink (Coke Machine)          │
│ Directory: /u0/drink              Shell: /u0/drink/shell/shell │
│ Office: NRH Hallway                                        │
│ Last login Wed Mar 31 18:08 (EST) on ttypb from nick.csh.rit.edu │
│ Plan:                                                      │
│     Balance:  $  0.00                                      │
│                                                            │
│     1) Lipton Iced Tea $ 0.50  Empty  (4/44)              │
│     2) Mountain Dew    $ 0.50  Full   (24/44)             │
│     3) Hawaiian Punch  $ 0.50  Full   (36/44)             │
│     4) Dr Pepper       $ 0.50  Full   (25/44)             │
│     5) Coke Classic    $ 0.50  Full   (20/44)             │
│                                                            │
│          Drink    3+ hrs   1-3 hrs   0-1 hrs    Total      │
│          :::::     :::::::   :::::::   :::::::    :::::     │
│ Lipton Iced Tea      4         0         0         4       │
│    Mountain Dew     24         0         0        24       │
│  Hawaiian Punch     36         0         0        36       │
│       Dr Pepper     25         0         0        25       │
│     Coke Classic    20         0         0        20       │
└──────────────────────────────────────────────────────────┘
```

Since I'm sure you're going to ask for it later if I don't include it now, here's a list of vending machines attached to the Internet:

coke@cs.wisc.edu
@coke.elab.cs.cmu.edu
mnm@coke.elab.cs.cmu.edu
bargraph@coke.elab.cs.cmu.edu
drink@csh.rit.edu

WAIS

WAIS (Wide-Area Information Server) is useful for searching through material on the Internet that has been indexed based on content. WAIS is somewhat analogous to Gopher. Both tools allow you to search for information without worrying about where the information is physically stored, but WAIS doesn't provide much in the way of browsing.

For example, WAIS indexes consist of every word in a document, and each word carries the same importance; there's no way to tell WAIS that "Macintosh" is more important than "and" in a search. This differentiation between the importance of words is called weighting, and WAIS doesn't support it.

Also, there is no context sensitivity within the WAIS environment. Searching for FrameMaker, for example, would return information about FrameMaker running on every computer platform; there's no way to limit the search to the just Macintosh version of FrameMaker, for instance.

You can download a copy of the current version of the Macintosh WAIS client (wais-for-mac-1.1.sea.hqx) by FTP from think.com in the /wais/ directory. Documentation is available in the same directory.

To initiate a WAIS search

1. Launch the WAIS for the Macintosh program by double-clicking on its icon. The Sources and Questions window will appear.

2. From the Source menu, select the Open Source… command. A standard Open File dialog box will be displayed.

3. Open the directory-of-servers file (located in the Sources folder inside the WAIS folder).

4. From the File menu, select the Save command. The directory-of-servers icon will be saved within the Sources window.

5. From the Question menu, select the New Question… command. The Question dialog box will appear, as shown in Figure 8-13.

Figure 8-13: WAIS
Question dialog
box.

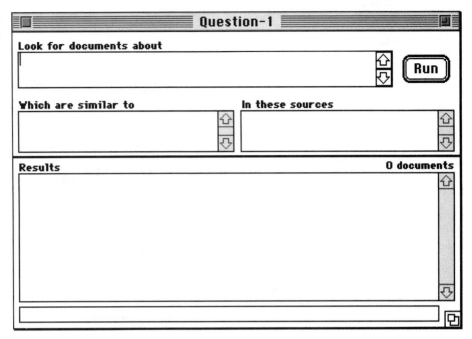

6. Enter your question using natural English structure in the Look for documents about box.

7. Drag the icons representing the Internet resources you want to search from the Sources window into the In these sources box.

8. Click the **Run** button. The results of the search will appear in the Results scrolling list. An example of the results of a search for "what is the chief export of Argentina" within the World Factbook is shown in Figure 8-14.

Figure 8-14: WAIS
search results.

Question-1

Look for documents about

what is the chief export of Argentina   [Run]

Which are similar to   **In these sources**

                                            ◉ world-factbook.src

Results   **15 documents**

📄 ▨	13K	Argentina Geography Total area: 2,766,890 km2; land area: 2,736,690
📄 ▨	5K	Cocos (Keeling) Islands (territory of Australia)
📄 ▨	13K	Belgium Geography Total area: 30,510 km2; land area: 30,230 km2
📄 ▨	10K	Antarctica Geography Total area: about 14,000,000 km2; land area: abo
📄 ▨	11K	Somalia Geography Total area: 637,660 km2; land area: 627,340 km2
📄 ▨	12K	Uruguay Geography Total area: 176,220 km2; land area: 173,620 km2
📄 ▨	5K	Atlantic Ocean Geography Total area: 82,217,000 km2; includes Baltic S
📄 ▨	13K	Bolivia Geography Total area: 1,098,580 km2; land area: 1,084,390 km
📄 ▨	8K	Falkland Islands (Islas Malvinas) (dependent territory of the UK)
📄 ▨	13K	Paraguay Geography Total area: 406,750 km2; land area: 397,300 km2

9. Double-click on any of the result icons to display their contents. If
   the icon is a source reference, select the Save command from the
   File menu to save the reference in your Sources folder. The source
   will also be added to the Sources window. The highlighted selection identifies meat, wheat, corn, oilseed, hides, and wool as
   Argentina's chief exports (as shown in Figure 8-15.)

Figure 8-15:
Contents of WAIS
search result.

Argentina Geography Total area 2,766,890 km2; land area 2,736,6

Inflation rate (consumer prices): 1,350% (1990)

Unemployment rate: 8.6% (May 1990)

Budget: revenues $12.2 billion; expenditures $17.3 billion,
including capital expenditures of $2.8 billion (1989)

Exports: $12.4 billion (f.o.b., 1990);

commodities--meat, wheat, corn, oilseed, hides, wool;

partners--US 12%, USSR, Italy, Brazil, Japan, Netherlands

Imports: $4.1 billion (c.i.f., 1990);

10. Repeat steps 6–9 to refine your search as necessary, adding or removing icons in the In these sources box.

World Wide Web (WWW)

World Wide Web (WWW), developed by the European Particle Physics Laboratory (CERN), is an online hypertext system that spans the Internet. Hypertext is a non-linear publishing method in which you can browse through passages of text, expanding items that interest you. When you expand an item, you are actually traversing a link to the new information.

A program that runs on your Mac (a WWW client), called MacWWW, is available by FTP from info.cern.ch in the /pub/www/ bin/mac/ directory.

To browse the World Wide Web

1. Launch MacWWW by double-clicking on its icon. You'll automatically be logged into the World Wide Web, or "web" as it's known on the Internet, as shown in Figure 8-16.

Figure 8-16: MacWWW initial login display.

2. Navigate through the web by double-clicking on any item that appears in boldface type. Clicking on the word help, for example, opens a linked window, as shown in Figure 8-17.

Figure 8-17:
MacWWW linked
window.

3. Continue to double-click on items that appear in boldface type. New linked windows will be opened as you traverse the hypertext links available.

CompactPro.
CompactPro and StuffIt continually vie for the top honors in Macintosh file compression. CompactPro can decode archived files in BinHex and StuffIt formats, as well as its own format. With CompactPro, you can create self-extracting files and segment files that are too large to fit on a single floppy disk. It's available by FTP from mac.archive.umich.edu in the /mac/util/compression/ directory.

In WWW, menus and other navigational aids appear as a list of links. Anything that is available via Gopher, WAIS or FTP is also available via WWW. Unfortunately, there is no easy way to find new information items.

Archie

Archie is an Internet service, originally developed at McGill University, that allows you to search indexes of available files on publicly-accessible FTP servers. In other words, you can ask Archie if a certain file exists on the Internet, and if so, where is it? Archie can be helpful in a number of circumstances. You can use it to search for files when you know their names. You can enter just part of a file's name, like "Eudora," to search for the popular e-mail program.

You search Archie's indexes by specifying a string of characters . Archie returns a list of filenames that match your search criteria, and the name of the FTP servers where they're located.

As a Macintosh user, you have three options for using Archie:

▓ You can TELNET to an Archie server and muddle through a command-line interface.

▓ You can use the Macintosh-specific Archie client. Chris McNeil's Archie client for the Macintosh (called, simply, Archie) is available by FTP from sumex-aim.stanford.edu in the /info-mac/comm/ directory.

▓ You can use TurboGopher to search the Archie database.

Figure 8-18 shows a list of Archie servers across the Net.

Figure 8-18:
Archie Servers.

Archie Server	Geographic Area
archie.ans.net	ANS Network sites
archie.au	Australia and Pacific Basin
archie.doc.ic.ac.uk	United Kingdom and Ireland
archie.funet.fi	Europe
archie.mcgill.ca	Canada
archie.rutgers.edu	Northeastern United States
archie.sura.net	Southeastern United States
archie.unl.edu	Western United States

Try to use the Archie server that is geographically closest to you. This will help balance network traffic.

Using the Macintosh Archie Client

Chris McNeil's Archie for the Macintosh is extremely easy to use.

1. Launch Archie by double-clicking on its icon. The Archie Query window will appear, as shown in Figure 8-19.

Figure 8-19: Archie Query window.

2. From the Prefs menu, select the Archie Server... command. The Archie Server dialog box will appear, as shown in Figure 8-20.

Figure 8-20: Archie Server dialog box.

3. In the Archie Server box, enter the domain address—in the domain.top-domain format—of the closest Archie server.

4. Click the **Save** button to dismiss the Archie Server dialog box. Your server configuration will be saved to disk.

5. In the Archie Query window's Search String box, enter the character string for which you want to search.

6. Click the **Search** button. The search will be initiated on the Archie server you specified, and the results will be returned in a new window.

Using TurboGopher for Archie Searches

Although Chris McNeil's Macintosh Archie client is easy to use, I find that using TurboGopher to search within the Archie database is just as easy and yields results somewhat faster.

1. Launch TurboGopher by double-clicking on its icon. (For more on obtaining and using TurboGopher, see Chapter 7, "Using Gopher.") TurboGopher comes pre-configured for use with the University of Minnesota's Gopher server, and the program will automatically login to the "mother" Gopher and display a Bookmarks window and a Home Gopher Server window, as shown in Figure 8-21.

Figure 8-21:
TurboGopher
initial display.

■ If you've already configured TurboGopher for use with another Home Gopher server, your screen will reflect the items available on that server.

2. Navigate to the Search FTP Sites with Archie folder.

■ If you're using the University of Minnesota's "mother" Gopher as your Home Gopher server, it's located inside the Internet file server (ftp) sites folder, as shown in Figure 8-22.

Figure 8-22: TurboGopher Archie Internet file server (ftp) sites folder.

3. Double-click on the Search FTP sites (Archie) folder. A new TurboGopher window will be opened displaying search icons, as shown in Figure 8-23.

Figure 8-23:
TurboGopher
Archie search
folder.

4. Double-click on the Exact search of archive sites on the Internet icon. The Search dialog box will appear, as shown in Figure 8-24.

Figure 8-24:
TurboGopher
Search dialog box.

5. Enter a word or series of words contained in the document or filename you wish to download.

6. Click the **OK** button. TurboGopher will search within the Archie database for documents and filenames matching the search words you specified. A new TurboGopher window will appear showing a list of the documents and files matching your search words, like the example of a search for "eudora" shown in Figure 8-25.

Figure 8-25:
TurboGopher
window with
search results.

An advantage of using TurboGopher for Archie searches is that the search results window contains "live" Internet resources. You can simply double-click on any item in the search results window to automatically login to an anonymous FTP archive or download a file.

RFCs

An RFC (Request for Comments) is a document that defines a specific part of the Internet itself. Because of the anarchic nature of the Internet, anyone can write an RFC. Most are highly technical, and relate to topics that are of little interest to the average user. Some RFCs, however, are veritable goldmines of useful information for real people. RFCs are always referred to by their number, and may be available in either text or PostScript formats (text versions have a .txt suffix; PostScript versions have a .ps suffix).

RFCs are available from many FTP archives, including the "official" depositories shown in Figure 8-26.

Figure 8-26: Official
RFC depositories.

FTP Site	Directory
nic.ddn.mil	/rfc/
nis.jvnc.net	/rfc/
nisc.sri.com	/rfc/
wuarchive.wustl.edu	/doc/rfc/
nnsc.nsf.net	/rfc/
src.doc.ic.ac.uk	/rfc/

Because all RFCs are available only by RFC number, it's a good idea to first download the index of RFC files (rfc-index.txt). This file contains a complete index of all currently available RFCs.

You can also obtain RFCs by e-mail with these steps:

1. Launch your e-mail program.
2. Create a new message to the address mail-server@nisc.sri.com.
3. Enter a one-line message consisting of send rfcxxx.txt (where xxx is the number of the RFC you want to receive).

   ▣ To receive the index, enter a one-line message consisting of send rfc-index.txt.

4. Send your e-mail message.

A list of some of the RFCs that are useful for average users is provided in Figure 8-27.

RFC	Title
1432	Recent Internet books
1402	There's Gold in them thar Networks! or Searching for Treasure in all the Wrong Places
1392	Internet Users' Glossary
1359	Connecting to the Internet: What connecting institutions should anticipate
1325	FYI on questions and answers: Answers to commonly asked "new Internet user" questions

Figure 8-27:
Useful RFCs.

RFC	Title
1296	Internet Growth (1981-1991)
1259	Building the open road: The NREN as test-bed for the national public network
1244	Site Security Handbook
1208	Glossary of networking terms
1207	FYI on Questions and Answers: Answers to commonly asked "experienced Internet user" questions
1192	Commercialization of the Internet summary report
1180	TCP/IP tutorial
1178	Choosing a name for your computer
1175	FYI on where to start: A bibliography of internet-working information
1167	Thoughts on the National Research and Education Network
1118	Hitchhikers guide to the Internet

FAQs

A FAQ (Frequently Asked Question) is a collection of questions (and their answers) most often asked by new Internet users. FAQs exist for all network news newsgroups and most mailing lists. Until you get your Internet legs, read the FAQ for the newsgroups you frequent. You can save yourself a lot of embarrassment by skimming FAQ files.

Most FAQs are posted to their related newsgroups on a monthly basis. In addition, FAQs for all the newsgroups are consolidated and posted to the news.answers newsgroup. You can also obtain FAQs by FTP from pit-manager.mit.edu in the /pub/usenet/ directory.

Internet Organizations

As the Internet has evolved from a project researching ways to ensure communications in the event of a nuclear attack into a research and business tool used by millions of individuals, a number of diverse and vital organizations have sprung up. The actions of two of these organizations—the Internet Society and the Electronic Frontier Foundation—have repercussions for every Internet user.

Electronic Frontier Foundation

On July 10, 1990, two unlikely cohorts announced they were forming a foundation to "address social and legal issues arising from the impact on society of the increasing pervasive use of computers as a means of communication and information distribution." Mitch Kapor is best known as the founder of Lotus Development Corporation, the publisher of the Lotus 1-2-3 spreadsheet program. John Perry Barlow is a sometimes lyricist for the Grateful Dead, one-time Congressional candidate and Wyoming rancher.

A number of factions are battling for control and influence over cyberspace, and the Electronic Frontier Foundation (EFF) is entrenched in the front lines of the battlefield. On one side of the battle lines are a number of government agencies, corporations and other entities that want to limit access to information and dictate what people can do in cyberspace. On the other side, there are those—like the members of the EFF— who want to widen (and deepen) everyone's access to information, and extend the rights most Americans enjoy in physical reality to cyberspace.

FTPd.

FTPd is a fully implemented FTP server and Gopher server for the Macintosh. Distributed as shareware, FTPd uses System 7's file sharing Users and Groups settings to restrict access to the server. MacBinary file transfer support is also provided. The program is available by FTP from mac.archive.umich.edu in the /mac/util/comm/ directory.

Kapor and Barlow came together when both were questioned by the FBI following an incident at Apple Computer where a group calling itself the NuPrometheus League had distributed the Color QuickDraw source code to members of the computer press and luminaries in the computer industry.

John Perry Barlow was amazed at the level of computer ignorance exhibited by the FBI agent who visited him in May 1990. Barlow had been a longtime member of the Internet-connected Whole Earth

'Lectronic Link (WELL), and describes himself as a "techno-crank." From the agent, Barlow learned that computer hackers—all computer hackers—were under suspicion as Evil Criminals. He also learned that the FBI was tracing anyone who had visited the Hackers Conference, an invitation-only affair begun in 1984 that drew attendees from the top levels of the computer industry, including executives, consultants, pundits and journalists.

It's important to draw the distinction between hackers (those who like to explore systems for the sake of learning something about those systems) and crackers (those who are out to wreak havoc by breaking into systems, deleting files and reaping financial gain illegally).

Barlow, alarmed at the implications of computer ignorance within the FBI (and the possibility of a high-tech witch hunt), sounded the alarm on the WELL. One of the many WELL inhabitants who took note of Barlow's outcry was Mitch Kapor, who had already endured being fingerprinted by the FBI.

Kapor flew to Barlow's Wyoming ranch in June 1990 to lay the groundwork for the EFF, and Barlow wrote "Crime and Puzzlement," an article announcing the pair's intention of forming a political organization intent on extending Constitutional rights to cyberspace.

The response from the computing community was astounding. Original funding for EFF was provided by Kapor and Apple cofounder Steve Wozniak. John Gilmore (one of the founders of Sun Microsystems) contributed, and others quickly followed.

The Electronic Frontier Foundation continues to fight for a careful balance of freedom, access and privacy throughout the networks, and they've even won a few battles.

You can download a wealth of information from the EFF's FTP or Gopher server at ftp.eff.org and gopher.eff.org respectively. Here's a sampling:

- Back issues of EFFector Online, the electronic newsletter of the EFF.

- Testimony of EFF staff and board members.

- Papers and articles by EFF staff and board members.

- EFF Newsnotes and informational postings.

- Papers and articles about cyberspace from such online luminaries as Bruce Sterling, John Perry Barlow and Dorothy Denning.

- Information about various legal issues affecting the Internet.
- Text of various laws and proposed laws relevant to the electronic frontier.

> Electronic Frontier Foundation
> 666 Pennsylvania Avenue, SE
> Suite 303
> Washington, DC 20003
> 202/544-9237
> 202/547-5481 (Fax)
> 617/576-4510 (Legal hotline)
> eff@eff.org

Internet Society

The Internet Society exists to encourage cooperation among the various networks that comprise the Internet, fostering a global communications infrastructure. The organization focuses on the future of the Internet and the emerging and established technologies that impact the Net . The Internet Society appoints a small group of members to the Internet Architecture Board—the closest thing the Internet has to a board of governors, although it's perhaps more accurate to think of the body as a group of tribal elders.

The Internet Architecture Board (IAB) is responsible for the technical management of the Internet. It adopts proposed standards and allocates addresses. The Internet Architecture Board also oversees two groups:

- The Internet Engineering Task Force (IETF) is responsible for the technical operation of the Internet.
- The Internet Research Task Force (IRTF) is responsible for research and development issues surrounding the Internet.

The Internet Society sponsors an annual conference, publishes a quarterly newsletter, and supports an electronic mail distribution list.

> Internet Society
> 1895 Preston White Drive
> Suite 100
> Reston, VA 22091
> 703/620-8990
> isoc@nri.reston.va.us

Neat Stuff

New information resources are added to the Internet every minute. It's impossible to keep up with everything on the Net—about the best you can do is seek out those things that specifically interest you. Keep in close touch with your friends and associates, tipping them off to new files, sites and resources that they might be interested in—and ask them to do the same for you. When you find something worth sharing, e-mail pointers (a "trail" through the Net) to each other. Exchange Gopher bookmarks.

The electronic updates that come with this book are another great way to keep up with what's new and worthwhile on the Internet. For more details, see Appendix A, "Electronic Updates."

As your tour guide, it's impossible for me to show you all of the Internet. (That's like trying to ride every ride at Disney World in just one day!) Because the Net is constantly changing, any collection of Internet resources is only a snapshot of what's interesting right now (Summer 1993). Of course, what's interesting to me may not be interesting to you at all, so I'm providing pointers of general interest.

Naturally, many of you will wonder why your favorite site or resource isn't listed with those that follow. The most likely answer is space limitations, but you should still e-mail your favorite Internet finds to me for inclusion in future editions and electronic updates. Send your useful, bizarre and otherwise enticing resources to me at: mfraase@farces.com.

Here's how the resource entries that follow are organized:

- The Type: field tells you what software tool or protocol you need to use to access the resource.

- The Address: field tells you the domain name address for the resource.

- The Pathname: field tells you the pathname for the directory or file of the resource.

- The Summary: field provides a brief description of the resource and any necessary login information.

Clearinghouse for Networked Information Discovery and Retrieval (CNIDR)

Type: FTP

Address: cnidr.org

Summary: The Clearinghouse for Networked Information Discovery and Retrieval is an organization dedicated to aiding Internet citizens in their searches for information throughout the network. CNIDR works with a number of other organizations to make information more accessible and standardized across the Internet.

Colorado Alliance of Research Libraries (CARL)

Type: TELNET

Address: pac.carl.org

Summary: The Colorado Alliance of Research Libraries provides access to a number of different academic and public library online catalogs, current article indexes, the Internet Resource Guide and the Academic American Encyclopedia. CARL also offers a service through which you can request (for a small fee charged to your credit card) a fax copy of any journal article in its catalog, as well as access to other services, such as Journal Graphics, which offers transcripts for popular news and public affairs television programs. A gateway to other library systems is also offered.

Computer Professionals For Social Responsibility (CPSR) Mailing List

Type: Mailing List

Address: listserv@gwuvm.gwu.edu

Summary: Send a one-line message in e-mail:

> subscribe CPSR *your name*

where *your name* is your full name (not your e-mail address).

Computer Professionals for Social Responsibility is an organization that concerns itself with the social and political aspects of computing. Mailing list subscribers will receive updates on CPSR's current Freedom of

Information Act (FOIA) requests, position statements and news releases on topics including privacy and cryptography.

Current Cites
Type: TELNET
Address: melvyl.ucop.edu
Summary: Provides a bibliography of current journal articles related to computers and information technology.

Enter **SHOW CURRENT CITES** at command prompt.

More information is available from drobinson@library.berkeley.edu

Dictionary Server
Type: TELNET
Address: cs.indiana.edu 2627
Summary: Provides access to an online Webster's Ninth Collegiate Dictionary.

Login as webster.

Enter **HELP** for online help system.

E-Mail Address Locator
Type: E-mail
Address: mail-server@pit-manager.mit.edu
Summary: In body of letter enter:

send usenet-addresses/name

where name is the name of the person you want to locate.

The service will return the e-mail address of the person in the username@domain.top-domain format. This service works only if the person you are looking for has posted an article to one of the USENET newsgroups.

Earthquake Information
Type: Finger
Address: quake@geophys.washington.edu
Summary: Reports recent earthquake information including location, magnitude and time.

Electronic Frontier Foundation (EFF) Mailing List

Type: Mailing List

Address: eff-request@eff.org

Summary: Send a brief e-mail message requesting to be added to the mailing list. The Electronic Frontier Foundation is a professional organization concerned with the legal, social, and political aspects of civilizing cyberspace. If you subscribe to the EFF mailing list, you'll receive copies of the EFFector Online electronic newsletter and news releases.

Electronic Serials List

Type: E-Mail

Address: listserv@uottawa.bitnet

Summary: An automated distribution server of a comprehensive list of electronic serials on various topics including computers, science, politcs, literature, etc.

Send the following lines in an e-mail message:

GET EJOURNAL1 DIRECTORY

GET EJOURNAL2 DIRECTORY

FTP Sites List

Type: FTP

Address: pilot.njin.net

Pathname: /pub/ftp-list/ directory (download the file ftp.list).

Summary: By checking the pub/ftp-list/ directory, you can download a file called ftp.list that lists scads of publicly accessible FTP sites throughout the Internet.

Geographic Server

Type: TELNET

Address: martini.eecs.umich.edu 3000

Summary: Provides geographic information, including population, elevation, latitude, longitude and more by city or area code. You navigate the information with on-screen menus.

Hot off the Tree (HOTT)

Type: TELNET

Address: melvyl.ucop.edu

Summary: Provides excerpts and abstracts of information technology articles from trade journals and online news services. HOTT is updated every week by the Technology Watch Information Group at the University of California at San Diego. Only two issues at a time are available online, so check this resource regularly if it's of interest to you.

Enter command **SHOW HOTT** at the command prompt. A menu of items will appear; enter your selection at the prompt. An example is shown in Figure 8-28.

Figure 8-28: HOTT example session.

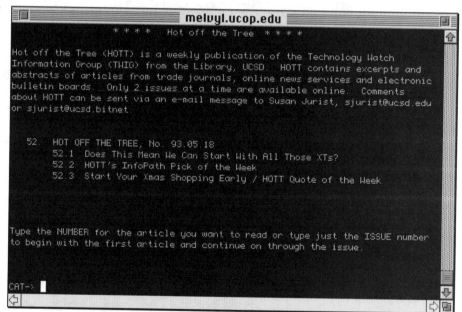

HPCwire

Type: TELNET

Address: hpcwire.ans.net

Summary: Provides menu-driven information searches related to high-performance computing and information services, from workstations to supercomputers.

Login as hpcwire. An example is shown in Figure 8-29.

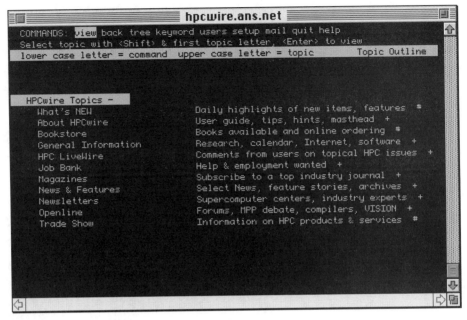

Figure 8-29:
HPCwire example
session.

Hytelnet Server

Type: TELNET

Address: access.usask.ca

Summary: Provides access to several university and library card catalogs. This is a useful way to search for books and journal articles on a specific topic, but you will not be able to access the full text of these resources via a remote Internet login.

Login as hytelnet.

Incomplete Guide to the Internet

Type: FTP

Address: ftp.ncsa.uiuc.edu

Pathname: /misc/ directory

Summary: An excellent guide to the Internet written by the NCSA Education Group. Contains coverage of SLIP connections and the use of the Eudora shareware e-mail program.

Internet Maps

Type: FTP

Address: ftp.merit.edu

Pathname: /maps/ directory

Summary: A collection of PostScript-format maps of the Internet. You must have a PostScript-capable printer to be able to print and view these maps.

Internet Monthly Report

Type: FTP

Address: nis.nsf.net

Pathname: /internet/newsletters/internet.monthly.report/ directory

Summary: Monthly Internet usage reports. The reports contain information from the Internet Research Group concerning the accomplishments and problems of the participating organizations. Each report usually contains an article from the Internet Architecture Board and a few Internet Engineering reports. Brief articles are also submitted by the various regional networks, and a calendar of upcoming events is included.

Internet Society Archive

Type: FTP

Address: nnsc.nsf.net

Pathname: /internet-society/ directory

Summary: Contains a collection of Internet Society materials, including status reports, position statements, etc.

InterNIC

Type: Organization

Address: info@ls.internic.net

Summary: A set of three organizations funded in part by the National Science Foundation dedicated to serving the needs of the NSFNET community. The InterNIC specializes in helping new users and in compiling registration, directory and database information. You can call their hotline at 800/444-4345 for more details.

Introduction to TCP/IP

Type: FTP
Address: topaz.rutgers.edu
Pathname: /tcp-ip-docs/ directory
Summary: An excellent guide to TCP/IP. This is one of the best and most clearly written references for installing, configuring, and administering a TCP/IP connection.

IP Address Resolver

Type: Directory Service
Address: resolve@cs.widener.edu
Summary: In body of e-mail message, enter:

site address

where address is the name of the site in the domain.top-domain format.
The service will return the IP address of the site.

Law Library

Type: TELNET
Address: liberty.uc.w lu.edu
Summary: Provides law libraries and legal research. Information on law library archives, White House electronic access, the United Nations, gay rights, adoption laws, privacy rights, copyright and much more is available, as shown in Figure 8-30. Login as lawlib.

Figure 8-30: Law Library example session.

```
                        liberty.uc.wlu.edu
1   Law-lib archive 1993-05 (May)  [text]                       2  6
2   Law-lib archive 1993-06 (June)  [text]                      2  6
3   White House Electronic Access FAQ (WWW)                     27  5
4   United Nations Justice Network (UNCJIN)                     25  5
5   St. Louis University, Law Library, Gopher                   21  5
6   Queer Resources Directory (WAIS db)                         10  5
7   Adoption Laws and Resources                                  9  5
8   University of Idaho, Library (IDA-                           9  5
9   Privacy Rights Clearinghouse, Bulletin Board Service         7  5
10  Uniform Commercial Code (WWW, Cornell Law School)            6  5
11  Indiana University, Law School, Gopher                       4  5
12  HONGKONGIANA ON-LINE (Journal Index, Articles on Hong Kong)  3  5
13  Copyright Registration Information (Lib. of Congress)        2  5
14  Federal Legislation (Bill Abstracts 1973- ) (Lib. of Congress)  2  5
15  Foreign Law (Abstracts / Article Citations) (Lib. of Congress)  1  5
16  Law-lib archive 1993-04 (April)  [text]                      1  5
17  LawNET - American Association of Law Libraries Information (Washburn U 29  4
18  Victorian Institute of Forensic Pathology, WWW              29  4
19  Int-law membership list  [text]                             26  4
20  Lexis/Nexis User Guides (University of Texas)               23  4
1-262  Search  Move  Next  Last  eXit  Color  Email
       Restrict set    Un-restrict    Back up one level  Arrange by name
                   &&& escapes interactive connections (Use if no exit instructions)
```

LawNet

Type: TELNET

Address: dessert.law.columbia.edu *or* lawnet.law.columbia.edu

Summary: Offers legal information and card catalog access. Columbia University's Law School library card catalog, information server, academic services and career services are all accessible, as shown in Figure 8-31.

Login as lawnet.

Figure 8-31: Lawnet example session.

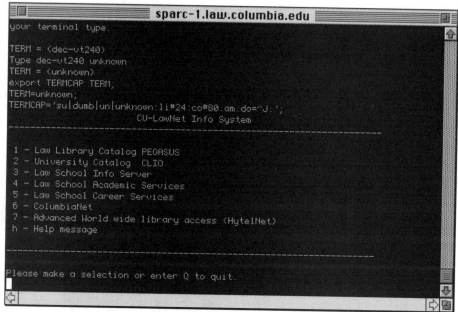

Library of Congress

Type: TELNET

Address: dra.com

Summary: Provides access to the catalog of the Library of Congress. Again, you won't be able to access the full text of the library's holdings, but this is a very useful resource when simply compiling a list of possible sources for a topic of research.

LIBS

Type: TELNET

Address: nessie.cc.wwu.edu

Summary: Provides gateway access to many TELNET services. Library card catalogs in various countries are accessible, as are several campus-wide information systems as shown in Figure 8-32. This service is referred to as a gateway because you can access other services through this portal.

Login as LIBS.

Figure 8-32: LIBS example session.

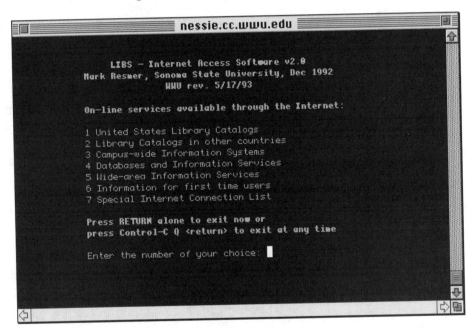

MacPGP v2.2 Encryption Utility

Type: FTP

Address: soda.berkeley.edu

Summary: MacPGP 2.2 is a data encryption utility that uses the IDEA cipher patented in Switzerland. This utility is of special interest because it has not been sanctioned for general use by the National Security Agency (NSA), which governs issues of coding and encryption in the United States. (This means that data encoded with

MacPGP is probably safer from prying eyes than it would be if you used a "government-approved" encryption method.)

Anonymous public key server sites:

pgp-public-keys@junkbox.cc.iastate.edu
tbird.cc.iastate.edu (/usr/explorer/public-keys.pgp)
pgp-public-keys@toxicwaste.mit.edu
toxicwaste.mit.edu (/pub/keys/public-keys.pgp)
pgp-public-keys@phil.utmb.edu
phil.utmb.edu (/pub/pgp/public-keys.pgp)

Mailing Lists List

Type: E-Mail

Address: listserv@vm1.nodak.edu

Summary: An automated distribution server of a comprehensive list of e-mail mailing lists. (For more on mailing lists, see Chapter 4, "Electronic Mail.")

Send the following line in an e-mail message:

LIST GLOBAL

MELVYL

Type: TELNET

Address: melvyl.ucop.edu

Summary: The MELVYL database contains the entire catalog of the University of California's monographs and periodicals. Several California state universities' holdings are accessible via MELVYL. The system also provides access to MEDLINE and Current Contents. Other systems are accessible by a gateway. Access to some resources is restricted by password.

MicroMuse

Type: TELNET

Address: michael.ai.mit.edu

Summary: MicroMuse is a text-only virtual environment under development at MIT. It's like the old-style text adventure games, with a politically correct spin. Education, cooperation and concern for the environment are stressed in this game-like environment. MicroMuse is something more easily experienced than explained; give it a try. A sample session screen is shown in Figure 8-33.

Login as guest

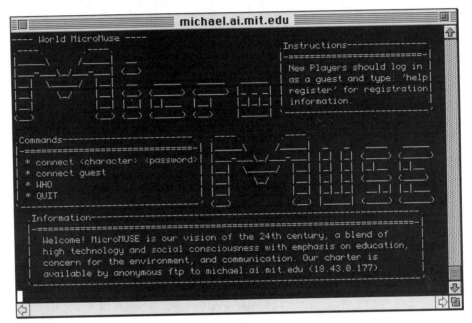

Figure 8-33: MicroMuse example session.

Mining the Internet

Type: FTP

Address: ucdavis.edu

Pathname: /ucd.netdocs/mining/ directory

Summary: This text file offers a good overview of the information resources offered on the Internet, using a mining metaphor.

Music Server

Type: FTP

Address: ftp.uwp.edu

Pathname: /pub/lyrics/ directory

Summary: This site is popular with college students. It provides lyrics, pictures, guitar chords and tablature for a wide array of popular music.

Network News Mailing List

Type: Mailing List

Address: listserv@vm1.nodak.edu

Summary: A collection of Internet resources and facts. Since this resource exists as a mailing list, you can expect fairly regular updates—and they will be mailed to you automatically until you revoke your subscription to the list. This is a handy tool for staying current with the Net's resources.

Send a one-line message in e-mail:

subscribe nnews *your name*

where *your name* is your full name (not your e-mail address).

New Users' Guide

Type: FTP

Address: nysernet.org

Pathname: /pub/resources/guides/ directory

Summary: New User's Guide to Unique and Interesting Resources on the Internet is authored by the New York State Education and Research Network (NYSERNet). It covers about 50 Internet resources in more than 145 pages.

NorthWestNet User Services Guide

Type: FTP

Address: ftphost.nwnet.net

Pathname: /nic/nwnet/user-guide/ directory

Summary: NorthWestNet User Services Internet Resource Guide (about 300 pages) covers electronic mail, FTP, remote login, supercomputer access and online library catalogs.

NREN Information

Type: FTP

Address: nis.nsf.net

Pathname: /nren/ directory

Summary: Collection of information on the National Research and Education Network (NREN).

Project Gutenberg

Type: FTP

Address: mrcnext.cso.uiuc.edu

Pathname: /etext/ directory

Summary: Project Gutenberg was formed to encourage the creation and distribution of electronic text, hoping to have one trillion volumes available by the end of 2001. Texts currently available include *Alice in Wonderland*, *Peter Pan*, Shakespeare's complete works and Milton's *Paradise Lost*.

Public Network News Servers

Type: Network News

Address: various, see Summary

Summary: These publicly-accessible network news servers are sites where you can login to read (and in some places, respond to) network news articles.

cc.usu.edu (read only)

etl.go.jp (read/post)

europa.eng.gtefsd.com (read only)

fconvx.ncifcrf.gov (read only)

gaia.ucs.orst.edu (read only)

hermes.chpc.utexas.edu (read only)

mailer.cc.fsu.edu (read only)

munnari.oz.au (read/post)

netnews.cc.lehigh.edu (read only)

news.funet.fi (read only)

news.unomaha.edu (read only)

news.yale.edu (read only)

news.ysu.edu (read only)

newshub.nosc.mil (read only)

newsserver.jvnc.net (read only)

newsserver.jvnc.net (read only)

quip.eecs.umich.edu (read/post)

sbcs.sunysb.edu (read/post)

sol.ctr.columbia.edu (read/post)

suntan.ec.usf.edu (read/post)

uicvm.uic.edu (read only)

umd5.umd.edu (read only)
usenet.coe.montana.edu (read only)
uunet.ca (read/post)
uwec.edu (read/post)
vax1.mankato.msus.edu (read only)
vaxc.cc.monash.edu.au (read/post)
willis1.cis.uab.edu (read only)

Special Internet Connections

Type: FTP

Address: csd4.csd.uwm.edu

Pathname: /pub/inet.services.txt

Summary: Scott Yanoff's excellent guide to Internet services. Also available by mailing list by sending a subscription request to yanoff@csd4.csd.uwm.edu, The list is also posted regularly to several USENET newsgroups including biz.comp.services and alt.internet.services.

Sports Schedules

Type: TELNET

Address: culine.colorado.edu

Summary: Provides daily schedules for a wide array of professional sporting events, including hockey, basketball and football.

TELNET to the specified port for the sport schedule you want:

NBA: culine.colorado.edu 859
NHL: culine.colorado.edu 860
MLB: culine.colorado.edu 862
NFL: culine.colorado.edu 863

Enter **HELP** for online help.
After login, press **Return** for today's schedules.

Travel Information

Type: FTP

Address: ccu.umanitoba.ca

Pathname: /pub/rec-travel/ directory

Summary: Provides worldwide travel information, including travel guides and FAQs. Here's a brief excerpt from Gary Fischman's entry for St. Maarten:

> "There isn't much in the way of tourist sights in St. Maarten/St. Martin. There is the old ruins of the fort in Marigot. It's up on a small hill next to the Marigot waterfront. The fort itself isn't much to see, but there is a great view of the northwest corner of the island."

University of North Carolina LaUNChpad

Type: TELNET

Address: launchpad.unc.edu

Summary: Provides access to a wide variety of Campus Wide Information Servers (CWIS). From LaUNChpad, you can also use a menu-driven interface to access a number of other Internet resources, including WAIS searches, Gopher servers, Supreme Court ruling databases, CARL and many of the other resources listed here. The advantage is that, as when working with Gopher, LaUNChpad automatically logs you in and out of each site—you don't have to memorize domain addresses and login passwords.

Login as launch

At the main menu, select item 3, "On-line Information Systems (LIBTEL)."

US State Department Travel Advisories

Type: FTP

Address: world.std.com

Pathname: /obi/US.StateDept/Travel/ directory

Summary: Foreign travel advisories provided by the State Department. The advisories are stored by country name, and each new advisory is appended to the end of the file.

VAX Manual

Type: FTP

Address: decoy.uoregon.edu

Pathname: /pub/vaxbook/vms.ps (make sure you also get the errata files which are updated on a regular basis).

Summary: Joe St. Sauver's excellent guide to the University of Oregon's VAX8000 system. At more than 300 pages, the guide provides information that is useful for general network users, not just VAX users.

Washington University Gateway

Type: TELNET

Address: wugate.wustl.edu

Summary: Provides gateway access to many TELNET services. Login as services

Weather Maps

Type: FTP

Address: vmd.cso.uiuc.edu

Pathname: /pub/wx/ directory

Summary: Provides current infrared weather maps and surface analysis.

Weather Service

Type: TELNET

Address: downwind.sprl.umich.edu 3000

Summary: Provides complete weather forecasts as well as other related information, such as earthquake reports, ski conditions and more.

White House E-Mail

Type: E-mail

Address: president@whitehouse.gov and vice.president@whitehouse.gov

Summary: Send e-mail to the leaders of the free world.

White House Press Releases

Type: E-mail

Address: clinton-info@campaign92.org

Summary: This e-mail server is not designed to answer e-mail letters, comments, or requests for specific information. It is designed solely to distribute press releases.

The e-mail server works by reading the subject line of your message and taking an appropriate action based on that subject line.

Subject: RECEIVE HELP
    Help file for the e-mail server.

Subject: RECEIVE ECONOMIC POLICY
Press releases related to the economy, including budget news, technology policy reviews, etc.

Subject: RECEIVE FOREIGN POLICY
Press releases related to foreign policy.

Subject: RECEIVE SOCIAL POLICY
Press releases related to social issues.

Subject: RECEIVE SPEECHES
All speeches made by the President and the most important speeches made by other Administration officials.

Subject: RECEIVE NEWS
Transcripts of White House Communications office press conferences.

Subject: RECEIVE ALL
All releases from all subject areas.

(More) White House Press Releases

Type: FTP

Address: sunsite.unc.edu

Pathname: /home3/wais/white-house-papers/ directory

Summary: News and press releases related to economic policy, foreign policy, social policy, press conferences and speeches.

Conclusion

So now you're a pro at practically all things Internet. What's that? You feel like we've just gone around the world in 80 days (or perhaps only eight)? You're still overwhelmed with all the things you can do, people you can meet and places you can visit? The secret to finding your way around the Internet is to forget about where you're going, and just go. Explore. Take a sidetrip. Have fun.

The good news is, you're not on your own. There are plenty of friendly people all over the Net who can offer you help whenever you need it. And just by buying this book, you'll get two electronic updates free. (For more details on taking advantage of the electronic updates, see Appendix A.)

But for now, you might want to get back out into the Net to check out a few of the resources listed in this chapter. And don't forget to drop me a line if you spot something extraordinary.

Appendix A
Electronic Updates & Visitors Center

New services are added to the Internet on a daily—sometimes hourly—basis. It's impossible for one person to keep up with everything that's happening on the Net.

I grew up in the 1960s, and I was constantly told by my elders that there was no such thing as a free lunch. I think the saying originated with signs that used to hang in taverns offering free lunches.

I've got good news for you: there is a free lunch. (OK, you had to buy this book to get the free updates, but you had to buy a drink or two to get a free lunch in the taverns of my youth!)

Because the Internet is in a constant state of flux, Ventana Press and Arts & Farces are offering you two *free* electronic updates to this book. The updates will include: reviews of the latest Internet client software releases, summaries of new information resources, tips and tricks for finding your way around the Net, news about trends and industry developments and much more.

Updates Are Just a Postcard Away

It's easy to make sure you receive your exclusive electronic updates, which are available only to owners of the *Tour Guide*. Updates will be distributed via e-mail. This way, they'll be sent directly to your electronic mailbox. To receive your free updates

- Fill out the response card bound into the back of the book. Make sure you've completed every portion of the card. (Incomplete cards will not be acknowledged and will not qualify for the two free updates.)

- Make certain you've included your Internet-accessible e-mail address in the standard format: username@domain.top-domain. (Addresses in any other format will not be acknowledged, and will not qualify for the two free electronic updates.)

- If you'd like to receive occasional informational mailings about other books and materials about the Internet and the Macintosh, simply check the appropriate box on the card.

- Note that the updates may be larger than can fit through the e-mail gateways of some of the commercial information services like CompuServe and MCI Mail. In this case, the updates will be sent to you in multiple segments.

The Electronic Visitors Center

It's always nice to have a "home base" when traveling in strange and foreign territory. The Visitors Center is a place where *Tour Guide* readers and others can stop and rest on their ramblings through the Net. And better still, it's where you'll find the latest versions of all the great freeware and shareware software discussed in the *Tour Guide*, as well as the latest updates, news, tips, tricks and other hot information.

Access *The Mac Internet Tour Guide* Visitors Center by FTP at ftp.farces.com.

Current versions of interesting Macintosh programs for use on the Internet are available via anonymous FTP. Special Read Me files and other goodies are available there. The Visitors Center is open to anyone, not just *Tour Guide* readers, so spread the word.

Also in the Visitors Center you'll find the latest versions of the programs discussed and demonstrated throughout the *Tour Guide*.

StuffIt Expander is a file decompression program that you'll need to process many of the files and other software resources you download from various sites on the Internet. The current version of StuffIt Expander is always available in the Visitors Center. **(This program is included on the companion disk.)**

Eudora is an e-mail program covered in Chapter 4, "Electronic Mail." You can use Eudora to send private messages to friends and associates. The most recent release of the freeware version of the program and complete documentation are available in the Visitors Center. **(This program is included on the companion disk.)**

Fetch is a File Transfer Protocol (FTP) program covered in Chapter 6, "Transferring Files." You can use Fetch to upload and download files at various archives on the Internet. The current version of Fetch is always available in the Visitors Center. **(This program is included on the companion disk.)**

TCP/Connect II is a commercial program available from InterCon Systems that provides e-mail, network news, FTP and TELNET services for the Macintosh. A time-limited demo version of this product is always available in the Visitors Center.

Nuntius is a network news reader program covered in Chapter 5, "Network News & Newsgroups." You can use Nuntius to read and post articles to any USENET newsgroup. The current version of Nuntius is available in the Visitors Center.

TurboGopher is a Macintosh Gopher program covered in Chapter 7, "Using Gopher." You can use TurboGopher to download files and browse information resources on various Internet Gopher servers. The most recent version of TurboGopher (and related Helper files) are always available in the Visitors Center.

NCSA TELNET is a terminal program, covered in Chapter 8, "Other Internet Resources," that you can use to login remotely to computers on the Internet. Many Internet resources are accessible via TELNET, and you can also use the program to login to any computer on which you have an account. The current version of NCSA TELNET is available in the Visitors Center.

How to Subscribe to a Full Year of Updates

Mac Internet Tour Guide electronic updates will be published and distributed on a quarterly basis. As a purchaser of this book, you'll receive the first two updates free of charge. If you want to subscribe to additional quarterly updates, the current subscription rate is $25 per year (4 issues).

To receive a full year of updates, simply send a check or money order for $25 (US funds only) payable to Arts & Farces to:

Arts & Farces
2285 Stewart Avenue
Suite 1315
Saint Paul, MN 55116

For more information on subscribing to future updates, send e-mail to:
tour-guide-request@farces.com

A Note about Privacy

The Internet is a place where privacy has to be balanced against the free flow of information. The real world is no different. You'll notice there's a good deal of information you're providing on *The Mac Internet Tour Guide* electronic update request postcards. But how that information is used is up to you. If, like many Internet and Macintosh enthusiasts, you like to stay informed about the latest publications and related materials that are relevant to your interests, simply check the appropriate box on the card. Otherwise, the information you provide is for use by Arts & Farces only. I don't sell, lend, or rent our mailing list. The transactional information you provide is between the two of us, and is no one's business but our own.

Glossary

access method—The rules that manage how all the computers and other devices on a network can send information through the same physical medium in an orderly fashion.

access privileges—The privileges to open and make changes to folders and their contents; they are given to or withheld from users. By setting access privileges, you can control access to confidential information stored in folders on a server.

Access Privileges window—When using the AppleShare file server, a window that displays the access privileges, owner, group and other information about a folder or volume. You use the Get Privileges command in the File menu of the Finder or the Access Privileges desk accessory in the Apple menu to display the window and to review, set or change access privileges for a folder or volume.

acronym—A word formed from the initial letter or letters of the main parts of a compound term, such as ROM (read-only memory).

activate—To make a nonactive window active by clicking anywhere inside it.

active window—The frontmost window on the desktop; the window where the next action will take place. An active window's title bar is highlighted.

addressing—A scheme, determined by network protocols, for identifying the sending device and destination device for any given item of information traveling on a network.

administrator—The person who sets up a network resource, registers users and their passwords, and maintains the resource.

alert—A warning or report of an error in the form of an alert box, a sound from the computer's speaker, or both. See also **alert box**.

alert box—A box that appears on the screen to give a warning or report an error message. Its appearance is usually accompanied by a sound warning, usually the selected system beep.

alias—(n.) An alternate name used to invoke or identify a command, a network host, a list of users or some other applicable entity. (v.) To provide an entity with an alternate name, or to make an alias of a file or folder.

American Standard Code for Information Interchange—See **ASCII**.

AppleTalk network system—The system of network software and hardware used in various implementations of Apple's communications network.

AppleTalk protocol—Apple Computer's network standard that defines how devices communicate with each other across a network.

Archie—A network service used for locating files that are publicly accessible by anonymous FTP.

ARPANET—A wide area network that linked government, academic and industrial installations around the world. Primarily connecting research sites, the ARPANET was developed in the 1960s by the Advanced Research Projects Agency of the U.S. Department of Defense.

ASCII—Acronym for American Standard Code for Information Interchange (pronounced "ASK-ee"). A standard that assigns a unique binary number to each text character and control character. ASCII code is used for representing text inside a computer and for transmitting text between computers or between a computer and a peripheral device.

asynchronous—Not synchronized by a mutual timing signal or clock. Compare **synchronous**.

asynchronous transmission—A method of data transmission in which the receiving and sending devices don't share a common timer, and no timing data is transmitted. Each information character is individually synchronized, usually by the use of start and stop bits. The time interval between characters isn't necessarily fixed. Compare **synchronous transmission**.

bandwidth—The range of transmission frequencies that a network can use. The greater the bandwidth, the greater the amount of information that can travel on the network at one time.

baseband—A transmission method in which a network uses its entire transmission frequency range to send a single communication or signal. Compare **broadband**.

baud—(1) A unit of data transmission speed: the number of discrete signal-state changes (signal events) per second. Often, but not always, equivalent to **bits per second**. Compare **bit rate**. (2) The maximum speed at which data can be sent down a channel, such as a telephone line; often confused with the actual speed at which the data is transmitted between two computers, measured in bits per second.

BBS—See **bulletin board system**.

bit—A contraction of **binary digit**. The smallest unit of information that a computer can hold. The value of a bit (1 or 0) represents a simple two-way choice, such as yes or no, on or off, positive or negative, something or nothing.

bit rate—The speed at which bits are transmitted, usually expressed as **bits per second**, or bps. Compare **baud**.

bits per second—See **bit rate**.

bridge—(1) A device that lets you connect two or more networking systems together. (2) A combination of hardware and software that connects two or more networks. Bridges are used to increase the number of devices and the distances covered in a network.

broadband—A transmission method in which the network's range of transmission frequencies is divided into separate channels and each channel is used to send a different signal. Broadband transmission is often used to send signals of different kinds simultaneously, such as voice and data. Contrast with **baseband**.

bulletin board system (BBS)—A computerized version of the bulletin boards frequently found in grocery stores—places to leave messages and to advertise things you want to buy or sell. One thing you get from a computerized bulletin board that you can't get from a cork board is free software.

bus topology—A layout scheme in which devices on a network are connected along the length of a main cable, or **bus**, rather than in a daisy chain or a loop.

byte—The number of bits used to represent a character. For personal computers, a byte is usually eight bits.

cable—An insulated bundle of wires with connectors on the ends. Examples are serial cables, disk drive cables and LocalTalk cables.

carrier—The background signal on a communication channel that is modified to carry information. Under RS-232-C rules, the carrier signal is equivalent to a continuous MARK (1) signal; a transition to 0 then represents a start bit.

CCITT—Abbreviation for **Consultative Committee on International Telegraphy and Telephony**; an international committee that sets standards and makes recommendations for international communication.

choose—To pick a command by dragging through a menu. You often choose a command after you've selected something for the program to act on; for example, selecting a disk and choosing the Open command from the File menu.

Chooser—A desk accessory that lets you configure your computer system to print on any printer for which there's a printing resource on the current startup disk. If you're part of an AppleTalk network system, you use the Chooser to connect and disconnect from the network and choose among devices connected to the network. You can also specify a user name that the system uses from time to time—when you're printing on a LaserWriter, for example.

CIX—Abbreviation for **Commercial Internet Exchange**; an agreement among Internet service providers that allows them to account for commercial network traffic.

Clear To Send—An RS-232-C signal from a DCE to a DTE that is normally kept false until the DCE makes it true, indicating that all circuits are ready to transfer data. See also **Data Communication Equipment**, **Data Terminal Equipment**.

click—(v.) To position the pointer on something and then press and quickly release the mouse button. (n.) The act of clicking.

client—A computer that has access to services on a network. The computers that provide services are called **servers**. A user at a client may request file access, remote log-in, file transfer, printing or other available services from servers.

communications protocol—See **protocols**.

configuration—(1) A general-purpose computer term that can refer to the way you have your computer set up. (2) The total combination of hardware components—central processing unit, video display device, keyboard and peripheral devices—that make up a computer system. (3) The software settings that allow various hardware components of a computer system to communicate with one another.

configure—To change software or hardware actions by changing settings. Configurations can be set or reset in software or by manipulating hardware jumpers, switches or other elements.

connect time—The amount of time you spend connected to an information service.

daisy chain—(n.) A colloquial term for a group of devices connected to a host device, where the first device in the "chain" is connected to the host, the second device is connected to the first, the third device is connected to the second, and so on. (v.) To link together sequentially.

daisy chain topology—A network topology where each device on the network is directly connected to the next with a modular extension cable and a connecting device.

data—Information, especially information used or operated on by a program. The smallest unit of information a computer can understand is a bit.

data bits—In the stream of bits being sent from your computer to a peripheral device or another computer, the bits that contain meaningful information; distinguished from bits used to indicate that a character is about to start, has stopped, or is correct.

Data Carrier Detect (DCD)—An RS-232-C signal from a DCE (such as a modem) to a DTE (such as a Macintosh) indicating that a communication connection has been established. See also **Data Communication Equipment, Data Terminal Equipment**.

Data Communication Equipment (DCE)—As defined by the RS-232-C standard, any device that transmits or receives information. Usually this device is a modem.

Data Set Ready (DSR)—An RS-232-C signal from a DCE to a DTE indicating that the DCE has established a connection. See also **Data Communication Equipment**, **Data Terminal Equipment**.

Data Terminal Equipment (DTE)—As defined by the RS-232-C standard, any device that generates or absorbs information, thus acting as an endpoint of a communication connection. A computer might serve as a DTE.

Data Terminal Ready (DTR)—(1) One of the handshake lines in a data transmission interface. See also **hardware handshake**. (2) An RS-232-C signal from a DTE to a DCE indicating a readiness to transmit or receive data. See also **Data Communication Equipment**, **Data Terminal Equipment**.

default—A value, action or setting that a computer system assumes, unless the user gives an explicit instruction to the contrary. Default values prevent a program from stalling or crashing if no value is supplied by the user.

Defense Data Network (DDN)—A single, wide area, packet-switching network that integrated the ARPANET research network and the MILNET defense network.

device—(1) A hardware component of a computer system, such as a monitor, disk drive or printer. Also called a **peripheral device**, because such equipment is often physically separate from, but attached to, the computer. (2) A part of the computer, or a piece of external equipment, that can transfer information. (3) Any piece of equipment that can be attached to a network—a computer, a printer, a file server, a print server or any other peripheral device.

dialog box—(1) A box that contains a message requesting more information from you. Sometimes the message warns you that you're asking your computer to do something it can't do or that you're about to destroy some of your information. In these cases, the message is often accompanied by a beep. (2) A box that a Macintosh application displays to request information or to report that it is waiting for a process to complete.

download—To transfer files or information from one computer to another.

electronic mail—A network service that enables users to send and receive messages via computer.

Ethernet—A high-speed local area network that consists of a cable technology and a series of communication protocols. The hardware (cable) provides the physical link to connect systems together. The TCP/IP protocol allows different computers to exchange information over a network. The Ethernet specification was developed by Digital Equipment Corporation, Intel Corporation and Xerox Corporation. Ethernet is a registered trademark of Xerox Corporation.

Ethernet backbone—A network topology with separate AppleTalk networks interconnected to Ethernet gateways that are, in turn, connected to a single, continuous Ethernet cable.

Ethernet cable system—A system of high-performance coaxial cables widely used in the communications industry. Ethernet cables can be part of an AppleTalk network system.

EtherTalk—A high-speed AppleTalk network system that uses the cables of an Ethernet network. Ethernet is a widely used communications network. The Apple software and interface card that allow AppleTalk networking protocols to run on high-speed Ethernet media at 10 megabits per second—more than 40 times faster than the standard rate supported by Macintosh computers of 230.4 kilobits per second.

even parity—The use of an extra bit set to 0 or 1 as necessary to make the total number of 1 bits an even number; used as a means of error checking in data transmission. Compare **MARK parity**, **odd parity**, **space parity**.

FAQ—Abbreviation for **Frequently Asked Question**; a list of frequently asked questions (and their answers). Most mailing lists and all network news newsgroups provide FAQ postings on a regular basis.

file—(1) Any named, ordered collection of information stored on a disk. Application programs and operating systems on disks are examples of files. You make a file when you create text or graphics, give the material a name, and save it to disk; in this sense, **file** is synonymous with **document**. A Macintosh file consists of a **data fork** and a **resource fork**.

(2) For UNIX operating systems, an array of bytes; no other structure is implied by UNIX systems as they even treat devices like files.

file server—(1) A network device, usually consisting of a computer and one or more large capacity disks, on which network users can store files and applications in order to share them. (2) A specially equipped computer that allows network users to store and share information. (3) A combination of controller software and a mass-storage device that allows computer users to share common files and applications through a network.

file transfer protocol—A protocol that exchanges files with a host computer.

flame—A noxious and usually personal attack against the author of a network news article. A **flame war** is a series of related flame messages exchanged back and forth between two **flamers**, usually resulting in messages that barely relate to the original topic which spawned them in the first place.

FTP—(n.) (1) Abbreviation for **File Transfer Protocol**; a protocol that determines how files are transferred from one computer to another. (2) A software program that transfers files using FTP. (v.) The act of transferring files using FTP.

full duplex—A four-wire communication circuit or protocol that allows two-way data transmission between two points at the same time. Compare **half duplex**.

full-duplex communication—A method of data transmission where two devices transmit data simultaneously. This method allows the receiving device to echo back each character of your message as it is received.

gateway—A device that connects networks that use different protocols. In effect, it translates between the protocols so that devices on the connected networks can exchange data.

Gopher—A menu-based means (and set of governing protocols) of exploring information resources.

half duplex—A two-wire communication circuit or protocol designed for data transmission in either direction but not both directions simultaneously. Compare **full duplex**.

half-duplex communication—A way of communicating between your computer and another computer or a peripheral device in which you can only send data or receive it at one time—not both. The other computer cannot echo back each character of your message as it is received.

handshaking—The exchange of status information between a **DCE** and a **DTE** used to control the transfer of data between them. The status information can be the state of a signal connecting the DCE and the DTE, or it can be in the form of a character transmitted with the rest of the data. See also **Data Carrier Detect**, **Data Set Ready**, **Data Terminal Ready**, **XOFF**, **XON**.

hardware handshake—A protocol that tells the computer to start or stop sending data by setting the DTR (Data Terminal Ready) line logic state. Also known as the Data Transfer Ready protocol. Compare **XON/XOFF**.

host computer—(1) A multi-user computer, such as a minicomputer or mainframe, that serves as a central processing unit for a number of terminals. (2) The computer that receives information from and sends data to terminals over telecommunication lines. The computer that is in control in a data communication network. The host computer may be a mainframe computer, minicomputer or microcomputer.

IAB—Abbreviation for **Internet Architecture Board**; the "council of elders" that makes decisions about Internet standards.

IETF—Abbreviation for **Internet Engineering Task Force**; a sub-group of the Internet Architecture Board that concerns itself with solving technical problems on the Internet.

internet—A network made up of two or more interconnected local area or wide area networks.

Internet—A worldwide, interconnected group of networks. Internally, the internet is composed of heterogeneous networks (such as ARPANET and CSNET) that use different message formats and protocols. Through the use of gateways that convert formats and protocols between networks, the internet appears externally as a single network, with hosts on interconnected networks appearing as interconnected hosts.

Internet address—(1) An address for a computer on a network. The Internet address consists of a network number and a host number that is unique for that network. (2) The AppleTalk address and network number of a socket.

ISOC—Abbreviation for the **Internet Society**; an organization formed to support a world-wide information network, and the governing body of the Internet Architecture Board.

kilobit (kbit)—A unit of measurement, 1024 bits, commonly used in specifying the capacity of memory integrated circuits. Not to be confused with **kilobyte**.

kilobyte (k)—A unit of measurement consisting of 1024 (2^{10}) bytes. Thus, 64k memory equals 65,536 bytes. The abbreviation **k** can also stand for the number 1024, in which case **kbyte** or **kb** is used for kilobyte. See also **megabyte**.

Knowbot—A knowledge robot; a software program that provides information retrieval.

LAN—See **local (lower case) area network**.

local area network (LAN)—A group of computers connected for the purpose of sharing resources. The computers on a local area network are typically joined by a single transmission cable and are located within a small area such as a single building or section of a building. Compare **wide area network**.

local system—The computer from which a user originates a network command. Compare **remote system**.

local system administration—Management of a single computer. This includes such functions as starting up and shutting down the system, adding and removing user accounts, and backing up and restoring data. Compare **network administration**.

LocalTalk cable system—A system of cables, cable extenders and connector boxes that connect computers and network devices as part of the AppleTalk network system.

LocalTalk connector—A piece of equipment consisting of a connection box, a short cable and a machine-specific connector, that enables an Apple computer to be part of an AppleTalk network system. Also called a **LocalTalk connector box**.

login—To identify yourself to a system or network and start to use it. Usually logging on requires a password, depending on the system. Same as **log on**; opposite of **log off**.

login name—In UNIX systems, the name of a user's account. Used for identification purposes.

login prompt—The prompt (usually login: on UNIX systems) by which a system tells you it is ready to accept your login name.

log off—To indicate to a system or network that you have completed your work and are terminating interaction.

MARK parity—A method of error checking in data transmission in which the most significant bit of every byte is set to 1. The receiving device checks for errors by looking for this value on each character. Compare **even parity**, **odd parity**, **space parity**.

megabit (mbit)—A unit of measurement equal to 1,048,576 (2^{16}) bits, or 1024 kilobits, commonly used in specifying the capacity of memory ICs. Not to be confused with **megabyte**.

megabyte (mb)—A unit of measurement equal to 1024 kilobytes, or 1,048,576 bytes. See also **kilobyte**.

modem—Short for **modulator/demodulator**; a peripheral device that links your computer to other computers and information services using the telephone lines.

modem command—An instruction to a computer system, usually typed from the keyboard, that directs a modem attached to the computer to perform some immediate action.

multi-user—(adj.) Characterizes a mode or ability of an operating system to support several people using the same computer at once.

multi-user system—An operating system, such as UNIX, that allows many users to access application software simultaneously.

name—The name presented to users of a network to identify a given network service.

naming protocol—A protocol used by AppleTalk to associate a name with the physical address of a network service.

network—A collection of interconnected, individually controlled computers, together with the hardware and software used to connect them. A network allows users to share data and peripheral devices such as printers and storage media, to exchange electronic mail, and so on.

network administration—Management of the software and hardware that connects computers in a network, including such functions as assigning addresses to hosts, maintaining network data files, and setting up internetwork routing. Compare **local system administration**.

network administrator—The person who is responsible for setting up and maintaining the network.

network connection—A combination of hardware and software that lets you set up a particular implementation of the AppleTalk network system, such as LocalTalk or EtherTalk.

network device—A computer, printer, modem, terminal or any other physical entity connected to a network.

Network File System (NFS)—A protocol suite developed and licensed by Sun Microsystems that allows different makes of computers running different operating systems to easily share files and disk storage.

network manager—The person responsible for maintaining and troubleshooting the network.

network number—A unique number to each network in an internetwork that has been assigned by a seed router.

network system—A family of network components that work together because they observe compatible methods of communication.

NFS—See **Network File System**.

NIC—Abbreviation for **Network Information Center**; an organization responsible for supplying information for any of the component networks that make up the Internet.

NOC—Abbreviation for **Network Operations Center**; an organization responsible for the day-to-day operation of the component networks that make up the Internet.

node—(1) A device that's attached to a network and communicates by means of the network. (2) Any network device that has an address on the network. (Some network devices, such as modems, may be connected to a network but not be a node themselves.)

node number—A number that distinguishes one node from all others on the network.

NREN—Abbreviation for **National Research and Education Network**; an effort to combine the networks operated by the U.S. government into a single high-speed network.

odd parity—The use of an extra bit in data transmission set to 0 or 1 as necessary to make the total number of 1 bits an odd number; used as a means of error checking. Compare **even parity**, **MARK parity**, **space parity**.

off-line—(adj.) Not currently connected to or under the control of the computer. Used to refer to equipment such as printers and disk drives, information storage media such as disks, and the information they contain. Compare **online**.

online—(adj.) Currently connected to and under the control of the computer. Used to refer to equipment such as printers and disk drives, information storage media such as disks, and the information they contain. Compare **off-line**.

OSI model—The Open Systems Interconnection (OSI) reference model for describing network **protocols**, devised by the International Standards Organization (ISO); divides protocols into seven **layers** to standardize and simplify protocol definitions.

packet—A unit of information that has been formatted for transmission on a network.

port—(n.) (1) A socket on the back panel of a computer where you plug in a cable for connection to a network or a peripheral device. (2) A connection between the central processor unit and main memory or a device (such as a terminal) for transferring data. (3) A unique number that identifies a particular Internet service. (v.) To move software from one hardware architecture to another.

PPP—Abbreviation of **Point to Point Protocol**; a protocol that enables a computer to communicate with other computers using TCP/IP over standard telephone lines and high-speed modems.

protocols—The rules that govern interaction on a network. Protocols determine where, when, and how information is transmitted.

random-access memory (RAM)—The part of the computer's memory that stores information temporarily while you're working on it. A computer with 512k RAM has 512 kilobytes of memory available to the user. Information in RAM can be referred to in an arbitrary or random order, hence the term random-access. (As an analogy, a book is a random-access storage device in that it can be opened and read at any point.) RAM can contain both application programs and your own information. Information in RAM is temporary, gone forever if you switch the power off without saving it on a disk or other storage medium. Compare **read-only memory**.

read-only memory (ROM)—Memory whose contents can be read but not changed; used for storing firmware. Information is placed into read-only memory once, during manufacture. It remains there permanently, even when the computer's power is turned off. Compare **random-access memory**.

remote—(adj.) At a distance. Unable to be connected directly using local wiring, but requiring communications devices. Compare **local**.

remote computer—A computer other than your own but in communication with yours through telephone lines, network wiring, or other communication links. A remote computer can be at any distance from your computer, from right beside it to thousands of miles away.

remote site—A computer or network that is accessed through a long distance communications medium, such as telephone lines, network wiring, ISDN or a satellite.

remote system—On a network, any computer other than the local system.

RFC—Abbreviation for **Request for Comments**; a collection of papers that define the Internet standards and proposed standards.

server—A computer that provides a service across a network. The service may be file access, login access, file transfer, printing and so on. Computers from which users initiate the service are called **clients**.

service—A specialized function that a network provides to users, such as file sharing and electronic mail.

service provider—An organization that provides connections to the Internet.

signature—A text file, usually five lines or less, containing your identification and contact information that is added to your network news articles and e-mail messages.

SLIP—Abbreviation for **Serial Line Internet Protocol**; a protocol that enables a computer to communicate with other computers using TCP/IP over standard telephone lines and high-speed modems.

socket—On a network, a communication mechanism originally implemented on the BSD version of the UNIX operating system. Sockets are used as endpoints for sending and receiving data between computers.

space parity—A method of error checking in data transmission in which the most significant bit of every byte is set to 0. The receiving device checks for errors by looking for this value on each character. Compare **even parity**, **MARK parity**, **odd parity**.

standard—A set of specifications for designing hardware or software that is recognized by multiple vendors, an official standards organization or both.

synchronous—Able to perform two or more processes at the same time, such as sending and receiving data, by means of a mutual timing signal or clock. Compare **asynchronous**.

synchronous transmission—A transmission process that uses a clocking signal to ensure an integral number of unit (time) intervals between any two characters. Compare **asynchronous transmission**.

TCP/IP—Abbreviation for **Transmission Control Protocol/Internet Protocol**; a suite of networking protocols developed at the University of California for the U.S. Department of Defense.

TELNET—A terminal emulation protocol that lets you login remotely to other computers on the Internet, using a command line interface.

terminal—A keyboard and display screen through which users can access a **host computer**.

terminal emulation—Software that enables a personal computer to communicate with a **host computer** by transmitting in the form used by the host's terminals.

topology—The physical layout of a network.

traffic—Transmissions travelling across a network.

tty—A terminal; abbreviated from teletypewriter, which was the first terminal device used on UNIX operating systems.

USENET—A network of about 3 million users (mostly UNIX users) who communicate using the UNIX to UNIX Copy Protocol (UUCP).

WAIS—Abbreviation for **Wide-Area Information Server**; an Internet service for looking up specific information in Internet databases.

WAN—See **wide area network**.

wide area network—Computers and/or networks connected to each other using long distance communication methods, such as telephone lines and satellites. Compare with **local area network**.

World Wide Web (WWW)—A hypertext-based Internet service used for browsing Internet resources.

XOFF—A special character used for controlling the transfer of data between a **DTE** and a **DCE**. When one piece of equipment receives an XOFF character from the other, it stops transmitting characters until it receives an XON. See also **handshaking, XON**.

XON—A special character used for controlling the transfer of data between a **DTE** and a **DCE**. See also **handshaking, XOFF**.

XON/XOFF—A communications protocol that tells the computer to start or stop sending data by sending the appropriate character: either an XON or an XOFF. Compare **hardware handshake**.

Bibliography

Benedikt, Michael. *Cyberspace: First Steps*. Cambridge, Massachusetts: MIT Press, 1991.

Brand, Stewart. *The Media Lab: Inventing the Future at MIT*. New York: Viking, 1988.

Cerf, Vinton G. "Networks," *Scientific American*, vol. 265, no. 3, pp. 72–81. New York: Scientific American, September 1991.

Comer, Douglas E. *Internetworking with TCPIP: Protocols & Architecture. Vol. I.* 2d ed. Englewood Cliffs, New Jersey: Prentice Hall, 1991.

Engelbart, Douglas C. "A Conceptual Framework for the Augmentation of Man's Intellect." In *Vistas in Information Handling*, edited by Howerton and Weeks. Washington, D.C.: Spartan Books, 1963.

Gibson, William. *Burning Chrome*. New York: Ace Books, 1987.

———. *Count Zero*. New York: Ace Books, 1986.

———. *Mona Lisa Overdrive*. New York: Bantam Books, 1988.

———. *Neuromancer*. New York: Ace Books, 1984.

Gore, Al. "Infrastructure for the Global Village," *Scientific American*, vol. 265, no. 3, pp. 150–53. New York: Scientific American, September 1991.

Greif, Irene, ed. *Computer-Supported Cooperative Work: Readings in CSCW*. San Mateo, California: Morgan Kaufman Publishers, 1988.

Hiltz, Roxanne. *Online Communities: A Case Study of the Office of the Future.* Norwood, New Jersey: Ablex Press, 1984.

Kapor, Mitchell. "Civil Liberties in Cyberspace," *Scientific American*, vol. 265, no. 3, pp. 158–64. New York: Scientific American, September 1991.

Karraker, Roger. "Highways of the Mind," *Whole Earth Review*, no. 70, pp. 4–11. Sausalito, California: Point Foundation, Spring 1991.

Krol, Ed. *The Whole Internet User's Guide & Catalog.* Sebastopol, California: O'Reilly & Associates, 1992.

LaQuey, Tracy, and Jeanne C. Ryer. *The Internet Companion: A Beginner's Guide to Global Networks.* Reading, Massachusetts: Addison-Wesley, 1992.

Laurel, Brenda, ed. *The Art of Human Computer Interface.* Reading, Massachusetts: Addison-Wesley, 1990.

Licklider, J. C. R., Robert Taylor, and E. Herbert. "The Computer as a Communication Device." In *International Science and Technology*, April 1978.

McLuhan, Marshall, and Eric McLuhan. *The Laws of Media: The New Science.* Toronto: University of Toronto Press, 1988.

McLuhan Marshall. *Understanding Media: The Extensions of Man.* New York: McGraw-Hill, 1965.

Quarterman, John S. *The Matrix: Computer Networks and Conferencing Systems Worldwide.* Burlington, Massachusetts: Digital Press, 1990.

Toffler, Alvin. *Powershift: Knowledge, Wealth, and Violence at the Edge of the 21st Century.* New York: Bantam Books, 1990.

Turoff, Murray, and Roxanne Hiltz. *The Network Nation: Human Communication via Computer.* Reading, Massachusetts: Addison-Wesley, 1978.

Index

A

Acceptable use policies   40–41
Account, establishing   14–22
   business users   17–18
   government users   16–17
   individual users   18–19
   university users   14–16
Addressing   35–39
Alice in Wonderland   29
Anonymous FTP   148
Archie   231–36
   Archie servers   231
   Archie for the Macintosh   232–33
   TurboGopher Archie searches   233–36
Archives
   See File transfer protocol
ARPAnet   8–9

B

Bandwidth   11–12
Baseball schedule   16
BBEdit   87
BinHex   152
Brandi, Ralph   78–79
Brin, David (Earth)   50

C

Cassady, Neal   3–4
Clearinghouse for Networked Information
   Discovery and Retrieval (CNIDR)   243
Clipper encryption chip   5
Colorado Alliance of Research Libraries
   (CARL)   243
Commercialization of the Internet   10

CompactPro   230
Computer Professionals For Social Responsi
   bility (CPSR)   243–44
Connections to the Internet, types of   19–22
   dedicated   19–20
   dial-in   22
   SLIP and PPP   20–22
   UUCP   22
Courtesy   42–43
CTerm   221
Current Cites   244

D

Dante   1
DDN Network Information Center   96–97
Dictionary Server   244
Disinfectant (John Norstad)   155–56
Domain names   35–39
   top-level domain   36, 37–38

E

Earth (David Brin)   50
Earthquake Information   244
Edwards, Don (California State
   Representative)   52
Electronic Frontier Foundation
   (EFF)   239–41, 245
Electronic mail
   See E-mail
Electronic mailing lists
   See Mailing lists
Electronic Serials   245
Ellerbee, Linda   52

E-mail   5, 45–108
    addressing   53–59
        America Online   56–57
        AppleLink   57–58
        AT&T Mail   57
        CompuServe   55
        finding e-mail addresses   94–98,
            204, 244
        MCI Mail   55–56
        quick reference guide   59
        UUCP   53–54
    bang-path address   54
    blind courtesy copies   70–71, 85, 111
    bounced e-mail   48
    courtesy copies   70, 85
    etiquette   48–52
        EmilyPost   50
    Eudora
        See Eudora
    file attachments   103–8
        receiving files   105–8
        sending files   103–4
    filters   74, 89–93
    gateway   7, 53
    mailing lists
        See Mailing lists
    MCI Mail   7
    privacy   50–52
    TCP/Connect II
        See TCP/Connect II
    uses   46–48
EmilyPost   50
Encryption   14
Etiquette   42–43, 170
Eudora   39, 59–76, 103–8
    configuring   60–66
    creating new e-mail   69–71
    deleting e-mail   75–76
    documentation   67
    file attachments   103–8
        receiving files   105–8
        sending files   103–4

    managing e-mail   73–76
    reading e-mail   68–69
    replying to e-mail   71–73
    resource requirements   60
    retrieving e-mail   67–68
    sending e-mail   73

F

FAQ (Frequently Asked Question)   238
Fetch   41, 156–70
    configuring   158–64
    downloading files   164–68
    uploading files   169–70
File transfer protocol (FTP)   6, 147–87, 245
    archives, list   245
    archives, Macintosh   187
    archives, mirror   187
File types   152–54
    BinHex   152
    extensions   152–54, 168
Finger   38, 94–95, 222–25
Flame wars   18, 72, 110, 119
FTP
    See File transfer protocol
FTPd   239

G

Geographic Server   245
Gopher   42, 185–209
    FTP alternative   187
    future (Gopher +)   208
    uses   186–87
    politics   194–95
    servers   206–7
    See also TurboGopher

H

Help desk   16, 18
Hillseth, Robert   52
Hot off the Tree (HOTT)   246
HPCwire   246–47
Hytelnet   247

I

Icons (navigational) 2–3
   found text excerpts 3
   hot spots and cool resources 3
   people profiles 3
   software reviews 3
Incomplete Guide to the Internet 247
Inferno (Dante's) 1
Info-Mac archive (Stanford University) 32
Information browsing 6
InterCon Systems Corporation 76
Internet
   account, establishing 14–22
     business users 17–18
     government users 16–17
     individual users 18–19
     university users 14–16
   addressing 35–39
     domain names 35–39
     IP addressing 35–36
     top-level domain 36, 37–38
   ARPAnet 8–9
   bandwidth 11–12
   benefits 5–6
     e-mail 5
     file transfer 5
     information browsing 5
     network news 5
   commercialization 10
   connections, types of 19–22
     dedicated 19–20
     dial-in 22
     SLIP and PPP 20–22
     UUCP 22
   ease of use 2
   future 10–12
   governance 7–8
     Internet Architecture Board 7
     Internet Engineering Task Force 7
     Internet Society 7, 241, 248
     Network Operations Center 8

   history 8–10
   information democracy 32
   Internet Architecture Board 7
   Internet Engineering Task Force 7
   Internet Society 7
   maps 248
   monthly report 248
   Merit Network Inc. 9–10
   National Science Foundation 9–10
   Network Operations Center 8
   NSFNET 9–10
   organizing principles 32
   privatization 11
   service providers 23–26
   virtual community 5
Internet/NREN Business Journal 66
InterNIC 248
InterSLIP (SLIP software) 20, 28
IP addressing 35–36
   IP Address Resolver 249
IRC (Internet Relay Chat) 113, 202

J

Jacoby, Paul 117

K

Kadie, Carl 54, 58
Kerouac, Jack 3–4
Kesey, Ken 4
Knowbots 221

L

Law Library 249
LawNet 250
Library of Congress card catalog 250
Library of Congress Information System
   (LOCIS) 27
LIBS 251

M

MacPGP (encryption software)   14, 251–52
MacPPP (PPP software)   21, 28
MacSLIP (SLIP software)   28
MacTCP   7, 28, 28–29
Magazines, electronic ('zines)   36
Mail
   electronic mail
     See E-mail
   Post Office mail   5
Mailing lists   99–103
   subscribing   100–102
   cancelling subscription   102–3
   list of mailing lists   252
MandelTV (fractal software)   21
MCI Mail   7
Meckler Publishing   124
MELVYL   252
Merit Network   9–10
Merry Pranksters   4
MicroMuse   252–53
Mining the Internet   253
MOOGopher   144
Music Server   253

N

National Science Foundation   9–10
NCSA TELNET   212–16
   configuring   212–14
   remote login   214–16
Netfind   221–22
Network news   5, 109–145
   article   110
   cross-posting articles   110
   etiquette   116–18
   followup (response articles)   110
   mailing list   254
   message thread   110
   newsgroups   111–16
     hierarchy   111–12
     moderated newsgroups   114
     top-level categories   112–13
   news server   111

   post   110
   public news servers   255–56
   topics   110
Network Operations Center   8
Newsgroups
   See Network news
New Users' Guide   254
NNTP (Network News Transfer
   Protocol)   111
NorthWestNet User Services Guide   254
NotePad++   217
NREN Information   254
NSFNET   9–10
Nuntius   40, 121–27, 132–37
   configuring   121–27
   posting news article   134–37
   reading network news   132–34

P

Passwords   41–42
Peer-to-peer networking   8
Performance Systems International
   (PSI)   97–98
Photograph archive (Smithsonian
   Institution)   47
Ph servers   81
POP3 (Post Office Protocol version 3)   60, 77
Popcorn (Aladdin Systems)   163
PowerPC   149
PPP (Point-to-Point Protocol)   15, 20–22,
   28, 152
   MacPPP (PPP software)   21, 28, 152
Privacy   50–52
Privatization of the Internet   11
Project Gutenberg   255

Q

Qualcomm Inc.   67

R

Resource requirements   26–29
   client application software   29
   Macintosh requirements   26

MacTCP   28–29
modem   28
   InterSLIP   28
   MacPPP   28
   MacSLIP   28
   network interface card   27
RFC (Request for Comments)   236–38
Router   20, 34

S

Security issues   41–42
   passwords   41–42
Service providers   23–26
Shakespeare, William   33
Shoars, Alana   52
Signatures   66
Simpson, John   52
SLIP (Serial Line Internet Protocol)   15,
   20–22, 28
   InterSLIP (SLIP software)   20, 28
Smileys   120
Smithsonian Institution photograph
   archive   47
Software resources   150–52
   commercial distribution   150
   freeware software   151
   public domain software   151
   shareware software   151–52
Special Internet Connections   256
Sports Schedules   256
StuffIt Deluxe (Aladdin Systems   153–54
StuffIt Expander (Aladdin Systems)   153
StuffIt Lite (Aladdin Systems)   192
Sumex-aim
   See Info-Mac archive

T

Talk   202
TCP/Connect II
   e-mail   76–93
      configuring   77–81
      creating new e-mail   83–84

file attachments   103–8
   receiving files   105–8
   sending files   103–4
filters   74, 89–93
   managing e-mail   88–93
      mailbox strategies   59
   reading e-mail   83
   replying to e-mail   86–87
   retrieving e-mail   81–82
   sending e-mail   84–85
FTP   170–82
   configuring   171–76
      FTP server configuration   171–74
      FTP client configuration   174–76
   downloading files   177–80
   uploading files   182
network news   127–30, 137–45
   configuring   127–30
   posting news article   143–45
   reading network news   137–42
TELNET   216–21
   configuring   216–19
   remote login   219–21
TCP/IP (Transmission Control Protocol/
   Internet Protocol)   6–7, 32, 33–34
   Introduction to TCP/IP   249
TELNET   212–21
   See also NCSA TELNET; TCP/Connect II
TeX   62
Travel advisories (US State
   Department)   35, 257
Travel Information   257
TurboGopher   42, 185–209
   Archie searches   233–36
   bookmarks   200–6
      creating   201–3
      exporting   204
      importing   205
      opening   205
   browsing information   193–94
   configuring   188–93
   downloading files   195–200
   tips for using   207

U

University of Michigan Macintosh
   archive   155
University of North Carolina
   LaUNChpad   257
UNIX
   what a Mac user needs to know
      about UNIX   7
USENET news
   See Network news
USENET user list   95–96
UUCP   22, 111

V

VAX Manual   258
Viruses   154–56

W

WAIS (Wide-Area Information
   Server)   226–29

Washington University Gateway   258
Wayfinding elements   2–3
   found text excerpts   3
   hot spots and cool resources   3
   people profiles   3
   software reviews   3
Weather Maps   258
Weather Service   258
White House E-Mail   258
White House Press Releases   259
White Pages   97–98
Whois   96–97
World Wide Web (WWW)   229–30

Z

'Zines (electronic magazines)   36
ZTerm   174

Colophon

The Mac Internet Tour Guide was produced on a Macintosh Quadra 700 using PageMaker 4.2. Body text is set in Adobe Palatino, sidebars are DTC Futura and Futura Bold and heads are DTC Kabel. The cover art was produced on a Macintosh Quadra 800 using Adobe Illustrator.

Page proofs were output to a LaserWriter IIg and final film output was produced using an Agfa ProSet 9800. Internet software was tested on a Macintosh IIci running System 7.0.1 and on a Macintosh Centris 610 running System 7.1, both using Hayes Optima 14400 FAX 144 modems.

DISK PREVIEW
The Mac Internet Tour Guide
Companion Disk

The software on the companion disk accompanying *The Mac Internet Tour Guide* is distributed with the permission of its authors and is provided here for evaluation purposes. You may try it without obligation, but if you decide to keep a program permanently, please check the Read Me file that is on the disk and make the appropriate shareware payment whenever applicable. Ventana Press and the author provide this software for your use as is and make no guarantee or warranty regarding its performance or compatibility.

Before you begin, we suggest making a careful backup of the contents of your hard drive and a backup of the companion disk. To install the software from the companion disk, you will need about 4mb of free space on your hard drive.

Eudora
Eudora is one of the best Internet e-mail programs available for the Macintosh. It is fully compatible with the POP3 mail server offered by most Internet service providers. To configure Eudora for use with your mail server see Chapter 4, "Electronic Mail."

Fetch
Fetch is a File Transfer Protocol (FTP) program. With Fetch you can quickly and easily download files from or upload files to a remote host on the Internet. Instructions for configuring Fetch are provided in Chapter 6, "Transferring Files."

InterSLIP
InterSLIP is a Control Panel that allows you to establish a connection to the Internet with a modem and an ordinary telephone line.

MacTCP
MacTCP is required to establish an Internet connection. It is a Control Panel that allows your Mac to communicate with other computers using the TCP/IP protocols on the Internet.

Stuffit Expander

Stuffit Expander is a file decompression program that you'll need for the files and other software resources you download from various sites on the Internet.

TurboGopher

TurboGopher allows you to browse through information resources on the Internet, translating complicated menu structures into familiar folder and file icons. TurboGopher is covered in Chapter 7, "Using Gopher."

Important Notes

The complete Eudora documentation set would not fit on the floppy disk that came with this book. You can FTP complete documentation—in Microsoft Word format—from Qualcomm Inc.'s server, or you can order a printed manual and distribution disk from the company for $30.

Your Internet service provider or network administrator will provide you with configuration instructions for MacTCP and InterSLIP. *Do not attempt to configure these programs yourself, unless you are absolutely sure you know what you are doing.*

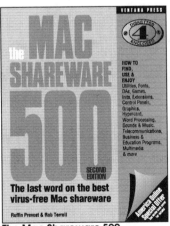

the
Ventana Press

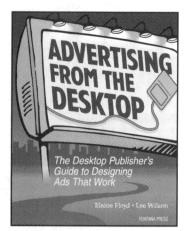

Desktop Design Series

To order these and other Ventana Press titles, use the form in the back of this book or contact your local bookstore or computer store. Full money-back guarantee!

Return order form to:
Ventana Press, P.O. Box 2468, Chapel Hill, NC 27515
☎**919/942-0220; Fax 919/942-1140**

Can't wait? Call toll-free, 800/743-5369 (U.S. Only)!

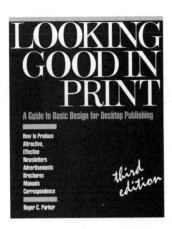

Newsletters From the Desktop
$23.95
306 pages, illustrated
ISBN: 0-940087-40-5
Now the millions of desktop publishers who produce newsletters can learn how to dramatically improve the design of their publications.

The Makeover Book: 101 Design Solutions for Desktop Publishing
$17.95
282 pages, illustrated
ISBN: 0-940087-20-0
"Before-and-after" desktop publishing examples demonstrate how basic design revisions can dramatically improve a document.

Advertising From the Desktop
$24.95
464 pages, illustrated
ISBN: 1-56604-064-7
Advertising From the Desktop offers unmatched design advice and helpful how-to instructions for creating persuasive ads. This book is an idea-packed resource for improving the look and effect of your ads.

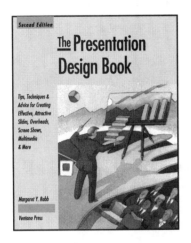

Looking Good in Print, Third Edition
$24.95
424 pages, illustrated
ISBN: 1-56604-047-7
With over 200,000 copies in print, **Looking Good in Print** is looking even better, with a new chapter on working with color, plus sections on photography and scanning. For use with any software or hardware, this desktop design bible has become the standard among novice and experienced desktop publishers alike.

The Presentation Design Book, Second Edition
$24.95
320 pages, illustrated
ISBN: 1-56604-014-0
The Presentation Design Book is filled with thoughtful advice and instructive examples for creating presentation visuals that have the power to communicate and persuade. For use with any software or hardware.

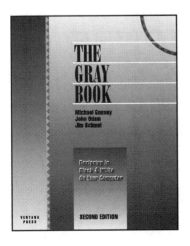

The Gray Book, Second Edition
$24.95
272 pages, illustrated
ISBN: 1-56604-073-6
This "idea gallery" for desktop publishers offers a lavish variety of the most interesting black, white and gray graphics effects that can be achieved with laser printers, scanners and high-resolution output devices.

TO OBTAIN YOUR FREE
ONE-MONTH TRIAL ACCOUNT

Simply fill in the form below and send it (or a fax) to:

Minnesota Regional Network (MRNet)
511 11th Avenue South, Suite 216
Box 212
Minneapolis, MN 55415

Attn: MacInternet Free Trial Account

Name ---
Address --
City/State/Zip ---

Phone --

User ID ---
(Choose your preferred Internet ID. Limit 10 characters)

You must return this page or a fax.

Quick-Reference Page

Use this page and its reverse side to keep track of important information about your Internet account. The information will always be close at hand, even when you aren't logged on to the Internet. You can also copy this page and fax or mail it to vendors and software developers to aid them in their technical support efforts.

Frequently Used Addresses & Other Information

User Name	_____
Computer Name	_____
Domain Name	_____
E-mail Address	_____
IP Address of Your Computer	_____
IP Subnet Mask of Your Computer	_____
IP Address of Domain Name Server	_____
IP Address of Domain Name Server	_____
IP Address of Local Gateway	_____
SLIP/PPP or Dial-Up Access Number	_____
Address of News Server	_____
Address of Mail Server	_____
Network Administrator E-mail	_____
Frequently Used E-mail Addresses	_____
Frequently Used E-mail Addresses	_____
Frequently Used E-mail Addresses	_____
Frequently Accessed Resources	_____
Frequently Accessed Resources	_____
Frequently Accessed Resources	_____

Popular Macintosh FTP Sites

Site	FTP Address	Notes
Stanford University	sumex-aim.stanford.edu	_____
University of Michigan	mac.archive.umich.edu	_____
University of Minnesota	boombox.micro.umn.edu	_____
Washington University (mirrors)	wuarchive.wustl.edu	_____
Apple Computer (general archive)	ftp.apple.com	_____
Arts & Farces (Visitors Center)	ftp.farces.com	_____

Technical Support Information

Software/Service	E-mail	Phone
Network Administrator	_____	_____
Connection Problems	_____	_____
Network Service Problems	_____	_____
TurboGopher	gopher@boombox.micro.umn.edu	612/626-4276
Eudora	eudora-info@qualcomm.com	N/A
MacSLIP	info@hydepark.com	512/454-1170
Fetch	fetch@dartmouth.edu	N/A
NCSA TELNET	mactelnet@ncsa.uiuc.edu	N/A
TCP/Connect II	support@intercon.com	703/709-9890

Mac Internet Tour Guide Visitors Center

Access *The Mac Internet Tour Guide* Visitors Center by FTP at:
ftp.farces.com

Current versions of interesting Macintosh programs for use on the Internet are available via anonymous FTP. The latest versions of all the key shareware and freeware programs discussed in this book will be available for downloading.

Author

Michael Fraase
Arts & Farces
2285 Stewart Ave., Suite 1315
Saint Paul, MN 55116
mfraase@farces.com

Publisher

Ventana Press
PO Box 2468
Chapel Hill, NC 27515
919/942-0220 (voice)
919/942-1140 (fax)

Notes

_____
_____
_____
_____
_____
_____
_____

TO ORDER additional copies of *The Mac Internet Tour Guide* or any Ventana Press title, please fill out this order form and return it to us for quick shipment.

	Quantity		Price		Total
Advertising From the Desktop	_____	x	$24.95	=	$_____
The Gray Book, Second Edition	_____	x	$24.95	=	$_____
Looking Good in Print, Third Edition	_____	x	$24.95	=	$_____
The Mac Internet Tour Guide	_____	x	$27.95	=	$_____
The Mac Shareware 500 Book/Disk Set	_____	x	$39.95	=	$_____
The Makeover Book	_____	x	$17.95	=	$_____
Newsletters From the Desktop	_____	x	$23.95	=	$_____
The Official America Online Membership Kit & Tour Guide: Mac Edition	_____	x	$34.95	=	$_____
The Presentation Design Book, Second Edition	_____	x	$24.95	=	$_____
The System 7 Book, Second Edition	_____	x	$24.95	=	$_____
Voodoo Mac	_____	x	$21.95	=	$_____

Shipping: Please add $4.50/first book, $1.35/book thereafter; $8.25/book "two-day air," $2.25/book thereafter. For Canada, add $6.50/book.   = $_____

Send C.O.D. (add $4.50 to shipping charges)   = $_____

North Carolina residents add 6% sales tax   = $_____

         Total   = $_____

Name _____

Company _____

Address (No PO Box) _____

City_____ State_____ Zip_____

Daytime Telephone _____

___ Payment enclosed ___VISA ___MC   Acc't # _____

Expiration Date_____ Interbank # _____

Signature _____

Please mail or fax to: **Ventana Press, PO Box 2468, Chapel Hill, NC 27515**
☎ **919/942-0220, FAX: 919/942-1140**

CAN'T WAIT? CALL TOLL-FREE ☎ 800/743-5369 (U.S. Only)!

PLEASE READ THIS LICENSE CAREFULLY BEFORE USING THE SOFTWARE. BY USING THE SOFTWARE, YOU ARE AGREEING TO BE BOUND BY THE TERMS OF THIS LICENSE. IF YOU DO NOT AGREE TO THE TERMS OF THIS LICENSE, PROMPTLY RETURN THE UNUSED SOFTWARE TO THE PLACE WHERE YOU OBTAINED IT AND YOUR MONEY WILL BE REFUNDED.

1. License. The application, demonstration, system and other software accompanying this License, whether on disk, in read only memory, or on any other media (the "Software") the related documentation and fonts are licensed to you by [Licensee Name]. You own the disk on which the Software and fonts are recorded but [Licensee Name] and/or [Licensee Name]'s Licensors retain title to the Software, related documentation and fonts. This License allows you to use the Software and fonts on a single Apple computer and make one copy of the Software and fonts in machine-readable form for backup purposes only. You must reproduce on such copy the [Licensee Name] copyright notice and any other proprietary legends that were on the original copy of the Software and fonts. You may also transfer all your license rights in the Software and fonts, the backup copy of the Software and fonts, the related documentation and a copy of this License to another party, provided the other party reads and agrees to accept the terms and conditions of this License.

2. Restrictions. The Software contains copyrighted material, trade secrets and other proprietary material. In order to protect them, and except as permitted by applicable legislation, you may not decompile, reverse engineer, disassemble or otherwise reduce the Software to a human-perceivable form. You may not modify, network, rent, lease, loan, distribute or create derivative works based upon the Software in whole or in part. You may not electronically transmit the Software from one computer to another or over a network.

3. Termination. This License is effective until terminated. You may terminate this License at any time by destroying the Software, related documentation and fonts and all copies thereof. This License will terminate immediately without notice from [Licensee Name] if you fail to comply with any provision of this License. Upon termination you must destroy the Software, related documentation and fonts and all copies thereof.

4. Export Law Assurances. You agree and certify that neither the Software nor any other technical data received from [Licensee Name], nor the direct product thereof, will be exported outside the United States except as authorized and as permitted by the laws and regulations of the United States. If the Software has been rightfully obtained by you outside of the United States, you agree that you will not re-export the Software nor any other technical data received from [Licensee Name], nor the direct product thereof, except as permitted by the laws and regulations of the United States and the laws and regulations of the jurisdiction in which you obtained the Software.

5. Government End Users. If you are acquiring the Software and fonts on behalf of any unit or agency of the United States Government, the following provisions apply. The Government agrees:

(i) if the Software and fonts are supplied to the Department of Defense (DoD), the Software and fonts are classified as "Commercial Computer Software" and the Government is acquiring only "restricted rights" in the Software, its documentation and fonts as that term is defined in Clause 252.227-7013(c)(1) of the DFARS; and

(ii) if the Software and fonts are supplied to any unit or agency of the United States Government other than DoD, the Government's rights in the Software, its documentation and fonts will be as defined in Clause 52.227-19(c)(2) of the FAR or, in the case of NASA, in Clause 18-52.227-86(d) of the NASA Supplement to the FAR.

6. Limited Warranty on Media. [Licensee Name] warrants the diskettes and/or compact disc on which the Software and fonts are recorded to be free from defects in materials and workmanship under normal use for a period of ninety (90) days from the date of purchase as evidenced by a copy of the receipt. [Licensee Name]'s entire liability and your exclusive remedy will be replacement of the diskettes and/or compact disc not meeting [Licensee Name]'s limited warranty and which is returned to [Licensee Name] or an [Licensee Name] authorized representative with a copy of the receipt. [Licensee Name] will have no responsibility to replace a disk/disc damaged by accident, abuse or misapplication. ANY IMPLIED WARRANTIES ON THE DISKETTES AND/OR COMPACT DISC, INCLUDING THE IMPLIED WARRANTIES OF MERCHANTABIL- ITY AND FITNESS FOR A PARTICULAR PURPOSE, ARE LIMITED IN DURATION TO NINETY (90) DAYS FROM THE DATE OF DELIVERY. THIS WARRANTY GIVES YOU SPECIFIC LEGAL RIGHTS, AND YOU MAY ALSO HAVE OTHER RIGHTS WHICH VARY BY JURISDICTION.

7. Disclaimer of Warranty on Apple Software. You expressly acknowledge and agree that use of the Software and fonts is at your sole risk. The Software, related documentation and fonts are provided "AS IS" and without warranty of any kind and [Licensee Name] and [Licensee Name]'s Licensor(s) (for the purposes of provisions 7 and 8, [Licensee Name] and [Licensee Name]'s Licensor(s) shall be collectively referred to as "[Licensee Name]") EXPRESSLY DISCLAIM ALL WARRANTIES, EXPRESS OR IMPLIED, INCLUDING, BUT NOT LIMITED TO, THE IMPLIED WARRANTIES OF MERCHANTABILITY AND FITNESS FOR A PARTICULAR PURPOSE. [LICENSEE NAME] DOES NOT WARRANT THAT THE FUNCTIONS CONTAINED IN THE SOFTWARE WILL MEET YOUR REQUIREMENTS, OR THAT THE OPERATION OF THE SOFTWARE WILL BE UNINTERRUPTED OR ERROR-FREE, OR THAT DEFECTS IN THE SOFTWARE AND THE FONTS WILL BE CORRECTED. FURTHERMORE, [LICENSEE NAME] DOES NOT WARRANT OR MAKE ANY REPRESENTATIONS REGARDING THE USE OR THE RESULTS OF THE USE OF THE SOFTWARE AND FONTS OR RELATED DOCUMENTATION IN TERMS OF THEIR CORRECTNESS, ACCURACY, RELIABILITY, OR OTHERWISE. NO ORAL OR WRITTEN INFORMATION OR ADVICE GIVEN BY [LICENSEE NAME] OR AN [LICENSEE NAME] AUTHORIZED REPRESENTA- TIVE SHALL CREATE A WARRANTY OR IN ANY WAY INCREASE THE SCOPE OF THIS WARRANTY. SHOULD THE SOFTWARE PROVE DEFECTIVE, YOU (AND NOT [LICENSEE NAME] OR AN [LICENSEE NAME] AUTHORIZED REPRESENTATIVE) ASSUME THE ENTIRE COST OF ALL NECESSARY SERVICING, REPAIR OR CORRECTION. SOME JURISDICTIONS DO NOT ALLOW THE EXCLUSION OF IMPLIED WARRANTIES, SO THE ABOVE EXCLUSION MAY NOT APPLY TO YOU.

8. Limitation of Liability. UNDER NO CIRCUMSTANCES INCLUDING NEGLIGENCE, SHALL [LICENSEE NAME] BE LIABLE FOR ANY INCIDENTAL, SPECIAL OR CONSEQUENTIAL DAMAGES THAT RESULT FROM THE USE OR INABILITY TO USE THE SOFTWARE OR RELATED DOCUMENTATION, EVEN IF [LICENSEE NAME] OR AN [LICENSEE NAME] AUTHORIZED REPRESENTATIVE HAS BEEN ADVISED OF THE POSSIBILITY OF SUCH DAMAGES. SOME JURISDICTIONS DO NOT ALLOW THE LIMITATION OR EXCLUSION OF LIABILITY FOR INCIDENTAL OR CONSEQUENTIAL DAMAGES SO THE ABOVE LIMITATION OR EXCLUSION MAY NOT APPLY TO YOU.
In no event shall [Licensee Name]'s total liability to you for all damages, losses, and causes of action (whether in contract, tort (including negligence) or otherwise) exceed the amount paid by you for the Software and fonts.

9. Controlling Law and Severability. This License shall be governed by and construed in accordance with the laws of the United States and the State of California, as applied to agreements entered into and to be performed entirely within California between California residents. If for any reason a court of competent jurisdiction finds any provision of this License, or portion thereof, to be unenforceable, that provision of the License shall be enforced to the maximum extent permissible so as to effect the intent of the parties, and the remainder of this License shall continue in full force and effect.

10. Complete Agreement. This License constitutes the entire agreement between the parties with respect to the use of the Software, the related documentation and fonts, and supersedes all prior or contemporaneous understandings or agreements, written or oral, regarding such subject matter. No amendment to or modification of this License will be binding unless in writing and signed by a duly authorized representative of [Licensee Name].

Yes! I Want to Stay Plugged In!
Send Me My Two Free Electronic Updates!

Navigating the strange and confusing highways and byways of the Internet can be a daunting proposition. New services spring up like fast food restaurants along the freeway. By sending in the card below, you'll receive two free updates via electronic mail and access to *The Mac Internet Tour Guide* Visitors Center. Your two free updates will feature the latest information about new Internet resources, file reviews, tips, tricks and pointers on finding and making the most of everything great on the Net.

Mac Internet Tour Guide electronic updates will be published and distributed on a quarterly basis. You'll receive the first two updates free of charge. After that, if you wish to continue receiving the updates, the yearly rate is only $25 for four issues. To subscribe now to a full year of updates (for a total of 6 issues), send a check for $25 (US funds only) payable to Arts & Farces to: Arts & Farces, 2285 Stewart Avenue, Suite 1315, Saint Paul, MN 55116. For more information, send e-mail to: tour-guide-request@farces.com

For more details, see Appendix A. To receive your two free updates, fill out the card below (be sure to fill it out completely) and return it to:

Ventana Press
Attention: Mac Internet Tour Guide
PO Box 2468
Chapel Hill, NC 27515

❏ Yes, please send me my two free editions of *The Mac Internet Tour Guide* electronic update. Here's my e-mail address (in the standard format of username@domain.top-domain):

_____

❏ Please keep me up-to-date on future offers and information about other Internet and Macintosh books and related materials.

Name _____

Organization or Company _____

Address _____

City _____State _____Zip _____

Ventana Press
Attention: Mac Internet Tour Guide
PO Box 2468
Chapel Hill, NC 27515

Place
Stamp
Here

Ventana Press

Attention: Mac Internet Tour Guide

PO Box 2468

Chapel Hill, NC 27515